MILTON STUDIES
XXXIV

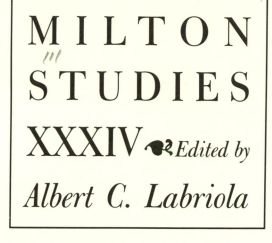

MILTON STUDIES

XXXIV *Edited by*

Albert C. Labriola

UNIVERSITY OF PITTSBURGH PRESS

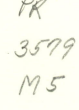

MILTON STUDIES

is published annually by the University of Pittsburgh Press as a forum for Milton scholarship and criticism. Articles submitted for publication may be biographical; they may interpret some aspect of Milton's writings; or they may define literary, intellectual, or historical contexts—by studying the work of his contemporaries, the traditions which affected his thought and art, contemporary political and religious movements, his influence on other writers, or the history of critical response to his work.

Manuscripts should be upwards of 3,000 words in length and should conform to the *Chicago Manual of Style*. Manuscripts and editorial correspondence should be addressed to Albert C. Labriola, Department of English, Duquesne University, Pittsburgh, Pa., 15282-1703. Manuscripts should be accompanied by a self-addressed envelope and sufficient unattached postage.

Milton Studies does not review books.

Within the United States, *Milton Studies* may be ordered from the University of Pittsburgh Press, c/o CUP Services, Box 6525, Ithaca, N.Y., 14851, 607-277-2211.

Published by the University of Pittsburgh Press, Pittsburgh, Pa. 15260

Copyright © 1997, University of Pittsburgh Press

Manufactured in the United States of America

Printed on acid-free paper

Library of Congress Catalog Card Number 69-12335

ISBN 0-8229-3958-4

US ISSN 0076-8820

A CIP catalogue record is available from the British Library.

Eurospan, London

CONTENTS

MILTON STUDIES
XXXIV

PARADISE LOST AND THE COLONIAL IMPERATIVE

Paul Stevens

And God blessed them, and God said unto them, Be fruitful, and multiply, and replenish the earth, and subdue it: and have dominion over the fish of the sea, and over the fowl of the air, and over every living thing that moveth upon the earth.

Genesis i, 28

Colonies . . . have their warrant from God's direction and command; who as soone as men were, set them to their taske, to replenish the earth and subdue it.

The Planter's Plea, 1630[1]

WHILE THERE HAS been a great deal of interest over the last several years in the relationship between Renaissance literature and the rhetoric of colonialism, and while at the same time there has been a dramatic renewal of interest in Milton's politics, surprisingly little has been written on Milton and colonialism. The most important exception is David Quint's recent book, *Epic and Empire* (1993). Quint, who approaches the issue through a somewhat ambivalently postmodern analysis of the political implications of genre, comes to the conclusion that the Milton of *Paradise Lost* is a poet against empire. In this essay I wish to challenge Quint's reading in order to suggest how exactly and to what extent *Paradise Lost* authorizes colonial activity even while it satirizes the abuses of early modern colonialism.[2]

I

Until fairly recently, "cultural" in the context of literary studies was understood as something which was by definition apolitical. It was, as Terry Eagleton in an uncharacteristically nostalgic mood has suggested, "the 'other' of political society—the realm of being as opposed to doing, the kingdom of ends rather than of means, the home of transcendental spirit rather than the dreary prose of everyday life."[3] For many scholars the exhilaration of professing literature lay precisely in the discipline's promise to transcend the quotidian. All that has clearly changed. After two or three decades of

3

"theory," for most active critics, the distinction between culture and politics has largely disappeared, and the net result for Renaissance studies as for most other areas of literary study is political criticism.

While the long-term consequences of this change may be significant, its immediate manifestations are rarely as radical or disturbing as the newspapers still like to claim.[4] What political criticism tends to mean—to use Thomas Kuhn's well-worn but still useful vocabulary—is that political readings of literary texts and the culture in which they were produced have become "normal science," that is, an institutionally sanctioned, normative practice.[5] While it is certainly true that many critics are well informed and passionate in their political commitment, at least as many simply acquiesce in the prevailing discourse and often allow the rhetoric of their critical practice to make them sound far more radical than they actually are. Political criticism in Renaissance studies seems to take two predominant forms. On the one hand, it seems to mean integrating literary texts into exciting new homologies of contemporary political issues, thus satisfying the critic's need not only to analyze but to act or effect an "intervention." On the other hand, it seems to mean simply figuring out the immediate political context of a literary work for no other purpose than a positivist determination to get at the "facts." In the first form, agency is much more likely to be granted to ideology or discourse; in the second, to local contingencies or the will of the individual. Even in the first form, however, ideology often figures, though certainly not always, as an increasingly limited or mannerist category. In this context, David Quint is especially interesting because, while routinely invoking ideology in *Epic and Empire*, he appears to be in transit from the first form of critical practice to the second, and in so moving helps to illustrate my point about the domestication of political criticism.

In *Epic and Empire*, Quint appears as a traditionally trained literary historian, simultaneously eschewing the "bad history" of new historicism's political homologies (pp. 14, 370) while busily adapting the well-tried methods of genre analysis to meet the discipline's apparently insatiable demand for political readings. Quint's first move in this process is to credit familiar literary genres with specific political or ideological implications. Literary history as the history of genres is thus represented as possessing a political life of its own. The two genres he is most interested in are epic and romance. Epic after Virgil, he feels, is the peculiar property of empire, and by *empire* he means the centralized, expansionist Western state, the Roman Empire and its various early modern heirs. Seen from the perspective of Virgilian epic, romance is the aimless, meaningless fate of the enemies of empire. "To the victors," so the *Aeneid* implies, "belongs epic, with its linear teleology;

to the losers belongs romance, with its random and circular wandering. Put another way, the victors experience history as a coherent, end-directed story told by their own power; the losers experience a contingency that they are powerless to shape to their own ends" (p. 9). But the power of romance is not mocked, and the contingency it articulates, so Quint argues, eventually comes to be seen by the defeated as a means of escaping, contesting, or subverting the power of the victors. To be specific, the contingency of romance enables the defeated to see all kinds of liberating possibilities beyond the totalizing and totalitarian closure of epic narrative.

Thus, in the same way that Patricia Parker in the 1970s—in the heyday of Yale deconstruction—made romance thematize Derridean *différance,* the distancing, difference, and deferral "intrinsic to language," so now Quint politicizes it.[6] Just as in Parker's account, to which Quint is immediately indebted, romance is understood as anticipating Derrida's critique of "Presence"—that is, "the metaphysical assumption of an ultimate Origin, Center, or End, and the various social and intellectual hierarchies it authorises" (p. 220)—so in Quint's account romance stands in opposition to what not surprisingly turns out to be a familiarly Foucauldian version of the imperial state's power. To the degree that Milton's great epic, for instance, turns to romance, so it may be construed, like its sequel *Paradise Regained,* as "a defense of the individual against the state, against its instruments of surveillance and control" (p. 324). It is difficult at this point not to feel that in Milton Quint is allegorizing his own commonsense belief in individual agency and his desire to distance himself from the Foucauldian moment of early new historicism. In a footnote he refers us to David Bromwich, who valorizes common sense and excoriates theory and "the erosion of [the] secular individualism" it signifies as "perhaps the worst intellectual disaster of the 1970s and 1980s."[7]

The place of *Paradise Lost* in Quint's story of politics and generic form is central. The logic of his literary history would seem to demand that Milton's great poem be consigned to the ash heap of beautiful but obsolete imperial epics. The poem is, however, saved by the "turn to romance" which Quint claims is the distinguishing feature of what he calls "the losers' epic" (p. 9), a subgenre inaugurated by Lucan's *Pharsalia.* In *Paradise Lost,* the triumphalist epic plot first given a specific ideological direction in Virgil's *Aeneid* and reproduced in Renaissance poems like Tasso's *Gerusalemme Liberata* and Camoëns's *Lusiads* is satirized by Milton in the way Satan's would-be colonial epic collapses into a "bad romance" (p. 248) and transumed in the way Adam and Eve's tragic story turns into a good romance. "Reserving the imperial typology of the Virgilian epic for its God alone,"

Quint concludes, "*Paradise Lost* effectively moves away from epic altogether" (p. 248). Like a more quietist version of the Romantic Milton of Wordsworth's sonnet or Masson's biography, Quint's Milton gradually emerges as a poet against empire, and his poem comes to be seen as "an indictment of European expansion and colonialism that includes his own countrymen and contemporaries" (p. 265). Most important, Milton emerges as an individual who seems so able to manipulate generic form that ideology seems to have little constraining force for him.

Despite Quint's impressive erudition and many brilliant local insights, this reading of *Paradise Lost* may be questioned on a number of grounds, all of them requiring the reader to step outside the narrow bounds of Quint's politically inflected literary history. Two points, both suggestive of Milton's lack of freedom from ideological constraint, immediately come to mind. *First,* that Satan's journey to the new world is not so much a satire on colonialism as on the abuses of colonialism. There is, for instance, no evidence to suggest that Milton ever felt the Protestant colonization of New England, Virginia, or Ulster, in principle at least, anything but admirable. Nor does reserving the imperial typology of Virgilian epic to God alone constitute a rejection so much as a displacement of an extraordinarily deep-rooted and tenacious will-to-order which is often hard to distinguish from a will-to-power. *Second,* that the representation of Adam and Eve in Paradise, especially in the way that representation both amplifies and idealizes the colonial imperative embedded in Scripture, confounds the postmodern distinction Quint wishes to make between the political implications of epic and romance. For the new world that Adam and Eve are commanded to replenish and subdue in Genesis—the world Milton calls their "neather Empire" (IV, 145)—is precisely the end that so many early modern colonialists desire and feel themselves duty-bound to seek.[8] In other words, the image at the heart of the poem of a paradise that is lost, the romance vision of a garden that is to be regained when "the Earth / Shall all be Paradise" (XII, 463–64), is central to the *mentalité* responsible for the building of European colonial empires. In drawing attention to the imperative of Genesis i, 28, Milton's contemporary, John White, for instance, offers a glimpse of the biblical origin of empire. If we allow, says White in *The Planter's Plea*, God's command to replenish and subdue the earth "to bind *Adam*, [then] it must binde his posterity, and consequently our selves in this age, and our issue after us, as long as the earth yields empty places to be replenished" (p. 2). As long as the earth yields empty places to be replenished. With the last clause, it suddenly becomes apparent that the endless deferral of fulfillment in romance is not the antithesis of empire but in the case of Western colonialism its scriptural genesis.

II

In order to develop these points let me begin with Satan's journey to the New World. As Martin Evans demonstrated in a brilliantly succinct analysis over twenty years ago, there is abundant evidence to suggest that the journey parodies a colonial venture.[9] The project that governs the poem's satanic plot is the discovery and colonization of a new land. It is true that in one version of this plan colonization is understood simply as a means of precipitating the land's destruction, but much more insistently it is imagined as a permanent settlement. Beelzebub talks of possessing "All as our own," of driving out "as we were driven, / The punie habitants" (II, 366–67). Satan imagines dwelling secure "in some milde Zone" where "the soft delicious Air" shall breathe her balm and heal his scars (II, 397–402). This satanic colonizing project is mediated through multiple frames of reference: classical, biblical, and of course, not least, contemporary. The journey to the New World is, for instance, repeatedly described in terms of recent overseas "adventures" for trade or settlement. As Satan approaches the gates of hell he is seen as a fleet of merchant ships returning from the East Indies, Bengal, or the Spice Islands (II, 636–42); as he approaches Paradise he is imagined on board ship, sailing from the Cape of Good Hope and cheered by the spicy odors of Arabia (IV, 159–65); and, most important, when he finally encounters the naked inhabitants of the New World, he speaks the words any patriotic Englishman in the late 1650s would expect a rapacious adventurer or conquistador to let slip:

> And should I at your harmless innocence
> Melt, as I doe, yet public reason just,
> Honour and Empire with revenge enlarg'd,
> By conquering this new World, compels me now
> To do what else though damnd I should abhorre.   (IV, 338–92)

In the event, in what seems like a ringing indictment of colonialist ambition, honor and empire are shown to mean fraud and dispossession; the poor natives are cheated of their birthright and fall prey to the ghastly hellhounds of Sin and Death.

At this point, it is important to emphasize that, despite Quint's assertion to the contrary, the early modern discourse of English colonialism was consistent in its efforts to distinguish legitimate from illegitimate activity.[10] Though much of this moralizing was of course disingenuous, much of it was agonizingly sincere, and in *The Reason of Church-government* (1642) Milton himself contributes to the debate when he deploys a colonial metaphor to distinguish himself from the Bishops. When it comes to bearing God's truth, the difference between the Bishops and himself is the difference between two kinds of colonial entrepreneur: on the one hand there are those false merchants who "abuse the people, like poor Indians with beads and glasses," while on the other there are those resolute adventurers who bear themselves honestly at the trading post, "uprightly in this their spiritual factory," offering stones of "orient lustre" at bargain prices, "at any cheap rate, yea for nothing to them that will" (CM III, pp. 229–30). Thus, at the same time that he is justifying himself for speaking out against the Bishops, he is also justifying colonial trade by distinguishing the true from the false. In effect, he is offering his own merchant class an idealized view of itself, tacitly accepting the legitimacy of establishing factories or trading colonies like those set up at Jamestown in Virginia (1607) or Surat in India (1612).[11]

The metaphor of treasure, the stones of "orient lustre," the pearl of great price (Matt. xiii, 45–46), is especially relevant because the image is a staple of those tracts and pamphlets whose main purpose is to demonstrate the lawfulness of colonization. As Milton gives this image of "heavenly traffic" a colonial setting to dramatize his religious vocation, so propagandists deploy it to lend the religious aspirations of their readers a colonial outlet. We offer native peoples "the incomparable treasure of the trueth of Christianity and of the Gospell," says Richard Hakluyt, "while we use and exercise common trade with their merchants." We "doe buy of them the pearles of the earth," says the Virginia Company's *True Declaration*, "and sell to them the pearls of heaven."[12] In practice, of course, the pearls of heaven often got lost in the rush for the pearls of the earth. In 1622, for instance, an English fleet from the East India Company's factory at Surat joined forces with a Moslem army from Persia to bloodily relieve the Christian Portuguese of that pearl of the orient, Ormus, the center of the Persian Gulf pearl trade.[13] For Milton such excess is to be censured, and it is precisely for reasons of excess that "the wealth of Ormus and of Ind" is associated with Satan (II, 1–5). Milton's pride in English colonial adventure and his disapproval of mercantile excess are simultaneously made explicit in his *Brief History of Muscovia* (1682): "The discovery of *Russia* by the northern Ocean, made first, of any Nation that we know, by *English* men, might have seem'd an enterprise almost heroick; if any higher end than the excessive love of Gain and Traffick, had animated the design" (YP VIII, p. 524).

The class into which Milton was born, it needs to be remembered, was mercantile. The parish of All Hallows, Bread Street, London, the first social group of which the poet became conscious, was largely composed of successful merchants, more than half of them dealers in cloth, and many, including Milton's maternal grandfather, members of the Merchant Taylors' Company.[14] His next-door neighbor, Ralph Hamor, was a merchant-tailor but also a member of the Virginia Company and his son, also called Ralph, wrote one of the best known defenses of the colony, *A True Discourse of the Present Estate of Virginia* (1615). The rector of the parish in 1626 was Samuel Purchas, whose great collection of colonizing voyages, *Purchas His Pilgrimes,* Milton combed through for his history of Russia and is said to have planned to abridge.[15] For people like this, whether domestic merchants or members of overseas companies, the commonplace shorthand or metonym for colonial excess was Spanish imperialism.

From the first English translation of Bartolomé de Las Casas's *Brevisima Relación de la Destrucción de las Indias* in 1583,[16] English colonialism had defined itself in opposition to Spain's excessive love of gain and traffic—a lust for land and treasure which, according to Las Casas, had led to a series of genocidal atrocities. Las Casas's detailed account of these cruelties enabled the English to represent themselves as a kinder, gentler type of colonialist, indeed as protectors of the Indians.[17] Throughout his 1596 tract, *The Discovery of Guiana,* for instance, Sir Walter Ralegh presents himself to his readers as a knight from Spenserian romance come to do Gloriana's bidding by protecting the Indians from the depredations of the Spanish:

I made them understand that I was a servant of a Queene, who was the great *Casique* of the north, and a virgin, and had more *Casiqui* under her then there were trees in their Iland: that she was an enemy to the *Castellani* in respect of their tyrannie and oppression, and that she . . . had sent me to free them. . . . I shewed them her maiesties picture which they so admired and honored, as it had beene easie to have brought [thought] them Idolatrous thereof.[18]

This self-representation is part of a continuous tradition of national propaganda from the 1580s to the late 1650s, and it impinges directly on Milton's career. Between 1655 and 1658, while Milton was still employed on government business, and at about the same time, according to his nephew Edward Phillips, that he was beginning work on *Paradise Lost,* the rhetoric of Spanish colonial abuse was redeployed in a concerted effort to justify Cromwell's Western Design—that is, his plan to carve out a colonial empire in the Caribbean.[19] In Sir William Davenant's 1658 masque, *The Cruelty of the Spaniards in Peru,* for instance, the New Model Army, complete with red coats, arrives to rescue the racked and tortured Incas in a vision of things to come. In *The Tears of the Indians,* the 1656 translation of Las Casas's pamphlet made by Milton's other nephew, John Phillips, Cromwell appears making ready to avenge the Indians—for they had been devoured by the Spanish, "not as if they had been their Fellow-Mortals, but like Death it self."[20] And in the official 1655 *Declaration Against Spain,* which may or may not have been written by Milton, the self-imposed English obligation to avenge the blood of so many slaughtered Indians becomes a warrant by which the English can legitimately inherit Indian land.[21]

Given the immediacy and intensity of this tradition, given Milton's social background and his participation in articulating government policy (including his work on an abortive colonial treaty with the Spanish), it seems unlikely that his critique of colonial abuses in *Paradise Lost* would be uninfluenced by what the Spanish in self-defense called the Black Legend. And indeed if it is uninfluenced by it, then the significance of Milton's explicit characterization of the Spanish as "*Geryons* Sons" (XI, 410) at the only moment in the poem when the politics of contemporary colonialism is directly referred to remains unclear. For there on the mountaintop of Speculation, as Adam is shown the future empires of the world, Milton rehearses the argument of Ralegh's *Discoverie of Guiana:* the riches of Mexico and Peru are juxtaposed with the "yet unspoil'd" riches of Guiana, "whose great Citie *Geryons* Sons / Call *El Dorado*" (XI, 409–11). In Spenser, Geryon's son is the monstrous progeny of Spanish imperialism devouring the children of the Netherlands; in Milton, "*Geryons* Sons" is an allusion to a specific historical example of the way contemporary colonialism may reenact the entry of Death itself into the world.[22]

John Phillips's description of Spanish excess as "Death it self," of the Spanish murdering Indians "to satisfie the contemptible hunger of their Hounds" (sig. A8r), suggests the degree to which the representation of Sin and Death in *Paradise Lost* continues the colonial critique. One of the distinguishing features of Las Casas's text is the recurrent reference to the Spanish use of war dogs, "which they teach and instruct to fall upon the Indians and devour them" (p. 130). In *Paradise Lost*, the denouement of Satan's conquest of the New World is the arrival of Sin and Death as hellhounds specifically charged by "the folly of Man" (X, 619) to devour the inhabitants: "See with what heat these Dogs of Hell advance / To waste and havoc yonder World," cries God the Father (X, 616–17). What is most important here is that Death and the havoc he causes are not the necessary outcomes of colonialism but of the perversion of colonialism, of excess, fraud, and dispossession, that is, of Sin. The extent to which the colonial triumph of Sin and Death is a counterfeit imitation of the good is suggested in the way their satanic charter is made to parody the colonial ideal of Genesis i, 28:

> right down to Paradise descend;
> There dwell and Reign in bliss, thence on the Earth
> Dominion exercise and in the Aire,
> Chiefly on Man, sole Lord of all declar'd,
> Him first make sure your thrall, and lastly kill.   (X, 398–402)

III

The strongest argument for doubting Milton's conversion to any kind of blanket anticolonial stand is not, as I have just tried to suggest, that his satire on colonialism can so easily be construed as a satire on its abuses, but that his depiction of Adam and Eve in Paradise turns out to be such a powerful representation of its ideal. And because that ideal has the quality of a romance, it undermines the explanatory force of Quint's binary opposition between the political implications of epic and romance.

The most obvious difference between Satan's colonial project and that of Adam and Eve is explained by Sir Francis Bacon: "I like a *Plantation* in a Pure Soile; that is, where people are not *Displanted*, to the end, to *Plant* in Others. For else it is rather an Extirpation, then a *Plantation*."[23] Satan does not have a pure soil; Adam and Eve do. Satan and his fellow adventurers are forced to rehearse various self-serving arguments to extirpate the territorial rights of the natives: they are "punie," *puis né*, born later, says Beelzebub (II, 367); "Into our room . . . advanc't," says Satan (IV, 359). Their very chthonic origins are turned against them: they are denigrated as people of clay, children of despite, as though they were tainted by the ground out of which they had come (IX, 176). Adam and Eve, however, have no need for such arguments. Not only do they have a pure soil, but the world they enter conforms in almost every way with the ideal of English colonial discourse. If the New World of that discourse is frequently recreated in the image of a biblical paradise, so Milton's biblical Paradise is indebted to his familiarity with colonial accounts of the New World.[24] The land Adam and Eve enter is gendered female, virginal, and stands ready to be husbanded. It is a place like Robert Johnson's Virginia, where "valleys and plaines . . . [stream] with sweete Springs, like veynes in a naturall bodie," where the soil is so strong and lusty that it "sendeth out naturally fruitfull vines running upon trees, and shrubbes." It is place like Samuel Purchas's Virginia of such "luxuriant wantonesse" that it is well "worth the wooing and loves of the best Husband."[25] Adam and Eve are imagined like the settlers of Virginia, not only as husbandmen, but paradoxically as the plants to be husbanded: they are rooted in the soil, "earth-born" (IV, 360), like the vine and the elm, indigenous, almost autochthonous. But most important, like Purchas's settlers, they have the charter of Genesis i, 28, "a Commission from . . . [God] to plant" (XIX, pp. 218–19). "Not only these fair bounds," says Milton's God to Adam, amplifying the biblical text,

> but all the Earth
> To thee and to thy Race I give; as Lords
> Possess it, and all things that therein live,

> Or live in Sea, or Aire, Beast, Fish, and Fowle.
> In signe whereof each Bird and Beast behold
> After thir kindes; I bring them to receave
> From thee thir Names, and pay thee fealtie
> With low subjection.   (VIII, 338–45)

What is most seductive about this fantasy of world dominion is that it articulates both the complete possession of power and its deferral. For in Milton's fiction not only Adam and Eve's nether empire but the Garden itself has to be replenished and subdued, that is, cultivated. Adam and Eve are confronted with "a Wilderness of sweets" where nature "Wantond as in her prime, and plaid at will / Her Virgin Fancies" (V, 294–96): as Eve explains,

> what we by day
> Lop overgrown, or prune, or prop, or bind,
> One night or two with wanton growth derides
> Tending to wilde.   (IX, 209–12)

Their struggle to cultivate the wilderness is, as in any other early modern colonial romance, a metonym for the struggle toward civility. Implicit in Adam's response to Eve's plan to divide their labors is the suggestion that she has overemphasized the vehicle at the expense of the tenor, the gardening at the expense of the civility it is meant to convey: "Yet not so strictly hath our Lord impos'd / Labour" (IX, 235–36) so as to debar them from the daily delights of civil intercourse—"whether food, or talk between, / Food of the mind, or this sweet intercourse / Of looks and smiles, for smiles from Reason flow" (IX, 237–39). As their ensuing quarrel indicates, with its carefully plotted account of the disintegration of the language of politeness, civility is understood not simply as refreshment or relief from work but as a different kind of work—a community-defining social practice that takes skill and energy, an art that needs to be joined to nature. Because this task is at the heart of their quest, the failure of Adam and Eve is causally linked to their subsequent moral and epistemological failures, that is, the collapse of civility is not accidental but central to Milton's representation of the Fall.

My point here is twofold: first, that what is frustrated or deferred in Milton's story of Adam and Eve is the desire for a culturally specific form of civility and the membership of the ideal, imagined community it signifies; and second, that this desire is the lack that most powerfully animates early modern colonial settlement at its most idealistic: "if bare nature be so amiable in its naked kind," wonders Robert Johnson of his brave new world, "what may we hope, when Arte and Nature both shall joyne, and strive together."[26] It is a solipsistic desire because it is a longing for the ideal form of a civility that already identifies colonists as English, Christian, European. It is a desire that renders the literary historian's distinction between epic's imagined completion of history and romance's imagined wandering toward that completion relatively insignificant. It is not clear, for instance, that Ralegh's digressive and ultimately fruitless Spenserian quest in *The Discoverie of Guiana*—as much a courtly demonstration of temperance as a search for El Dorado[27]—is any less a manifestation of Western imperialism's will-to-power than the *Aeneid* or the *Lusiads*. Both epic and romance are perfectly capable of articulating an imperial ideology.[28]

If one of the ways in which ideology may be understood is as "identity-thinking," that is, as the network of "discursive formations" that give a particular culture or community its coherence or integrity, then ideology in *Paradise Lost* may be most usefully approached through the discourse of civility.[29] The civility that constitutes the daily practice of Adam and Eve is, however, more than just a discourse in the sense of one particular tradition; it is more like a master code that generates and demands adherence to a series of moral and epistemological rules so deeply ingrained as to be hardly open to question—rules such as the need to restrain the luxuriant growth of wanton fancy, to subdue sensual appetite, and to maintain the sovereignty of reason (IX, 1127–31).[30] These imperatives are aestheticized in art's power "to allay the perturbations of the mind, and set the affections in right tune" (*The Reason of Church-government*, CM III, p. 238). As Ferdinand in *The Tempest*, in what many claim to be Shakespeare's colonial romance, unwittingly bears witness, such civility so aesthetically conceived is precisely the end of Prospero's art: the magician's strange and rare music crept by him on the waters, he says, "Allaying both their fury and my passion / With its sweet air" (I, ii, 392–94).[31] For both Milton and Shakespeare, civility so understood is not relative, particular, or contingent, but absolute and universal, in Milton's case especially empyreal and imperial.

What needs to be emphasized at this point is the degree to which the early modern discourse of civility *is* contingent, from our perspective both culturally specific and solipsistic. In colonial narratives this may be seen most tellingly in those moments of wonder when what is discovered is not the disconcerting strangeness of the other so much as an idealized form of the familiar in the midst of the other. Contrary to Stephen Greenblatt's argument, in epiphanies of wonder ideology is just as likely to be reasserted as resisted.[32] What most moves Ralegh, for instance, is not the incomprehensibility or alterity of Guiana, but marvellous moments of recognition like this:

On both sides of the river, we passed the most beautiful countrie that ever mine eies beheld: and whereas all that we had seen before was nothing but woods, prickles, bushes, and thornes, heere we beheld plaines of twenty miles in length, the grasse short and greene, and in divers parts groves of trees by themselves, as if they had been by all the art and labour in the world so made of purpose and stil as we rowed, the Deere came downe feeding by the waters side, as if they had been used to a keepers call. (p. 48)

The same discovery of a civility so wonderful because of its unexpected familiarity is recounted by George Percy as he and his companions negotiate the labyrinthine woods of Nevis in the West Indies:

We past into the thickest of the Woods where we had almost lost our selves, we had not gone above half a mile amongst the thicke, but we came into a most pleasant Garden, being a hundred square paces on every side . . . we saw the goodliest tall trees growing about the Garden, as though they had beene set by Art, which made us marvel very much to see it.[33]

In *Paradise Lost,* Milton's immersion in colonial discovery narratives is evident in the way he reproduces the same wonderful moment of recognition. What we discover in his Paradise, so remote in time and exotic in location, is not so much a transcendent ideal as an idealized English quotidian. Following Satan, traveling east of Eden, beyond the undergrowth "so thick entwin'd" of "shrubs and tangling bushes," the "new wonder" that greets us is "A happy rural seat of various view" (IV, 174–76, 205, 247)— "almost laughably," says John Broadbent, registering his own moment of recognition, "the England of Penshurst, Cooper's Hill, and Appleton House."[34] The civility Adam and Eve seek and lose is precisely what Milton himself cannot give up. It is a discourse so pervasive and constitutive of other discourses—moral, epistemological, aesthetic—that it functions as his *habitus;* that is, in Pierre Bourdieu's explanation of ideology, the complex of "principles which generate and organize practices and representations that can be objectively adapted to their outcomes without presupposing a conscious aiming at ends"—in Eagleton's words, "the relay or transmission mechanism by which mental and social structures become incarnate in daily social activity."[35]

If the implication of Adam and Eve in a colonial romance is as deep rooted as I am suggesting, then one might expect their failure to be represented in terms of the ultimate colonial failure of civility, that is, of "going native." The fear that animates English colonial texts as diverse as Spenser's *View of the Present State of Ireland,* or John Rolfe's letter explaining his marriage to Pocahontas, is the fear of degeneration, of becoming savage, of being excluded from the civil community.[36] And that is, of course, exactly the fate that overtakes Adam and Eve. In their fall, the first settlers are metamorphosed into Indians. The difference between guilt and shame is the difference between moral failure on the one hand and social transgression and exclusion on the other.[37] At their most intense moment of shame, Adam and Eve are excluded from the community into which they were born: "How shall I behold the face / Henceforth of God or Angel," cries Adam, "O might I here / In solitude live savage" (IX, 1080–81, 1084–85). In attempting to cover their "uncleanness" with fig leaves, they only confirm their excluded, degenerate status: "O how unlike / To that first naked Glorie," comments the poet. Now in their shame they look like the American Indians "*Columbus* found . . . so girt / With featherd Cincture, naked else and wilde / Among the Trees on Iles and woodie shores" (IX, 1114–18). For Milton, guilt and shame seem inseparable. That the Fall, the original moral failure of all humankind, is imagined in terms of what for many of us now is largely a matter of the cultural difference of a specific part of humankind suggests the degree to which moral failure in Milton cannot be imagined in terms other than those of the failure of civility or community transgression. Adam and Eve have not only broken God's commandment, but they have become the defining other of English or European culture. Covered with fig leaves, they imagine themselves back within the community—"Thus fenc't, and as they thought, thir shame in part / Coverd" (IX, 1119–20)—when in fact they are still outside the fence, beyond the pale: "distemperd," "estrang'd," "tost and turbulent" (IX, 1131, 1132, 1126).

To the extent that Adam and Eve are capable of regeneration, however, so the colonial quest can continue, and, as the evidence of American colonial writers like Cotton Mather suggests, the image of these first settlers will inspire generations of English colonists on their errand into the wilderness. In his *Magnalia Christi Americana* (1702), for instance, Mather imagines the garden as New England overgrown and threatened by Satan and his followers in the form of the Indians:

About this time *New-England* was miserably *Briar'd* in the Perplexities of an *Indian War;* and the Salvages, in the *East* part of the Country, issuing out from their inaccessible *Swamps,* had for many Months made their Cruel Depredations upon the poor *English* Planters, and surprized many of the Plantations on the Frontiers, into Ruin. . . . They [the English] found, that they were like to make no weapons reach their Enswamped Adversaries, except Mr. *Milton* could have shown them how

> To have pluckt up the Hills with all their Load,
> Rocks, Waters, woods, and by their shaggy tops,
> Up-lifting, borne them in their Hands, therewith
> The Rebel Host to've over-whelm'd.[38]

IV

Milton as a poet against empire is too easy. In his "Digression on the Long Parliament," which he sought to publish with his *History of Britain* long after the Restoration in 1670, Milton urges his readers to learn the lessons of political failure.[39] Unless the conduct of affairs is given to "men more then vulgar," he says, men "bred up . . . in the knowledge of Antient and illustrious deeds, invincible against money, and vaine titles," men whose minds are "well implanted with solid & elaborate breeding," then "wee shall else miscarry still and com short in the attempt of any great enterprise" (YP V, p. 451). Though this was written in 1649, the fact that Milton wanted it published in 1670 does not suggest that he was someone who had given up on England's need to cultivate its nether empire. This is even more apparent in his last polemical pamphlet, *Of True Religion* (1673), in which he proudly recalls England's defining act of independence in throwing off the "*Babylonish* Yoke" of the pope's authority and happily joins in the common work of the nation in hindering "the growth of this Romish Weed": "I thought it no less then a common duty to lend my hand, how unable soever, to so good a Purpose" (YP VIII, pp. 430, 417–18).

The *locus classicus* for the quietist Milton's rejection of empire is Jesus' excoriation of the Roman Empire's corruption in *Paradise Regained* (1671). But Jesus' rejection of Rome turns out to be highly ambiguous. First, the rejection comprises a traditional, humanist civility argument. Jesus makes it clear that though Rome has become degenerate, it had actually started out well: the Romans "who once just, / Frugal, and mild, and temperate, [had] *conquer'd well*" (IV, 133–34; my emphasis). Thus, presumably, for a state or people bound by the civil imperatives of justice, frugality, mildness, and temperance, it was still possible to conquer well. Second, the affective attraction of power is evident in Jesus' intensely threatening millenarian prophecy:

> Know therefore when my season comes to sit
> On *David's* Throne, it shall be like a tree
> Spreading and over-shadowing all the Earth,
> Or as a stone that shall to pieces dash
> All Monarchies besides throughout the world
> And of my kingdom there shall be no end.   (IV, 146–51)[40]

The anger of the dispossessed in this apocalyptic passage makes it difficult not to recall D. H. Lawrence's comments on the Book of Revelation: "For Revelation, be it said once and for all, is the revelation of the undying will-to-power in man, and its sanctification, its final triumph." And as Laura Knoppers has recently shown, the allusions to the Book of Daniel in this prophecy had immediate, aggressively political, "Fifth Monarchy" ramifications for Restoration England.[41]

The strongest evidence in *Paradise Lost* (1674) for Milton's rejection of empire is Michael's quietist admonitions, but the poem's closing books are an act of public humiliation and it is in this context that the archangel's admonitions are best understood. Even then they are every bit as ambiguous as Jesus' rejection of Rome. It is true that Michael encourages Adam to focus on obedience rather than what he once possessed in Paradise, "all the rule, one Empire" (XII, 581), but at the same time Adam makes it clear that the imperial imperative of Genesis i, 28, has not lapsed: "that right we hold / By his donation" (XII, 68–69). It is true, we are somewhat belatedly told, that the imperative was never meant to legitimize "Dominion absolute" of "Man over men" (XII, 68–70), but in Michael's nostalgic glance back at what might have been, Adam's empire is imagined as a patriarchal dominion in which the garden might have been

> Perhaps thy Capital Seate, from whence had spred
> All generations, and hither come
> From all the ends of th'Earth, to celebrate
> And reverence thee thir great Progenitor.   (XI, 343–46)

And outside the poem, it is clear that Milton does not stop believing in the necessity for a civil community in which some people will be subject to others: the vulgar will still have to be led, the corrupt punished, the Romish weeded out, the savage civilized, and so on. There is, for instance, no evidence to suggest that Milton ever felt the need to revise his view that the Irish were degenerate and had merely proved their obdurate willfulness by refusing to take advantage of England's "civilizing Conquest" to "improve and waxe more civill" (*Observations upon the Articles of Peace*, YP III, p. 304). Finally, it is true that Michael urges Adam to concentrate on the "paradise within thee, happier farr" (XII, 587), but, if my argument is true, then that admonition to turn inward and forget the expansiveness of the Genesis imperative will be undermined by the logic of daily practice—the quotidian demands of early modern civility. Not least, it will be undermined by the extraordinary, affective power of those demands' ideal representation in Milton's version of Paradise, and the consequent longing or lack that that aesthetic achievement creates in the readers of Milton's great poem.

As all his writings testify, Milton was an intensely idealistic and moral man, and what is most challenging about him, like Las Casas and other putative early modern anticolonialists, is that it is his very virtue, his desire for civility and his refusal of any thoroughgoing relativism, that makes it so difficult for him to stand outside the discourse of colonialism. To argue otherwise is to underestimate the power of ideology and to continue the work of diluting the truly important insights of the political criticism that we associate with cultural materialism and the now much-denigrated new historicism.

Queen's University, Canada

NOTES

1. John White, *The Planter's Plea* (London, 1630; rpt. New York, 1968), p. 1.

2. David Quint, *Epic and Empire: Politics and Generic Form from Virgil to Milton* (Princeton, 1993). Other works on Milton and early modern colonialism include Robert Ralston Cawley, *Milton and the Literature of Travel* (Princeton, 1951); James H. Sims, "Camoëns' 'Lusiads' and Milton's 'Paradise Lost': Satan's Voyage to Eden," in *Papers on Milton*, ed. Philip Mahone Griffith and Lester F. Zimmerman (Tulsa, 1969); *John Milton: Paradise Lost: Books IX–X*, ed. J. Martin Evans (Cambridge, 1973), esp. pp. 46–47; I. S. MacLaren, "Arctic Exploration and Milton's 'Frozen Continent,'" *N&Q*, new ser. XXXI, no. 3 (1984), 325–26; Gordon Campbell, "The Wealth of Ormus and of Ind,"*MQ* XXI, no. 1 (1987), 22–23; V. J. Kiernan, "Milton in Heaven," in *Reviving the English Revolution*, ed. Geoff Eley and William Hunt (London, 1988), pp. 161–80; Thomas N. Corns, "Milton's *Observations upon the Articles of Peace:* Ireland Under English Eyes," in *Politics, Poetics, and Hermeneutics in Milton's Prose*, ed. David Loewenstein and James Grantham Turner (Cambridge, 1990), pp. 123–34; Andrew Barnaby, " 'Another Rome in the West?': Milton and the Imperial Republic, 1654–70," *Milton Studies* XXX, ed. Albert C. Labriola (Pittsburgh, 1993), pp. 67–84; Paul Stevens, " 'Leviticus Thinking' and the Rhetoric of Early Modern Colonialism," *Criticism* XXXV, no. 3 (1993), 441–61; "Spenser and Milton on Ireland: Civility, Exclusion, and the Politics of Wisdom," *ARIEL* XXVI, no. 4 (1995), 151–67; and David Armitage, "John Milton: Poet Against Empire," in *Milton and Republicanism*, ed. David Armitage et al. (Cambridge, 1995). I should also mention three unpublished papers: Paul Brophy, " 'So Many Signs of Power and Rule': Colonial Discourse, Pastoralism, and the Representation of Autochthony in *Paradise Lost*," 1990; Balachandra Rajan, "Banyan Trees and Fig Leaves: Some Thoughts on Milton's India," 1991; and Bruce McLeod, "The 'Lordly Eye': Milton's Imperial Imagination," 1995.

3. Terry Eagleton, "Discourse and Discos," *Times Literary Supplement*, 15 July 1994, p. 3.

4. See Peter Brooks, "Frighted with False Fire," *Times Literary Supplement*, 26 May 1995, pp. 10–11.

5. Thomas S. Kuhn, *The Structure of Scientific Revolutions*, 2nd ed. (Chicago, 1970), esp. pp. 10–34.

6. Patricia A. Parker, *Inescapable Romance: Studies in the Poetics of a Mode* (Princeton, 1979), p. 220.

7. David Bromwich, *A Choice of Inheritance: Self and Community from Edmund Burke to Robert Frost* (Cambridge, Mass., 1989), p. 279. For Quint's praise of Bromwich's "searching" critique, see *Epic and Empire*, p. 370.

8. Milton's poetry is quoted from *The Works of John Milton*, ed. Frank Allen Patterson et al., 18 vols. (New York, 1931–38), and his prose, unless otherwise indicated, from *Complete*

Prose Works of John Milton, ed. Don M. Wolfe et al., 8 vols. (New Haven, 1953–82). Hereafter cited as CM and YP, respectively.

9. Evans, *Paradise Lost: Books IX–X,* pp. 46–47.

10. See Quint, *Epic and Empire,* p. 169: "Unlike the other European nations engaged in imperial and colonial expansion in the New World, the Spaniards seriously worried about the legality and morality of their project."

11. Much more pointedly, he may also be offering his readers an idealized view of those smaller, domestic merchants who were excluded from overseas commerce by the increasingly Royalist "great Marchants" of the chartered companies. For the rivalry between the two groups, see Robert Brenner, *Merchants and Revolution: Commercial Change, Political Conflict, and London's Overseas Traders, 1550–1653* (Princeton, 1993), esp. pp. 83–89.

12. Richard Hakluyt the younger, Epistle Dedicatory, *The Principal Navigations of the English Nation,* Vol. II of *The Original Writings & Correspondence of the Two Richard Hakluyts,* ed. E.G.R. Taylor, 2 vols. (1589; rpt. Nendeln, Liechtenstein, 1967), p. 400; *A True Declaration of the State of Virginia,* vol. V of *New American World: A Documentary History of North America to 1612,* ed. D. B. Quinn, 5 vols. (New York, 1979), p. 250.

13. "And so the Inhabiters of Hormuz doe say, that all the world is a ring, and Hormuz is the stone of it." "Relations of Ormuz," in vol. X of Samuel Purchas, *Hakluytus Posthumus, or Purchas His Pilgrimes* (1625), 20 vols. (1905–07; rpt. New York, 1965), p. 324. See also Campbell, "The Wealth of Ormus," pp. 22–23, Cawley, *Milton and the Literature of Travel,* pp. 78–79, and Sir William Foster, *England's Quest of Eastern Trade* (London, 1937), pp. 295–313.

14. See William Riley Parker, *Milton: A Biography,* 2 vols. (Oxford, 1968), vol. I, pp. 6–8; vol. II, pp. 698–701.

15. See YP VIII, p. 459.

16. M.M.S., *The Spanish Colonie* (London, 1583); rpt. in Purchas, *Hakluytus Posthumus,* vol. XVIII, pp. 83–180.

17. Richard Hakluyt the younger sets the tone in his *Discourse of Western Planting* (London, 1584); rpt. in *Original Writings,* ed. Taylor, vol. II, pp. 211–326, esp. pp. 257–65. See also Richard Helgerson, *Forms of Nationhood: The Elizabethan Writing of England* (Chicago, 1992), pp. 151–91, esp. p. 185.

18. Sir Walter Ralegh, *The Discoverie of the Large, Rich, and Bewtiful Empyre of Guiana* (1596; rpt. New York, 1968), p. 7. On Ralegh's Spenserian self-representation, see Louis Montrose, "The Work of Gender in the Discourse of Discovery," *Representations* XXXIII (1991): 177–217, esp. 187. See also Mary C. Fuller, "Ralegh's Fugitive Gold: Reference and Deferral in *The Discoverie of Guiana," Representations* XXXIII (1991), 42–64.

19. On the propaganda for the Western Design, see Karen Ordahl Kupperman, "Errand to the Indies: Puritan Colonization from Providence Island through the Western Design," *William and Mary Quarterly,* 3rd ser., XLV, no. 1 (1988): 70–99, and Janet Clare, "The Production and Reception of Davenant's *Cruelty of the Spaniards in Peru," MLR* XXXIX, no. 4 (1994): 832–41.

20. Sir William Davenant, *The Cruelty of the Spaniards in Peru,* in *The Works of Sir William Davenant,* 2 vols. (1673; rpt. New York, 1968), vol. II, pp. 103–14, esp. pp. 111–14. John Phillips, *The Tears of the Indians* (1656; rpt. Stanford, n.d.), sig. A8ᵛ.

21. CM XIII, pp. 509–63, esp. pp. 517, 555. Since J. Max Patrick's rejection in YP V, pp. 711–12, the tide of critical opinion has turned against Milton's authorship of the *Declaration.* While Kiernan, "Milton in Heaven," p. 175, and Clare, "Production and Reception," p. 835, seem unaware that there is an issue, Kupperman, "Errand to the Indies," p. 94, concludes that the manifesto "was written by a committee headed by Nathaniel Fiennes." Robert T. Fallon, *Milton in Government* (University Park, Pa., 1993), pp. 99–100, follows Patrick, and

Dustin Griffin, *Regaining Paradise: Milton in the Eighteenth Century* (Cambridge, 1986), p. 279, persuasively argues that Thomas Birch's attribution of the Manifesto to Milton in 1738 was conditioned by impending hostilities with Spain and the parliamentary opposition's desire to enlist the prestige of Milton's name in its attacks on Walpole's reluctance to go to war.

22. See Fallon, *Milton in Government*, pp. 88–100, 229–46; *The Faerie Queene* V, x, 8ff.

23. Sir Francis Bacon, "Of Plantations," in *The Essayes or Counsels, Civill and Morall*, ed. Michael Kiernan (1625; rpt. Oxford, 1985), p. 106. The same point, but with the added authority of Genesis i, 28, is made in the *Declaration Against Spain*: "The best Title, that any can have to what they possess in those parts of America, is Plantation and Possession, where there were no Inhabitants, or where there were any, by their consent, or at least in such waste and desolate parts of their Countries, as they are not able in any measure to plant, and possesse; (God having made the world for the use of men, and ordained them to replenish the same.)" (CM XIII, p. 555).

24. Compare Cawley, *Milton and the Literature of Travel*, and Joseph E. Duncan, *Milton's Earthly Paradise: A Historical Study of Eden* (Minneapolis, 1972), esp. pp. 188–233, 234–42.

25. Robert Johnson, *Nova Britannia* (London, 1609), in Quinn, *New American World*, vol. V, p. 239. Compare Annette Kolodny, *The Lay of the Land: Metaphor as Experience and History in American Life and Letters* (Chapel Hill, 1975), esp. pp. 10–25. "Virginias Verger," in Purchas, *Hakluytus Posthumus*, vol. XIX, pp. 243, 242.

26. Quinn, *New American World*, vol. 5, p. 238. On the centrality of civility, see, for instance, Nicholas Canny's seminal article, "The Ideology of English Colonization: From Ireland to America," *William and Mary Quarterly*, 3rd ser. XXX (1973): 575–98.

27. Compare Montrose, "The Work of Gender," 186–88.

28. For a different way of interpreting the colonial uses of romance, see Stephen Greenblatt, *Marvelous Possessions: The Wonder of the New World* (Chicago, 1991), esp. pp. 132–33.

29. Especially suggestive is Terry Eagleton's critique of Adorno in *Ideology: An Introduction* (London, 1991), esp. pp. 126–27, 221–24, and Fredric Jameson, *The Political Unconscious: Narrative as a Socially Symbolic Act* (Ithaca, N.Y., 1981), pp. 103–50.

30. Compare Paul Stevens, *Imagination and the Presence of Shakespeare in "Paradise Lost"* (Madison, 1985), pp. 11–45, esp. pp. 21–22.

31. Quoted from *The Tempest*, ed. Stephen Orgel (Oxford, 1987). For *The Tempest* as a colonial romance, see especially Paul Brown, " 'This Thing of Darkness I Acknowledge Mine': *The Tempest* and the Discourse of Colonialism," in *Political Shakespeare: New Essays in Cultural Materialism*, ed. Jonathan Dollimore and Alan Sinfield (Manchester, 1985), pp. 48–71.

32. Greenblatt, *Marvelous Possessions*, pp. 17–19: "The experience of wonder seems to resist recuperation, containment, ideological incorporation."

33. George Percy, "A Discourse of the Plantation of the Southern Colonie in Virginia" (1606–07), in Quinn, *New American World*, vol. V, p. 268.

34. John B. Broadbent, *Some Graver Subject: An Essay on "Paradise Lost"* (1960; rpt. London, 1967), p. 184.

35. Pierre Bourdieu, *The Logic of Practice*, trans. Richard Nice (Stanford, Calif., 1990), p. 53; Eagleton, *Ideology*, p. 156.

36. Compare Edmund Spenser, *A View of the Present State of Ireland*, ed. W. L. Renwick (Oxford, 1970), esp. pp. 63–69, and John Rolfe, "Letter to Sir Thomas Dale," in Ralph Hamor, *A True Discourse of the Present Estate of Virginia* (1615; rpt. New York, 1971), pp. 61–68.

37. On the difference between moral rules and pollution rules, see Mary Douglas, *Purity and Danger: An Analysis of Concepts of Pollution and Taboo* (London, 1966), esp. pp. 129–39.

38. Compare *Paradise Lost* VI, 644–47. Cotton Mather, *Magnalia Christi Americana*, Books I and II, ed. Kenneth B. Murdock (Cambridge, Mass., 1977), p. 298. George F. Sensabaugh, *Milton in Early America* (Princeton, 1964) is the strongest advocate for the shaping influence of Milton in colonial America. Sensabaugh's views are contested by Keith W. F. Stavely, especially in "The World All Before Them: Milton and the Rising Glory of America," *Studies in Eighteenth-Century Culture* XX (1990): 147–64. However, in his effort to distance the poet, whom he considers increasingly antimillenarian and antinationalist, from the imperialism of American revolutionary rhetoric, Stavely inadvertently reveals just how imperial a poem many colonial Americans took *Paradise Lost* to be. Their "misreading," if it is one, constitutes eloquent testimony to the poem's ideological force.

39. The "Digression" was written in 1649 and, according to Edward Phillips, could not pass the licensor in 1670. For the complex but fascinating political and textual history of the "Digression," see Nicholas von Maltzahn, *Milton's "History of Britain": Republican Historiography in the English Revolution* (Oxford, 1991), pp. 1–21, 22–48, esp. pp. 45–46.

40. Compare Barnaby, "Milton and the Imperial Republic," pp. 78–81.

41. Lawrence, *Apocalypse* (1931; rpt. London, 1972), p. 13; Knoppers, *Historicizing Milton: Spectacle, Power, and Poetry in Restoration England* (Athens, Ga., 1994), pp. 123–41, esp. pp. 137–41.

MILTON, GALILEO, AND SUNSPOTS: OPTICS AND CERTAINTY IN *PARADISE LOST*

Amy Boesky

How to see? Where to see from? What limits to vision? What to see for? Whom to see with? Who gets to have more than one point of view? . . . What other sensory powers do we wish to cultivate besides vision?

Donna Haraway, Simians, Cyborgs, and Women (1991)

R EADERS OF MILTON have long been intrigued and puzzled by what has come to be called "the Galileo question" in *Paradise Lost*. Galileo is the sole contemporary to be mentioned in the epic, once by name and twice "pronominally." As a symbol (perhaps *the* symbol) of augmented vision in the poem, Galileo can be read as a human counterpart to the archangel Raphael, a seer whose vision points beyond the bars of mortal knowledge to things divine. Conversely, Galileo may be seen as subtly satanic in the epic, connected to "the conflict of vision, sight, appearance, illusion and belief [that] is the key to the fall of man."[1] In this essay I will suggest that Galileo is an overdetermined figure for Milton, representing both the powers of mortal vision and its fallibility. Moreover, I will offer a new source for the astronomer's equivocal presentation in *Paradise Lost*, proposing that Milton's multivalent allusions to Galileo refer repeatedly to his *Letters on Sunspots* (1613), an epistolary sequence which itself takes the rival claims between certainty and uncertainty for subject.

Galileo is alluded to three times in *Paradise Lost*. In each case his name is mentioned in conjunction with the instrument which secured his fame: the optic glass or telescope. This connection has been widely acknowledged, but what has not been remarked is that each of the three passages in which the astronomer is mentioned concludes its representation of observation with the image of a "spot" or "spottiness." Galileo is first introduced in *Paradise Lost* in Book I as the Bard describes Satan's shield, hanging from his shoulder "like the Moon," whose orb

> Through Optic Glass the *Tuscan* Artist views
> At Ev'ning from the top of *Fesole*,

> Or in *Valdarno*, to descry new Lands,
> Rivers or Mountains in her spotty Globe.   (288–91)[2]

What we are introduced to here, as Julia Walker points out, is both a new way of seeing and a new visual field, and what is observed in this instance is not merely the moon, but the spottiness of its surface. The spots on the moon, as Galileo described them in *Sidereus Nuncius*, were discolorations or shadows which he distinguished from the "large" or "ancient" spots detected since antiquity. The new, smaller, and more numerous spots, according to Galileo, argued against the static perfection of heavenly bodies maintained by so many contemporary scientists and philosophers:

> The latter spots had never been seen by anyone before me. From observations of these spots repeated many times I have been led to the opinion and conviction that the surface of the moon is not smooth, uniform, and precisely spherical as a great number of philosophers believe it (and the other heavenly bodies) to be, but is uneven, rough, and full of cavities and prominences, being not unlike the face of the earth, relieved by chains of mountains and deep valleys.[3]

While similarities between earth and heavenly bodies could be seen as ennobling, spots on the moon's face argued against its perfection; by association, earth was understood to be similarly "spotty," rough, and pocked, a face less than perfect (see fig. 1). Milton's conjunction between observation, telescopes, and spottiness is reiterated in Book III of *Paradise Lost* when Satan lands on the sun before beginning his descent to Mount Niphates and on to Eden. Here the Bard compares the fallen angel to a sunspot: "There lands the Fiend, a *spot* like which perhaps / Astronomer in the Sun's lucent Orb / Through his glaz'd Optic Tube yet never saw" (588–90, italics mine). This passage has provoked interest because of the complexities of the phrase "yet never saw," a phrase that disqualifies the image that precedes it. As such, it is part of a larger pattern in the poem discussed by Stanley Fish in *Surprised by Sin:* the function of the allusion is not to secure materiality, but to occlude it. Has the astronomer seen commensurate spots at all? Maybe and maybe not; the reader is asked to call up this image only to find it challenged. "The implication is personal," Fish claims. "The similes and many other effects say to the reader: 'I know that you rely upon your senses for your apprehension of reality, but they are unreliable and hopelessly limited.' " Fish adds that it is significant for Galileo to have been introduced at this point, for "the Tuscan artist's glass represents the furthest extension of perception, and is not enough." In a footnote, Fish points out that Galileo's association with visual imperfection is further supported by the consistent pattern of details that recurs each time the astronomer is alluded to in the

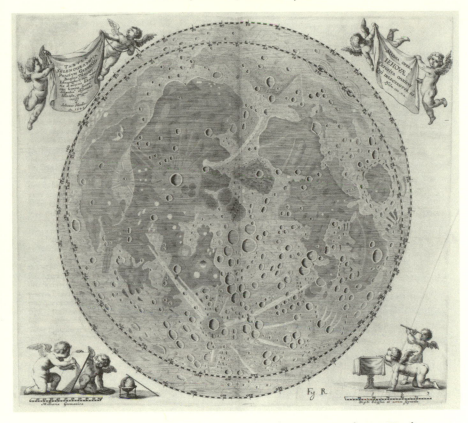

Fig. 1. The spotty surface of the moon, as seen through a telescope. From Johannes Hevelius, *Selenographia* (1647). By permission of Houghton Library, Harvard University.

epic, a pattern comprising "Galileo, the moon, spots (representing an unclear vision), etc."[4]

That "pattern" appears frequently and complexly enough in the epic to warrant further consideration. In Book I Satan's shield is compared to the "spotty Globe" of the moon; in Book III the fiend lands on the sun's lucent orb like "a spot," and finally, in Book V, Galileo's name is directly introduced in a passage that describes powerful observation culminating in the discovery of "a cloudy spot":

> As when by night the Glass
> Of *Galileo*, less assur'd, observes
> Imagind Lands and Regions in the Moon:
> Or Pilot from amidst the *Cyclades*

Delos or *Samos* first appearing kenns
A cloudy spot.   (261–66)

In this passage the power of Galileo's "glass" is linked to the power of exploration as it charts new lands and regions, a bit like the colonial excursions
of Satan in Book II, where Satan seeks a "new world" (II, 403), "happy Ile"
(II, 410), or "some mild Zone" (II, 397) in order to establish a new empire.
In *Sidereus Nuncius*, Galileo also describes telescopic vision in imperial
terms, first in his dedication to Cosimo II, where he suggests the stars can
be seen as "human monuments" and the heavens as a site for the inscription
of man's wit, and again in the opening passages of his *Astronomical Message:*
"Surely," he argues, "it is a great thing to increase the numerous host of
fixed stars previously visible to the unaided vision, adding countless more
which have never before been seen, exposing these plainly to the eye in
numbers ten times exceeding the old and familiar stars." While such visual
aggrandizement is recalled by the Bard's description of Raphael's descent
in Book V, it is at the same time suggestively challenged in Milton's passage,
both by the qualifying phrase "less assur'd" and by the problematic adjective "imagin'd." As Donald Friedman points out, this passage draws on what
some of Galileo's students have called "the ambiguity that was characteristic
of [Galileo's] work as productive scientist":

Thus the Tuscan artist sees "Imagined lands" in the moon, perhaps because he
imagines them, or because the telescope presents images of them, or because his
readers and believers imagine them, or because, finally, others have imagined them
and Galileo has succeeded in observing them truly. Milton resolves this tangle no
more definitively than Raphael decides between the two great systems of cosmology.

The word *spot* contributes importantly to this sense of ambiguity, and the
recurrence of the word in conjunction with Galileo and his optic glass bears
further consideration, especially as it complicates the passages in Book VIII
which the Galileo allusions build toward: Adam's instruction from Raphael
concerning celestial movement, and the poem's pronouncement on scientific curiosity and the limits of knowledge. Five times in *Paradise Lost* the
word *spot* is associated with optic lenses, astronomical investigation, and the
risks of curiosity and of certitude, and in each instance the word is associated both with uncertainty and with temptation.[5]

For Milton, the word *spot* most often suggests a blemish or stain.[6] So
Adam assures Eve in Book V of *Paradise Lost* that "evil into the mind of
God or Man / May come and go, so unapprov'd, and leave / No spot or
blame behind" (117–19). The speaker of *Sonnet XXIII* imagines his "late
espoused saint" brought back from the grave, washed clean of the "spot of

childbed taint," and in *Sonnet XXII,* writing to Cyriack Skinner on his blindness, Milton describes the way his eyes have "forgot" seeing, "though clear / To outward view of blemish or of spot." In Milton's prose as well,[7] "spot" often implies a stain or blemish, as opposed to the "Spotlesse Truth" (*Of Reformation,* YP I, p. 535), or the "Spotlesse, and undecaying robe of Truth" (*Of Prelatical Episcopacy,* YP I, p. 639). In *Of Reformation,* Milton seeks a force powerful "enough to wash off the originall Spot without the Scratch" (YP I, p. 523); in *Reason of Church-Government* he demurs lest "any wrincle or spot should be found in presbyterial government" (YP I, p. 834), and in *An Apology Against a Pamphlet,* he protests lest "on my garment the least spot, or blemish in good name" should appear (YP I, p. 871). The word *spot* could mean a location or a site as well as a blemish in the seventeenth century, as it does today.[8] But for Milton even this usage carries pejorative connotations, as the Attendant Spirit complains in *Comus* when sent down from heaven to visit the "smoak and stirr of this dim spot, / Which men call Earth" (5–6). Even when "spot" as a place appears to have positive associations, they are subtly undermined. At the end of Book III in *Paradise Lost,* Uriel, "the sharpest sighted spirit of all in Heav'n" (691), points Satan to Eden: "That spot to which I point is *Paradise,* / *Adams* abode, those loftie shades his Bowr" (733–34). Prelapsarian Eden is seen as a spot here, but it is Satan (through Uriel) who identifies it as such. The second and last time Eden is described in the epic as a spot, Satan's perspective is more sinisterly employed and scopic vision more clearly revealed as treacherous. This is the moment just before the Fall in Book IX when Satan, in serpent form, undulates through the flowers, "now hid, now seen," to find Eve "separate" from Adam (436, 423). Satan weaves:

> Among thick-wov'n Arborets and Flowrs
> Imborderd on each Bank, the hand of *Eve:*
> Spot more delicious than those Gardens feign'd
> Or of reviv'd *Adonis,* or renownd
> *Alcinous,* host of old *Laertes* Son
> . . . .
> Much hee the Place admir'd, the Person more.   (437–41, 444)

Satan's conjunction in this passage between the place of Paradise and the person of Eve is strengthened by the proximity between the words *Eve* and *spot,* a proximity interrupted only by Eve's "hand": this hand (glossed by Shawcross, as by Hughes, Orgel, and Goldberg as "handiwork") has created beauty, but Satan anticipates it will soon be stained: "So saying, her rash hand, in evil hour / Forth reaching to the Fruit, she pluck'd, she eat" (IX,

780–81). In Milton's writing, then, "spots" signify a stain or blemish, or are suggestively associated with sites (spots) of temptation, with the incitement to improved or higher knowledge.[9]

Why, then, is Galileo's optic glass so firmly associated with spots in Milton's epic? The answer may be partly that Galileo's vision is problematic in *Paradise Lost*, intended as a foil for the vision of the Bard as well as the reader. We are asked, that is, to oversee the preliminary or partial vision represented by the skilled astronomer and his special instrument. The spots detected through the astronomer's optic glass are at once flaws in vision's subject and vision's subject itself, for it is the "cloudy spot" in the Aegean which first alerts the Pilot that land is near, and the spots in the moon may in fact be "new lands / Rivers or Mountains," not imagined, but real. These spots point to new implications for Galileo's recurrence in the epic. By taking seriously what Fish brushes off as Milton's "implied equality between spot and fiend" in Book III, the passages in which "spot" and observation appear together can be seen to comprise a complex conceit in which vision, enlargement, and edification are importantly connected. In other words, Milton's "implied equality between spot and fiend" may point to something more in the epic than just another reminder that human vision is inferior to that of God.

In *Areopagitica*, Milton relays that he met Galileo in 1638 during his extended travels in Italy, before he was recalled to England by the first stirrings of the Civil War. Milton was twenty-nine and just beginning his career; Galileo was old, infirm, and under house arrest: "There it was that I found and visited the famous Galileo, grown old, a prisoner to the Inquisition for thinking in astronomy otherwise than the Franciscan and Dominican liscensers thought" (YP II, p. 538). It is difficult to read this passage without recognizing the potency for Milton of Galileo as a symbol, a martyr, as Julia Walker puts it, "to the cause of intellectual freedom." But even this brief relation has provoked debate. In 1918, S. B. Liljegren contended that Milton's visit was a fiction, and while Liljegren's charge has been rebutted, some uncertainty remains; as Donald Friedman observes, "the absence of any mention of the Arcetri visit by Milton, Galileo, or their friends in any surviving document remains puzzling, especially since, in a letter to Lukas Holste written from Florence, Milton at least refers to other Italians whose acquaintance distinguished his visit to Rome."[10]

Perhaps the most interesting issue at stake in this debate is whether Milton knew then or later of Galileo's blindness, a fact which a meeting with the astronomer in 1638 clearly would have provided.[11] Milton makes no mention of Galileo's blindness either in *Areopagitica* or in *Paradise Lost*, where, Stanley Fish argues, the "Tuscan Artist" possesses "the furthest extension of human perception." A. N. Wilson, who does not question that the famous meeting took place, suggests that Milton "forgets" the astronomer's blindness "for poetic purposes" in *Paradise Lost*. But in an epic whose Bard bemoans his own blindness with painful detail, and whose allusions to Galileo emphasize exceptional (if humanly limited) powers of vision, such forgetting would be especially puzzling. If Milton did in fact meet with Galileo in 1638, and not just with his students, we must assume that Galileo's blindness is implicitly encoded in his allusions in *Paradise Lost*—part of what John Guillory calls the poem's "repressed content." In *Paradise Lost*, then, Galileo is a reminder of mortal blindness as much as a symbol of "augmented vision." His presence in the poem, as Schwartz puts it, "invites not only speculation about astronomy, then, but also questions about power and its abuses, desire and its frustrations."[12]

For modern readers, "the Galileo question" has become a debate about epistemology as much as about history and evidence. Do the allusions to Galileo suggest an astronomically conservative or resistant Milton, reluctant to entirely repudiate the Ptolemaic universe already long refuted by many of his contemporaries? Or instead are the allusions intended to suggest Milton's identification with Galileo's intellectual courage, his enthusiasm for "the implications of the new philosophy" despite Raphael's reluctance in *Paradise Lost* to throw his support behind one scientific theory or another? Even the most sanguine interpreters of Galileo's role in the epic have conceded that Milton is equivocal elsewhere about the use of optic lenses; for instance, it is Satan in *Paradise Regained* who proffers the Son his "aery microscope" to magnify the false visions of Athens and Rome.[13] In this uneasiness, Milton shared contemporary ambivalence toward the new optical lenses.[14] Concern about the accuracy as well as the morality of telescopic lenses was fairly widespread in the Restoration; some saw the telescopic lens, like the *camera obscura*, as a contrivance to trick or deceive the senses. In the second part of *Hudibras* (1663–64), Samuel Butler satirizes Sidrophel, a "conj'rer" and "profound gymnosophist," for constructing a telescope only "to know / If the moon shine at full or no." By the 1660s the new lenses were gaining widespread popularity as toys or trifles. Samuel Pepys, an enthusiast for every scientific novelty, describes in his diary a dinner party in 1665 at which each guest purchased a "pocket glasse" from "a Perspective glasse maker." For Pepys, the scopophilic pleasure of the pocket telescope was hardly subtle. From a church pew, he used his "glass" to ogle women: "I did entertain myself with my perspective glass up and down the church, by which I had the great pleasure of seeing and gazing at a great many very fine women; and what with that, and sleeping, I passed away the time till sermon was done."[15] The pocket glass gratified the visual curiosity Augustine referred to as "the lust of the eye." By the 1690s "perspective glasses" began to be advertised for sale to the English public in almanacs, but the popularity of such lenses in certain spheres (particularly with the middle classes and with women) helped to discredit them in others; Robert Hooke, for example, complained that the decline of microscopic studies in the late seventeenth century was a consequence of the instrument's use "for Diversion and Pasttime, and that by reason it is become a portable Instrument, and easy to be carried in one's pocket." Some feared the new lenses; others feared they were being degraded into mere toys (see figs. 2 and 3).[16]

For Milton, the telescope appears to be an overdetermined symbol, a magnification of vision that is at once an augmentation and a distortion, what Donna Haraway calls a "god-trick." I do not think that Milton forgets Galileo's blindness in *Paradise Lost;* rather, blindness becomes associated for him with the telescope, an instrument Milton suspected not because he was less prescient than his contemporaries, but because he questioned the scopic power represented by Galileo's optic glass (Pepys's "great pleasure of seeing and gazing") even as he applauded it. In Schwartz's terms, the "aggression of the voyeur" is repeatedly challenged in *Paradise Lost* rather than reductively assigned, not the least importantly because the reader engages in the scopophilic pleasures Galileo's optic glass invites. Situating Milton's astronomical allusions in *Paradise Lost* more precisely in Galileo's writings will emphasize the extent to which these allusions are concerned both with the potentialities and dangers of visual curiosity. As Friedman points out, "every allusion in the poem to Galileo and to his major discoveries, although clearly intended still to contribute to a sense of intellectual courage, its motives and implications, is also shadowed by implied doubts, or at least uncertainties, about the subject of scientific hypotheses, the validity of empirical observation, and particularly about the spiritual and psychic sources of invention." Like Galileo's *Sunspot Letters,* Milton's multivalent allusions to Galileo and to the telescope take the rival claims between certainty and uncertainty for subject.[17]

On May 12, 1612, Galileo sent Frederico Cesi a copy of the first of his letters on sunspots, accompanied by a covering letter in which he declared that he had finally concluded (and believed he could now demonstrate) that sunspots were "contiguous to the surface of the solar body, where they are continually generated and dissolved, just like clouds around the earth, and are carried around by the sun itself, which turns on itself in a lunar month with a revolution similar [in direction] to those others of the planets." Gali-

Fig. 2. Cherubs using optical instruments. From *La Dioptrique oculaire*, Père Cherubin d'Orleans (1671). By permission of Houghton Library, Harvard University.

Fig. 3. Angels giving the gift of telescopes to man, with the injunction "Videte opera domini." From *La Dioptrique oculaire*, Père Cherubin d'Orleans. By permission of Houghton Library, Harvard University.

leo clearly recognized the revolutionary nature of his claims. His news, he continued to Cesi, "will be the funeral, or rather the extremity and Last Judgment of pseudophilosophy."[18] But he could not have anticipated the crisis these letters would create both in his own career and in contemporary relations between the church and the new science. At issue in the sunspot letters was a series of controversial questions: is the sun subject to mutations and change, as is the earth? Can the sun have spots or "blemishes" on its surface? And if the sun does have spots, and if their motion can be tracked mathematically, what are the implications for prior and current theories of celestial motion?

Galileo's *History and Demonstrations Concerning Sunspots and Their Phenomena* was addressed to a wealthy merchant named Welser who solicited it after having received a separate series of letters on the same subject by a Jesuit professor from Ingolstadt, Christopher Scheiner. Scheiner, a neo-Aristotelian, argued that the sunspots were actually planets or "fixed stars," and not "blemishes" on the surface of the sun. While systematically refuting Scheiner's claims, and hastening to assert his own priority in having discovered spots on the sun, Galileo takes up larger questions in the sunspot letters as well, questions such as what enables scientific certainty, what can be proven and what cannot, and what subjects are appropriate for scientific study. Like Adam's exchange with Raphael in Books V–VIII of *Paradise Lost,* Galileo's exchange with Welser is modeled on the Platonic dialogue. "With response to these solar spots," Welser begins the correspondence, "please do me the favor of telling me frankly your opinion—whether you judge them to be made of starry matter or not; where you believe them to be situated, and what their motion is."[19]

Despite his confidence in disproving Scheiner's claims, Galileo's first letter begins cautiously, almost hesitantly. He warns that he of all people must be circumspect in his claims: "I, indeed, must be more cautious than most other people in pronouncing upon anything new." Claiming that it is much harder to "discover the truth than to refute what is false," he says it is his intention to prove what he calls "a negative case," rather like Milton's "negative similes" (the sunspots "never seen") for he can be more certain of knowing "what sunspots are not than what they really are." The rhetoric of the first sunspot letter is clouded with qualification and equivocation: "I am not affirming or denying that the spots are located on the sun; I merely say that it is insufficiently proved that they are not" (*Letters,* p. 95). Galileo deliberately holds back from affirming "any positive conclusion about their nature": "The substance of the spots might be any of a thousand things unknown and unimaginable to us, while the phenomena commonly observed in them—their shapes, their opacity, and their movement—may lie partly or wholly outside the realm of our general knowledge" (p. 98). Like Milton's Raphael, Galileo relies on accommodated language to express the ineffable essence of these spots: "Let them be vapors or exhalations, then, or clouds, or fumes sent out from the sun's globe or attracted there from other places; I do not decide on this—and they may be any of a thousand other things not perceived by us" (p. 112). The material of sunspots is amorphous, vaporous, in constant flux. They are "variable in shape and size . . . they are movable to some extent by little irregular motions; and . . . they are all generated and dissolved, some in longer and some in shorter times" (p. 100). The spots, like Milton's angels, are the essence of mutability; they constantly change their characteristics, shrinking and enlarging:

some are always being produced, and others dissolved. They vary in duration from one or two days to thirty or forty. For the most part they are of most irregular shape, and their shapes continually change, some quickly and violently, others more slowly and moderately. They also vary in darkness, appearing sometimes to condense and sometimes to spread out and rarefy. In addition to changing shape, some of them divide into three or four, and often several unite into one. (p. 106)

Given their indeterminate nature, the spots must be described by simile: "I liken the sunspots to clouds or smokes. Surely if anyone wished to imitate them by means of earthly materials, no better model could be found than to put some drops of incombustible bitumen on a red-hot iron plate" (p. 140). Like Raphael in Book V of *Paradise Lost*, Galileo is acutely aware of the inadequacy of language in describing "the secrets of another world" (569). So, like Raphael, Galileo likens "spiritual to corporal forms" (V, 573). In the face of the Aristotelian belief that the surface of the sun must be "perfect," immutable, and unblemished, Galileo argues that these "dense, obscure, and foggy materials" are produced even in "that part of the sky which deserves to be considered the most pure and serene of all—I mean in the very face of the sun" (*Letters*, p. 119). "The sun itself," he writes to Cesi, "indicates [mutations] to us with most manifest sensible experiences."[20] Against Scheiner, Galileo maintains that the spots are in constant flux and cannot possibly be "fixed stars": "The solar stars cannot be said to be fixed, for if they did not change with respect to one another it would be impossible to see the continual mutations that are observed in the spots, and the same patterns would always return":

Hence anyone who wished to maintain that the spots were a congeries of minute stars would have to introduce into the sky innumerable movements, tumultuous, uneven, and without any regularity. But this does not harmonize with any plausible philosophy. And to what purpose would it be done? To keep the heavens free from even the tiniest alteration of material. Well, if alteration were annihilation, the Peripatetics would have some reason for concern; but since it is nothing but mutation, there is no reason for such bitter hostility to it. . . . If the earth's small mutations do not threaten its existence (if, indeed, they are ornaments rather than imperfections in it), why deprive the other planets of them? Why fear so much for the dissolution of the sky as a result of alterations no more inimical than these?[21]

In 1612 Galileo asked Carlo Cardinal Conti how the church felt about admitting changes in the heavens. He was told that the Bible did not support Aristotle's belief in celestial perfection and immutability, and, if anything, suggested the contrary. But as Stillman Drake points out, Conti warned Galileo to be careful before drawing conclusions about the motion of sunspots.[22] In fact, Galileo was to conclude far more from his observations of these spots than that the heavens are mutable. The motion of sunspots, which Galileo was able to chart and to document through his telescope, left him "no doubt about the orbit of Venus. With absolute necessity we shall conclude, in agreement with the theories of the Pythagoreans and of Copernicus, that Venus revolves about the sun as do all the other planets" (*Letters*, pp. 93–94). This was Galileo's first published support of the Copernican theory of planetary motion. In the final paragraphs of his third sunspot letter, Galileo included remarks on his recent observations of the planet Saturn, whose moons had recently seemed to vanish. In 1614, Galileo theorized, the moons would reappear, confirming their harmony "with the great Copernican system." Once again Galileo uses the word "cloud" as a metaphor: "To the universal revelation of which doctrine [the Copernican system], propitious breezes are now seen to be directed towards us, leaving little fear of clouds or crosswinds" (*Letters*, p. 144). But here his early caution, like those clouds, seems to have disappeared, as if certainty itself were a kind of spot beneath the cloud of hesitancy and self-protection. In other words, Galileo moves in the sunspot letters from a position of caution and circumspection to a daring public defense of the Copernican theory of planetary motion. Sunspots may be the manifest subject of these letters, but embedded within them a series of competing subjects can be detected: chiefly, the possibilities and hazards of scientific certainty.

Critics have long observed the prominence of the astronomical debate in Book VIII of *Paradise Lost*. Throughout the epic the motion or fixity of the stars introduces a conjunction for Eve and for Adam between the ideas of beauty, spots, temptation, and the limits of vision. In Book VIII, Adam rephrases for Raphael a question Eve had asked of him in Book IV, wondering for whom the stars shine at night "when sleep hath shut all eyes?" (IV, 658). Strikingly, Adam had then "answered" the question he now paraphrases for Raphael, revealing the conditional and qualified status of the response as an utterance. After Raphael has relayed the story of Satan's fall and the War in Heaven, Adam thanks the "Divine Historian" for having allayed his thirst for knowledge, but admits that "something yet of doubt remains" (VIII, 13):

> When I behold this goodly Frame, this World
> Of Heav'n and Earth consisting, and compute,
> Thir magnitudes, this Earth a spot, a grain,
> An Atom, with the Firmament compar'd
> And all her numberd Starrs, that seem to rowl
> Space incomprehensible (for such
> Thir distance argues and thir swift return
> Diurnal) meerly to officiate light
> Round this opacous Earth, this punctual spot,
> One day and night; in all thir vast survey
> Useless besides, reasoning I oft admire,
> How Nature wise and frugal could commit
> Such disproportions.   (15–27)

What Adam wonders is how "Nature wise and frugal" could commit "with superfluous hand" so many millions of stars to orbit around the "sedentarie Earth," "that better might with farr less compass move." Who watches these stars? Who is watched by them? What is the center and what is the margin? In asking this question, Adam twice refers to the earth as a spot—"this Earth a spot, a grain" (17) and "this opacous Earth, this punctual Spot" (23), as if imagining how earth must appear from the sun, rather than the other way around. In the first sunspot letter Galileo had imagined the same phenomenon: "There is no doubt that if the earth shone with its own light and not by that of the sun, then to anyone who looked at it from afar it would exhibit congruent appearances" (*Letters*, p. 99). Like Galileo, Adam tries to imagine earth from another perspective, an earth decentered; his "spot," in other words, not as a place to look out from, but as a place to look to. This moment in the poem crucially connects vision with knowledge, with temptation, and with absence; it is here, for instance, that Eve absents herself from the dialogues, stepping away ostensibly to be "sole Auditress" later on, preferring "Her Husband the Relater," and consequently leaving the scene before Raphael is able to answer the question that had first been her own.[23]

Raphael's response for Adam seems at first a disappointment. It contradicts not only the letter but the spirit of Galileo's treatise on sunspots. After delineating several competing theories of celestial motion, Raphael concludes that it is not Adam's place to chose one or another:

But whether thus these things, or whether not,
Whether the Sun predominant in Heav'n
Rise on the Earth, or Earth rise on the Sun.
·········
Sollicit not thy thoughts with matters hid,
Leave them to God above, him serve and fear.
·········
Heav'n is for thee too high
To know what passes there; be lowlie wise:
Think onely what concerns thee and thy being;
Dream not of other worlds, what Creatures there,
Live, in what state, condition, or degree,
Contented that thus farr hath been reveal'd
Not of Earth onely but of highest Heav'n.

(VIII, 159–61, 167–68, 172–78)

This is a jarring moment in the dialogues and in the epic at large, an interdiction which is difficult to square with Milton's lifelong defense of intellectual freedom. Raphael's censure seems directly to contradict Galileo's final sunspot letter, in which he sets forth a defense of scientific curiosity. In comparison, Raphael's response seems all the more confining. Here is Galileo:

In my opinion we need not entirely give up contemplating things just because they are very remote from us, unless we have indeed determined that it is best to defer every act of reflection in favor of other occupations. . . . But if what we wish to fix in our minds is the apprehension of some properties of things, then it seems to me that we need not despair of our ability to acquire this respecting distant bodies just as well as those close at hand—and perhaps in some cases even more precisely in the former than in the latter. Who does not understand the periods and movements of the planets better than those of the waters of our various oceans? Was not the spherical shape of the moon discovered long before that of the earth, and much more easily? . . . Hence I should infer that although it may be vain to seek to determine the true substance of the sunspots, still it does not follow that we cannot know some properties of them, such as their location, motion, shape, size, opacity, mutability, generation, and dissolution. . . . And finally, by elevating us to the ultimate end of our labors, which is the love of the divine Artificer, this will keep us steadfast in the hope that we shall learn every other truth in Him.[24]

While Galileo, like Raphael, defends the right to read "this greate book of the universe"; ("For Heav'n / Is as the Book of God before thee set"), he construes the borders of that book less narrowly than does Raphael. But it is important to remember here that Raphael, allied as he is both with God and the Bard, is not identical to them, nor to Milton himself. Raphael may not know the answer to Adam's question; he may not be permitted to answer

it other than as he does. Manifestly, Adam, "cleerd of doubt," could not be
further from the daring rhetoric of Galileo on enquiry and curiosity:

> How fully hast thou satisfi'd mee, pure
> Intelligence of Heav'n, Angel serene,
> And freed from intricacies, taught to live
> The easiest way, nor with perplexing thoughts
> To interrupt the sweet of Life, from which
> God hath bid dwell farr off all anxious cares,
> And not molest us, unless we our selves
> Seek them with wandring thoughts, and notions vain. (VIII, 180–87)

But is Adam really "cleerd of doubt" here? What he tells Raphael, before
firmly turning the subject to his own autobiography, is that "the Mind or
Fancie is apt to rove," subject to motions ("wandring") as strong as the
motions of any sunspot:

> to know
> That which before us lies in daily life,
> Is the prime Wisdom; what is more, is fume,
> Or emptiness, or fond impertinence,
> And renders us in things that most concern
> Unpractis'd, unprepar'd, and still to seek.   (VIII, 192–97)

There is something too rote here in Adam's summation of what he now
knows, and it is interesting that he ends this part of his response, before
suggesting "a lower flight" from this "high pitch," with the suggestive
phrase "still to seek." It is true that Adam here dismisses more knowledge
as "fume," from the Latin *fumus*, or smoke. Galileo in the first of the sunspot
letters had also chosen the word *fume* to describe his sunspots: "Let them
be vapors or exhalations, then, or clouds, or fumes sent out from the sun's
globe." The mind or fancy is subject (like Galileo's sun) to imperfections, to
smokes or exhalations, vapors that rise from it and wander. While it is possible to see Adam's dismissal of such "fumes" securing Milton's skepticism
for Galileo's theories, Adam's certainty is subsequently proven by the poem
to be premature. He cannot yet be cleared of doubt, for he is about to fall;
the "fume" of wanting to know more is still present in him, as it is in Eve.
His "Fancie," as he puts it, is still subject to mutation, to "spots," to the
roughness and blemish of change.

How, then, are we to understand the resonance in *Paradise Lost* of
these multiple allusions to Galileo's optic glass and to sunspots?[25] The intertextual connection I am proposing might seem by now only to further complicate "the Galileo question." Why should Milton draw on the sunspot
letters, in which Galileo for the first time openly declared his support for

the Copernican theory of planetary motion, only to make heaven's emissary equivocate on this very question?

In the proem to Book III of *Paradise Lost*—the book of Milton's epic most centrally concerned with tropes of vision (dominated by images of foresight, oversight, and perspective, its first and last phrases containing the word *light*), Milton's Bard famously laments his blindness. Addressing the sun ("Hail holy light"), the Bard employs an astronomical conceit, comparing his blind eyes to stars "unvisited" by light:

> thee I revisit safe,
> And feel thy sovran vital Lamp; but thou
> Revisit'st not these eyes, that rowl in vain
> To find thy piercing ray, and find no dawn;
> So thick a drop serene hath quencht thir Orbs,
> Or dim suffusion veild.   (21–26)

Both "rowl" and "Orbs" here point ahead to Raphael's discussion of celestial movement in Book VIII, as does the "Book of knowledge fair" brought up by the Bard at line 47. But in this instance, the orbs of the Bard's eyes are occluded by cloud, a "dim suffusion veild," and the book of knowledge threatens to become a "Universal blanc," a "fume" or "emptiness." Because of his blindness the Bard asks "Holy light" to provide him with a different kind of vision, extraordinary and inward, a kind of knowledge facilitated rather than impeded by blindness:

> So much the rather thou Celestial light
> Shine inward, and the mind through all her powers
> Irradiate, there plant eyes, all mist from thence
> Purge and disperse, that I may see and tell
> Of things invisible to mortal sight.   (51–55)

Through the special power of "Celestial light," the Bard will be granted (literally) *insight*, the power to "see and tell / Of things invisible." Unlike Galileo's vision, which could be identified as the kind of "conquering gaze from nowhere" rejected by recent critics of Western technology, the Bard asks for inward vision, for knowledge which must be and in fact can only be situated within his own being. This embodied or situated knowledge, to use Donna Haraway's terms, differs from the technologically assisted "power to see and not be seen, to represent while escaping representation." Like Eve, the Bard sees himself seeing; his inward vision itself becomes a subject of his and of our own scrutiny.[26]

Dayton Haskin has argued that Raphael's response to Adam is intended less to curtail knowledge than to problematize it, less to give the wrong answer than to suggest that any specific and limited answer to Adam's question would be wrong.[27] In this way, as Herz maintains, Galileo's presence in the poem does emphasize the narrator's dedication to the ideals of enquiry, investigation, and to learning, but not in the sense we might expect. Paradoxically, it is Milton's subtle challenges to Galileo's optics which most strongly confirm his dedication to the open-endedness of scientific enquiry. If Galileo is intended merely as a symbol for mortal vision at its most powerful, why would Milton so repeatedly occlude his allusions with ambiguities? Instead, Galileo must be seen from two perspectives at once, for in *Paradise Lost* he represents not merely the power to see, but the ambiguities that such power elicits. His power to stimulate curiosity may not be commensurate with his power to supply answers. In fact, our desire for answers, like Adam's, becomes part of the subject of the poem's concluding books; if we read the epic's answers carefully, we should expect to be disappointed—redirected, we might say—more than consoled.[28] As Barbara Lewalski maintains, Raphael declines to answer Adam's question about celestial movement in Book VIII and instead "invents a form that will not resolve the issue but that will provide a model for scientific enquiry, then and later." This model of enquiry and open-endedness is very close to Haraway's utopian vision of "situated knowledge" in which "science becomes the paradigmatic model not of closure, but of that which is contestable and contested. . . . A splitting of sense, a confusion of voice and sight, rather than clear and distinct ideas, becomes the metaphor for the ground of the rational."[29]

Galileo's "spots" in *Paradise Lost*, then, are at once sites of certainty, courage, and genius, and contradictorily blind spots, markers for the limits and dangers of scopic power. Adam's declaration that he is satisfactorily "cleer'd of doubt" in Book VIII is a signal that he has not yet learned the complexities of divided or doubled vision. Even after Michael purges his eyes with "Euphrasie and Rue" (XI, 413), Adam has not yet learned the "nobler sight" of what is contestable and contested. Adam's fall is continuous, his punishment both that he must look and that he cannot see. However terrible the specular vision Michael offers, the most painful consequence of the Fall for Adam remains the fear that he will become a spectacle ("for this we may thank Adam"); or, like the captive Samson, a "gaze" (*SA* 568). Michael's prophetic visions work like a perspective glass for Adam, as Milton's epic does for its readers. Lacking his careful instruction, we must surmise that our work, far more than that of Adam, is impeded; we can see no more than one spot at a time.

Boston College

NOTES

1. Judith Scherer Herz, " 'For whom this glorious sight?' ": Dante, Milton, and the Galileo Question," in *Milton in Italy: Contexts, Images, Contradictions,* ed. Mario A. Di Cesare (Binghamton, 1991), pp. 147–57; Donald Friedman uses the term *pronominally* to discuss Galileo's introduction into the epic in "Galileo and the Art of Seeing," in ibid., p. 160; Neil Harris, "Galileo as Symbol: The 'Tuscan Artist' in *Paradise Lost,*" *Annali del'Instituto e Museo di Storia della Scienza di Firenze* X, no. 2 (1985): 20–21. For another satanic reading of Galileo in the poem, see Roy Flannagan, "Art, Artists, Galileo and Concordances," *MQ* XX, no. 3 (1986): 103–05. Flannagan points out that the word *artist* in the phrase "Tuscan artist" is the only occurrence in Milton's poetry, and that the word *artist* had strong associations to black magic and conjuring in the period. Among the critics who see Galileo as a symbol of intellectual courage for Milton are Julia Walker, "Milton and Galileo: The Art of Intellectual Canonization," in *Milton Studies* XXV, ed. James D. Simmonds (Pittsburgh, 1989); Herz, " 'For whom this glorious sight?' "; Harinder Marjara, *Contemplation of Created Things: Science in Paradise Lost* (Toronto, 1992); and Dayton Haskin, *Milton's Burden of Interpretation* (Philadelphia, 1994). Regina Schwartz, "Through the Optic Glass: Voyeurism and *Paradise Lost,*" in *Desire in the Renaissance: Psychoanalysis and Literature,* ed. Valeria Finucci and Regina Schwartz (Princeton, 1994), pp. 146–66, suggests that Galileo's "optic glass" works in the epic to suggestively critique scopophilic pleasure and to destabilize the conjunction between voyeurism and sadism.

2. *The Complete Poetry of John Milton,* ed. John T. Shawcross (New York, 1971), p. 258. All quotations from Milton's poetry will be cited from this edition.

3. Walker, "Milton and Galileo," pp. 110–11; Galileo, "The Starry Messenger," in *Discoveries and Opinions of Galileo,* trans. Stillman Drake (New York, 1957), p. 31.

4. Stanley Fish, *Surprised by Sin: The Reader in "Paradise Lost"* (Berkeley and Los Angeles, 1969), pp. 29n1, 28.

5. David Quint discusses the rhetoric of colonialism in Satan's voyage in *Epic and Empire: Politics and Generic Form From Virgil to Milton* (Princeton, 1993), pp. 253–56; Galileo, "The Starry Messenger," p. 27; Friedman, "Galileo and the Art of Seeing," p. 167.

6. This is the first meaning of the word supplied by the *OED,* which defines *spot* as "a moral stain, blot, or blemish; a stigma or disgrace."

7. Milton's prose works are from *Complete Prose Works of John Milton,* 8 vols., ed. Don M. Wolfe et al. (New Haven, 1953–82), hereafter referred to in the text as YP.

8. This is the eighth meaning supplied by the *OED:* "a particular place or locality of limited extent."

9. Along these lines, *spot* in the middle and later seventeenth century was also a kind of cosmetic. The beauty spot or "patch" was widely used in the period; in fact, Pepys complains about Margaret Cavendish's use of spots or patches to conceal blemishes. A helpful study of cosmetics in the period can be found in Frances Dolan, "Taking the Pencil Out of God's Hand: Art, Nature, and the Face-Painting Debate in Early Modern England," *PMLA* CVIII, no. 2 (1993): 224–39. Though her article does not directly discuss beauty spots, Dolan includes an image from John Bulwer, *A View of the People of the Whole World* (London, 1654), p. 233, in which two women are portrayed sporting "spots" or patches, "varied into all manner of shapes and figures." Strikingly, these figures are astronomical, consisting chiefly of stars and moons.

10. Walker, "Milton and Galileo," p. 109; S. B. Liljegren, *Studies in Milton* (Lund, 1918), 23–36; Friedman, "Galileo and the Art of Seeing," p. 153. Marjorie Nicolson reviews and dismisses Liljegren's charge in "Milton and the Telescope," in *Critical Essays on Milton from ELH,* ed. (Baltimore, 1969), pp. 22–23.

11. As Liljegren remarks, "About half a year before Milton's arrival, Galileo became blind. He therefore implored the Pope to let him move into the city, in order to try to cure his disease. The Inquisitor at Florence was questioned about the matter and confirmed the fact that Galileo was in a very sad condition, totally and irremediably blind, ill, and helpless" (*Studies in Milton*, p. 27).

12. Fish, *Surprised by Sin*, p. 28; Wilson, *The Life of John Milton* (Oxford, 1983), p. 91; D. Guillory, *Poetic Authority: Spenser, Milton, and Literary History*. New York: Columbia University Press, p. 157; Schwartz, "Through the Optic Glass, p. 148.

13. Nicolson, "Milton and the Telescope," pp. 21, 29.

14. See, for example, Joseph Glanvill, "Modern Improvements of Useful Knowledge" (1676), cited in I. Bernard Cohen, *Revolution in Science* (Cambridge, Mass., 1985), p. 143. Cohen summarizes the response to Galileo in the later seventeenth century, pp. 136–45.

15. Butler qtd. in Marjorie Hope Nicolson, *Pepys' Diary and the New Science* (Charlottesville, 1965), pp. 126–27; Pepys, May 26, 1667, cited in Nicolson, *Pepys' Diary*, pp. 22–23.

16. "Lust of the eye" cited by Schwartz, "Through the Optic Glass," p. 148; Hooke qtd. in Michael Hunter, *Science and Society in Restoration England* (Cambridge, 1981), pp. 84–85; see also Guillory, *Poetic Authority*, p. 157. In *Science and Society*, Hunter discusses contemporary reservations about optic lenses on p. 68. See Nicolson, *Pepys' Diary*, p. 22, for a discussion of Pepys's dinner party. Margaret Cavendish, in Gerald Dennis Meyer, *The Scientific Lady in England, 1650–1760*, articulated profound distrust for the optic glass and its "visions," complaining that "concave and convex glasses, and the like . . . represent the figure of an Object . . . very misformed and misshaped: also a Glass that is flaw'd, crack'd, or broke . . . will present numerous pictures of one Object." She concluded that "the best Optick is a perfect natural Eye, and a regular sensitive Perception, and the best Judg, is Reason; and the best Study, is Rational Contemplation joyned with the Observations of Regular Sense, but not deluding Arts; for Art is not only gross in comparison to Nature, but, for the most part, deformed and defective."

17. Haraway, *Simians, Cyborgs, and Women: The Reinvention of Nature* (New York, 1991), p. 191; Schwartz, "Through the Optic Glass," esp. p. 153–; Friedman, "Galileo and the Art of Seeing," p. 166.

18. Stillman Drake, *Galileo at Work: His Scientific Biography* (Chicago, 1978), p. 183.

19. *History and Demonstrations Concerning Sunspots and Their Phenomena, Contained in Three Letters, Written to the Illustrious Mark Welser, Duumvir of Augsburg and Counselor to His Imperial Majesty* (1613), in *Discoveries and Opinions of Galileo*, p. 89. Hereafter referred to in the text as *Letters. An Account of Her Rise, with Emphasis on the Major Roles of the Telescope and Microscope* (Berkeley: University of California Press, 1955), p. 4.

20. Drake, *Galileo at Work*, p. 183.

21. Ibid., pp. 201–02.

22. Ibid., p. 189.

23. To my mind, Eve's withdrawal at the beginning of Book VIII has not yet been satisfactorily explained, and I would surmise that its revaluation will further complicate what I am identifying as the conditional nature of questions and answers both in this Book and in Book IV.

24. *Galileo at Work*, pp. 199–200.

25. Based on references to Galileo in Milton's work, Judith Herz, " 'For whom this glorious sight?' " p. 155n14, maintains that Milton knew the sunspot letters.

26. Haraway, *Simians, Cyborgs, and Women*, pp. 188, 192.

27. Haskin, *Milton's Burden of Interpretation*, pp. 200–04.

28. Stanley Fish, "Transmuting the Lump: *Paradise Lost*, 1942–1979," in *Doing What*

Comes Naturally: Change, Rhetoric, and the Practice of Theory in Literary and Legal Studies (Durham, 1989), pp. 247–93.

29. Lewalski, *"Paradise Lost" and the Rhetoric of Literary Forms*, p. 46; Haraway, *Simians, Cyborgs, and Women*, p. 198.

JOHN MILTON'S *PARADISE LOST* AND *DE DOCTRINA CHRISTIANA* ON PREDESTINATION

Paul R. Sellin

W HEN IN THE summer of 1991 William Hunter questioned the authorship of *De doctrina Christiana*, he set, as British colleagues like to say, the cat among the pigeons. Although there has been a shower of replies striving to refute him, much has been in vain because proving him wrong does not in itself clinch the attribution as automatically as many seem to think. For tough-minded book people, at least, the burden of proof is on those affirming the attribution, not on Hunter, and until the matter of authorship is settled, the received wont of reading *Paradise Lost* or Milton's other works in light of *De doctrina Christiana* stands on ground less firm than before. On the other hand, if Hunter can be shown to be right, the issue would be resolved. However, few elements in his arguments, whether on in- or external matters, have been accepted, and while efforts are underway to develop external bibliographical or stylistic criteria, these have not yet reached fruition. In the meantime, it might be helpful if someone isolated a doctrinal issue large enough and central enough to both *Paradise Lost* and the treatise that it could be used as a decisive litmus to determine whether the two documents are in fact as compatible as much scholarship maintains.[1]

Of the various answers to William Hunter, Barbara Lewalski's best steers us toward a broad issue of the kind needed: namely, predestination. In seeking to establish the "tract's consonance" with *Paradise Lost*, she states that

in terms which recall *De Doctrina* I, iii–iv, Milton has God himself deny predestination and insist that his conditional decrees guarantee human liberty:

> nor can justly accuse
> Thir maker, or thir making, or thir Fate;
> As if Predestination over-rul'd
> Thir will, dispos'd by absolute Decree
> Or high foreknowledge; they themselves decreed
> Thir own revolt, not I: If I foreknew,
> Foreknowledge had no influence on their fault,

45

Which had no less prov'd certain unforeknown.
So without least impulse or shadow of Fate,
Or aught by me immutably foreseen,
They trespass, Authors to themselves in all.[2]

Apart from the fact that the passage quoted refers not, as the pronominal plurals make abundantly clear, to human "liberty" but to that of the fallen angels, the assertion is puzzling that in *Paradise Lost* God "denies" predestination in "terms which recall *De Doctrina.*" As we shall see, *De doctrina Christiana* does anything but deny predestination. On the contrary, it conceives of predestination as a divine decree, as does virtually all Reformed debate rooted in Augustine, and like any theologian in that tradition, the author offers a formal definition of the term followed by an extensive chapter explaining it lemma by lemma, all of course justified with habitual scriptural proofs.[3] As for *Paradise Lost*, surely it is even more difficult to argue that "God himself" denies "predestination" or that in the passage quoted, he "insist[s]" that his "conditional decrees guarantee human liberty." In fact, the very speech that Lewalski inappropriately quotes culminates in God issuing the decree of predestination itself right before our nose (III, 56–134). Bending down his "eye, His own works and their works at once to view" and thereby beholding Satan wending toward Paradise in order to corrupt man, the Father in eternity ("High Thron'd above all highth") begins the episode with an act of "foreseeing." Anticipating that Adam will "hark'n to" Satan's "glozing lyes, / And easily transgress the sole Command," thus effecting his fall and that of "his faithless Progenie," God ruminates first on "ingrate" man whom he created "just and right, / Sufficient to have stood, though free to fall," and then on "the high Decree / Unchangeable, Eternal," that "ordain'd" the similar freedom of the fallen angels. Observing that the evil angels ("the first sort") "by their own suggestion fell, / Self-tempted, self-deprav'd" and therefore deserve no mercy, He justifies extending clemency to "Man" because, unlike the angels, he "falls deceiv'd / By the other first." Then follows the grand deed to which all the foregoing has been meant to lead: namely, public proclamation of his short, simple, yet eternal and absolute decree of predestination expressed in a pair of thundering imperatives:

> Man therefore shall find grace,
> The other none: in Mercy and Justice both,
> Through Heav'n and Earth, so shall my glorie excel,
> But Mercy first and last shall brightest shine.   (III, 131–34)

Lest readers miss what the Word of God here hath wrought, remarkable effects ensue to mark the event: "Ambrosial fragrance" fills all heaven, a sense of *"new* joy ineffable" diffuses "in the blessed Spirits elect," and "beyond compare the Son of God" appears "Most glorious, in him all his Father shon / Substantially express'd, and in his face / Divine compassion visibly appeer'd, / Love without end, and without measure Grace" (III, 135–43; italics mine). Prompted by the Son's questions regarding the dilemma of either allowing Satan his revenge or unmaking creation, the Father proceeds to a series of auxiliary decisions specifying the means by which the newly issued decree of predestination is to be carried out. These consist of a number of secondary proclamations establishing, among other things, the psychological powers of fallen man, the incarnation of the Son, his surrogacy for Adam's sin, his kingship, the Second Coming, the Last Judgment, the shutting of hell, and all eschatology to follow until "God shall be All in All" (III, 143–341). The episode then ends with the commanded adoration of the Son by the "multitude of Angels" surrounding the living throne and the narrator's description of their mighty hymn of praise (III, 341–410).

In short, *Paradise Lost* does not "deny predestination" any more than *De doctrina Christiana.* Rather, the uttering of the decree as impersonated in Book III forms one of the most dramatic moments in all literature—*pace* those who find God a bore—and the moment of its promulgation is pivotal, not simply for the scene in heaven but for the plotting of the entire epic to follow. Some might perhaps accept Barbara Lewalski's assertion if by "predestination" she meant "reprobation," but that would not be quite right either. The treatise indeed denies that reprobation constitutes any part of predestination. (It describes the "angeli mali" as "ad poenam reservati," but does so quite apart from the context of human predestination [CM XV, p. 106]). However, the decree as dramatized in *Paradise Lost* explicitly includes both absolute election of a special class of mankind and absolute reprobation of the fallen angels. Whether the election of the other class of men to conditional grace is as successful as Milton would like in posing as a kind of election rather than as a form of reprobation is a topic to which we shall return later.

Since both *De doctrina Christiana* and *Paradise Lost* treat predestination as a decree in traditional Reformed manner, the question is whether these two documents entail schemes of predestination that are like or different. If they essentially agree, the similarity will support Milton's authorship of *De doctrina Christiana.* If they differ significantly, then something is wrong, and William Hunter needs to be heeded.

In order to gain some perspective on the problem, let us begin by describing standard orthodox Reformed views of predestination and then compare them with the predestination that we find in the treatise and in

Paradise Lost (see table 1). Building on convenient paradigms developed many years ago by the *gereformeerde* Dutch scholar Klaas Dijk, I shall examine each system in terms of (1) end, or purpose of the decree; (2) the position of predestination among the other divine decrees preceding or following it; (3) the object of, or creature subject to the decree; and (4) the nature of the acts of election and reprobation that the decree entails.[4] These elements provide apt seamarks for comparison, especially as they derive straight from terminology and concepts which obtained during the quarrels about predestination that raged within the Reformed world during the late sixteenth century and during all of Milton's lifetime in the seventeenth. Naturally, treating predestination in terms of chronological or temporal priorities is but a figurative means—as Reformed divines (including the author of *De doctrina Christiana*) usually point out—of grasping logical interrelationships within the mind of God.

The first kind of predestination accepted by Calvinist orthodoxy is the "extreme" (in the eyes particularly of Melancthonian Lutherans and various heirs of Jacobus Arminius) supralapsarianism that was severely questioned but ultimately tolerated at the international Calvinist Synod of Dort in 1619. In this arrangement, God's end in issuing the decree is primarily to display his glory through the manifestation of mercy and justice. Regarding the order of divine decrees and the place of predestination among them, the deity issued the decree of predestination *before* the creation and *before* the Fall of Man, with sin a subsequent and necessary means to the end. Hence the decrees affecting Creation and Fall are instrumental to the antecedent decree of predestination, God deciding to create man and permit the Fall as means of executing the edict. Accordingly, the object of or creature subject to the great decree is *homo creabilis et labilis*—man not yet created, yet capable of falling—and the decree envisions humankind as its target, not serpents or fallen angels. With respect to election and reprobation, supralapsarianism presents a system of double predestination in which God reveals his mercy and justice in the eternal salvation or damnation of his creatures with respect to which he either elects or rejects them. Election and reprobation are thus acts not so much of mercy and justice per se as of divine will and pleasure, and they primarily manifest God's power and unrestricted sovereignty. As free will or actual sin in the creature plays no role with respect to preordaining salvation, this view is commonly attacked for making God the author of sin. Rooted in Luther, Zwingli, Calvin, and Beza, it is associated with theologians such as Whitaker, Zanchius, Perkins, Piscator, Trelcatius the elder, Trigland, and, above all, its leading proponent before and during the Synod of Dort, Franciscus Gomarus, Arminius's nem-

TABLE 1. COMPARATIVE APPROACHES TO THE DECREE OF PREDESTINATION

	Supra-lapsarian	Infra-lapsarian	CD	PL	Arminius	Junius
Ends						
Manifest	Mercy, justice	Virtues in general	Mercy, grace, wisdom	Mercy, justice	Mercy, justice	Mercy, grace, justice, goodness, wisdom
Order						
Creation	Before	After	Before	After	After	After
Fall	Before	After	Before	Before	After	Before
Object						
Homo	Creabilis and labilis	Creatus and lapsus	Creandus and lapsurus	Creatus & labilis	Creatus and lapsus	Creatus and labilis
Angelus				Creatus & lapsus		
Election						
Act of	Sovereignty	Mercy	Mercy	Mercy	Mercy	Mercy, wisdom, sovereignty
Reprobation						
Act of	Sovereignty	Justice	—	Justice	Justice	Justice
Applications	Particular	Particular	General	Particular and general	General	Particular
Free will	No	No	Yes	No and yes	Yes	No

esis at the University of Leiden. I omit mention of Father Mapple and Captain Ahab.[5]

The other view, which was embraced by the majority of orthodox Calvinists in Milton's time, is the infra- or sublapsarian. Although this system allows no more free will to the elect or reprobate than the supralapsarian, it differs sharply from the "extremists" in essential respects. Instead of illumination of the glory of God as manifested in mercy and justice, the aim behind the decree is to display the divine virtues in general, including of course mercy and justice. To do this, God decides to create man and for unknown reasons to permit the Fall, although foreknowing full well that this is certainly going to happen; hence the really significant difference between this position and that promulgated by the supralapsarians. In the infralapsarian view, specifically, the decree of predestination is held to *follow*, not precede, *both* the Creation and the Fall. As the decree thus cannot be responsible for the Fall—evil being now a condition precedent to the edict— the arrangement frees divine predestination from the charge of serving as an instrument to sin.

Accordingly, infralapsarians differ fundamentally from the "extreme" predestinarians with respect to the objects of the decree. Instead of applying to *homo creabilis et labilis*, the decree takes as its subject *homo creatus atque lapsus*—man already created and also fallen *before* the decree was proclaimed. Under such circumstances, reprobation becomes an act of pure justice, leaving the *massa damnata* in (if nothing else) Adam to their deserved fate, while election turns into an act of incomprehensible, totally undeserved mercy bestowed through the gracious will and inscrutable pleasure of the Father. Later divines commonly associated with this mainstream view are generally scions of Bullinger: Maresius, Turretin, Rivetus, Walaeus, Pierre Du Moulin, Friedrich Spanheim, Wollebius, and many, many others.[6]

How, then, do the treatise and *Paradise Lost* compare with Calvinist orthodoxy and with each other on this matter of predestination? Regarding the ends of the decree, *De doctrina Christiana* is quite specific: namely, "ad gloriam misericordiae, gratiae, sapientiaeque suae patefaciendam" ("in order to manifest the glory of his mercy, grace, and wisdom") (CM XIV, p. 90). One sees immediately in both the wording of the definition and the contents of the scriptural texts cited as proof that the "summus praedestinationis finis" places its emphasis on divine glory and virtues in rather a supralapsarian manner (pp. 90, 102). A glance at the order in which the relevant decrees occur instantly confirms that the treatise tilts entirely toward the supralapsarian, not the infralapsarian view. *De doctrina Christiana* is precise and explicit in laying down that predestination "ad salutem aeternam" took place in eternity *ante iacta mundi fundamenta*—that is, "before the foundations of the world were laid" (p. 90). Such a stand on sequence amounts to nothing less than classical supralapsarianism in that the decree of predestination *precedes* those effecting Creation and Fall, and it necessarily takes precedence over them.

Such an order of decrees also affects the object of the decree radically. Again, the subject creature turns out to be outspokenly supralapsarian: namely, *homo creandus et lapsurus*—man who has to/needs to/must be created and is going to fall.[7] Indeed, note how the touch of determinism that lurks in the Latin modifiers renders almost oxymoronic the addendum *sua sponte* ("man who is going to fall of his own free will") (CM XIV, p. 100). Note also that the decree applies to humankind alone, just as in traditional supralapsarian and infralapsarian schemes.[8]

Only with respect to election and reprobation does the treatise depart significantly from the supralapsarian position. In effect it denies double predestination, substituting a single predestination instead. As Lewalski observes, *De doctrina Christiana* rejects reprobation entirely, denying that this act constitutes any part of predestination (CM XIV, pp. 97, 99, 101). Predestination entails election only, and such election is not an absolute and particular but only a contingent, general election of "*eos qui credituri essent atque in fide permansuri*" ("those who are going to believe and continue steadfast in their faith") (p. 106). *De doctrina Christiana* is, in short, a clever, Ramicized piece of supralapsarianism that joins many predecessors in attempting to soften the traditional stand on reprobation and refute the standard accusation that such a form of predestination necessarily makes God the author of sin. Essentially the treatise converts double into single predestination and (without regard to actual sin or merit) makes election contingent on choices that the elect are foreseen as exercising in the future.

The crucial question, then, is to what extent does the scheme of predestination informing *Paradise Lost* resemble or differ from that presented in *De doctrina Christiana?* As dramatized by Milton, God the Father is presented as very self-conscious of his ends, and he is careful publicly to share his meditations on this point with the Son and the attendant angels. "In Mercy and Justice both," he is made to state explicitly, "Through Heav'n and Earth, so shall my glorie excel, / But Mercy first and last shall brightest shine" (III, 132–34). Clearly the emphasis is on glory as manifested in justice and mercy, rather like the *finis ultimus* that supralapsarians stress. Nevertheless, while the posture of *Paradise Lost* regarding ends is perhaps not as expansive as that outlined in *De doctrina Christiana*, it does nonetheless include a specific concern with divine justice in the context of predestination and reprobation that is lacking in the treatise.

When one turns to the order of decrees, the difference between *Para-*

dise Lost and *De doctrina Christiana* becomes glaring. The epic in fact adopts a position that, for want of a better term, I shall call "prelapsarian." Instead of placing the decree of predestination *before* the Creation ("ante iacta mundi fundamenta"), *Paradise Lost* runs exactly counter to *De doctrina Christiana* in that it puts the decree (to parody the language of the treatise) *POST iacta mundi fundamenta—after*, in other words, the *creation* of the universe, including the earth, Paradise, and the human couple toward which Satan is journeying at the moment that the decree is pronounced in Book III. This is, to say the least, at sharp variance with the uncompromising supralapsarianism informing the treatise on this point. At the same time, we should recognize that the poem is equally at odds with the infralapsarians, for while *Paradise Lost* sets the decree after the creation, it is even more remarkable for presenting it as *antecedent* to the Fall, which will not take place until Book IX, after the education of Adam. It is as if the "prelapsarianism" of *Paradise Lost* strives to avoid the shoals of the "supras" on the one hand and the rocks of "infras" on the other by rejecting both, yet incorporating a bit of each. With respect to the crucial matter of the order of decrees, then, the difference between *Paradise Lost* and *De doctrina Christiana* is both essential and undeniable.

What about the object of the decree, the creature subject to it? Like both the supralapsarians and the infralapsarians, the author of *De doctrina Christiana* envisions predestination as applying solely to humankind, as we have seen. The objects in Milton's poem are utterly different, for they involve two orders of creatures, not one: (1) *angelus creatus atque lapsus*—evil angels that have already undergone creation but also effected their own fall—and (2) *homo creatus sed labilis*—man that has already been created, not yet fallen, but capable of such fall. Needless to say, Milton's position in the epic regarding fallen angels as objects of predestination seems unusual. Not only is it a far cry from either of the orthodox notions of the objects of predestination, but in this regard the epic and the treatise clash irreconcilably.

The difference between *Paradise Lost* and *De doctrina Christiana* becomes even more pronounced when one considers election and reprobation, even though superficially both documents evince concern with free will and contingent election. Whereas the treatise rejects reprobation entirely, *Paradise Lost* does not. The decree as proclaimed in Book III explicitly denies grace to the fallen angels from this point on in the epic. Obviously, the reprobation of the rebel spirits on the ground that they fell self-corrupted is the sole act in the scheme that fulfills the declared end of manifesting the virtue of God's justice, albeit deriving from an object other than the one that predestinarians usually entertain.[9] Election, on the other hand, becomes an act primarily of mercy, much as the infralapsarians hold. However, instead of the familiar double predestination of the supralapsarians or the single predestination of the treatise, the epic in fact confronts us with a *triple* predestination. That is, in addition to reprobation of the evil angels, the poem develops two distinct acts of election. One is evidently particular and absolute (III, 183–84: "Some I have chosen of peculiar grace / Elect above the rest; so is my will"). It seems to take place solely at the unbound will and pleasure of the deity, and it is apparently extended without regard to actual sin or merit in the as yet unfallen object. The difference between this Miltonic class of absolute particular elect and the absolute particular elect that both the supralapsarians and the infralapsarians put forward is, to my thinking, moot. Does the creature blessed with such election in the epic have the power to reject it any more than the elect proposed by the orthodox? Hence, whereas mainstream Calvinists might well endorse *Paradise Lost* on this kind of election, the mind behind the treatise could not possibly do so.[10]

Only with respect to the third creature subject to reprobation and election—namely, "the" so-called "rest," who "shall hear me call, and oft be warnd / Thir sinful state, and to appease betimes / Th'incensed Deitie while offerd grace / Invites" (III, 185–88)—do the treatise and the epic bear a resemblance. The second kind of "election" posited by the epic, unlike the first, embraces a general election, not a particular one, and it is contingent on the will and behavior of the creatures so elected. However, because of the difference in order of decrees, the predicaments of the elect in the treatise and the epic are not the same. Indeed, the venerable Arminius himself would be likely to indict the author of *Paradise Lost* for foisting off what may really be a conservative form of human reprobation in the guise of election. Despite the claims for free will, the position is open to at least two challenges that Arminius actually makes against schemes like this. First, in contrast to the privileged class of absolute elect, the second group of contingently elect necessarily suffer under some form of preterition, in that God at some "time" decided on them "de ghenade, die noodich was, om de sonde te mijden, *niet* mede te deylen" ("*not* to bestow on [them] the grace that was necessary to avoid sin" [emphasis mine]).[11] Secondly, they also suffer under the threat of a predamnation that results in induration—one thinks of the irreversible hardening of the heart that Milton describes, once the day of "grace" goes "neglected or scorned" (III, 198–202)—an induration that in Arminius's eyes will have been visited upon the reprobate willy-nilly without regard to actual sin since God foresaw and decreed such conditions *before* the fall of Adam and the sinfulness ensuing.[12] Whether the treatise eludes this reef better than *Paradise Lost* others must judge (compare CM XIV, p. 102). Suffice it here to say that while it is difficult enough to try to argue that the treatise and the poem are entirely compatible even in the one area of election in which they come closest to overlapping, to proceed further and baldly claim that "Milton's views on predestination and free will, on reprobation, on God's foreknowledge of what men freely decide, are alike in both works" flies irresponsibly in the face of the evidence.[13]

For all the loose talk about Milton's "Arminianism," the Dutch theologian's views on predestination are very different from those forming the basis of the plot underlying *Paradise Lost*. This is *not* immediately apparent in specification of ends. Arminius habitually uses language such as "in laude gloriosae gratiae Dei" ("in praise of the glorious grace of God") and "justiti[a]e ipsius" ("of justice itself"), and a variety of passages shows that he basically thinks of the decree as displaying the same virtues of mercy and justice that the infra- and supralapsarians hold in common with Milton's poem.[14]

When one turns to the sequence of decrees, though, the gulf between Arminius and *Paradise Lost* becomes unbridgeable. In general, the Oudewater divine adopts not the order of decrees that we find in *Paradise Lost* but that espoused by the infralapsarians. That is, not merely creation (Arminius holds the "decretum de creando" to be "omnium decretorum Dei primum" ["the decree of creation the first of all God's decrees"]) but also the Fall of Man precedes the decree of predestination, quite unlike what happens in *Paradise Lost,* obviously.[15] This is by no means all, however. The difference between Arminius's theory of predestination—the essence of his genius, one should say—and the position of the infralapsarians is that between the Fall of Man and the decree affecting election and reprobation he introduced three other "precijs ende absoluyt" ("exact and absolute") decrees "om den sondighen mensche salich te maecken" ("in order to bestow salvation on sinful mankind"). According to Arminius, these edicts *precede* and govern predestination, not the other way around.[16] The first is God's appointment of his Son "tot eenen Middelaer, Verlosser, Salichmaecker, Priester ende Coninc" ("as a mediator, redeemer, savior, priest and king"). The second is his decision "de ghene die hen bekeeren ende ghelooven in ghenade te ontfangen" ("to receive in grace those who repent and believe") and "de onbekeerlicke, ende ongheloovige, inde sonde end onder den toorne te laten, ende te verdoemen als vreemt van Christo" ("leave the unrepentant and unbelieving in sin and under wrath, and damn them as alien to Christ"). The third is a decree "de middelen ter bekeeringhe, ende gheloove noodich, ghenoechsaem, ende crachtich, te beleyden" ("to bestow the means necessary for repentance and belief sufficiently and powerfully"). Then, in the last place, and only then, follows his decision "om sekere bysondere persoonen salich te maken, ende te verdoemen" ("to save and damn certain special persons") whom God in eternity foreknows as believers who will persevere or as unbelievers who will not.[17]

What is remarkable in *Paradise Lost* is that these latter decrees occur in virtually reverse order to that posed by Arminius. Predestination to salvation *precedes* (III, 131–34) the secondary decrees determining the means of carrying out the primary edict (III, 173–202), and these themselves in turn *precede*—to use the language of the argument to Book III—the Father's acceptance of the Son as "a Ransome for Man," his ordaining the "incarnation," his pronouncing of the Son's "exaltation," and his commanding angelic adoration. While aesthetically the sequence permits the episode to end in a grand climax, its elements stand in almost flagrant defiance of the very order of the decrees that constitute the heart of a brilliant theology that we perhaps all too readily presume Milton knew and approved.[18]

Arminius would also disagree with both the treatise and the poem about election and reprobation. Whereas the treatise denies reprobation, Arminius embraces it as a necessary counterpart to election, viewing the former as an act of justice, the latter as an act of mercy, just like the infralapsarians.[19] Since Arminius will hear nothing of an election or reprobation that takes no regard of sin as something perpetrated and of individual people as actual sinners, there can be of course no class of particular, special individuals elected absolutely before the Fall at the arbitrary pleasure of the Divine Will as there in fact is in *Paradise Lost*. As for the general election of the "rest" of humankind, as Milton puts it, which both Arminius and the poem make contingent on belief and unbelief foreseen in eternity beforehand, *Paradise Lost* may appear at first glance to resemble Arminius on this point. But as I indicated above, it is unlikely that, given the order of decrees in the poem, Arminius would have thought of such Miltonic "election" as anything other than a covert form of reprobation masquerading as its opposite. Mere endorsement of "free will" does not in and of itself mean much. What counts is the way one reasons toward it, and the order of decrees has probably more to do with determining a theologian's stand on human "liberty" than the other way around.

There remains the question of Milton's originality in *Paradise Lost*. Is the notion of the "prelapsarian" predestination dramatized in the epic unique to Milton or does it too have roots in Reformed controversies? In attacking traditional schemes of predestination, both the *Amica collatio cum Fr. Junio* of the early 1590s and the mature *Verklaring* of 1608 describe three approaches to predestination of which Arminius disapproves. The first is Beza's supralapsarian view; the third, the infralapsarian. The second, though, is a prelapsarian theory that constitutes nothing less than an obvious analogue to the arrangement that appears in *Paradise Lost*.[20] Arminius calls it "Thomas's" predestination, for he recognizes that the idea descends from "Aquinas's school" ("[sententia] altera: Thomae et sectatorum"), albeit his opponent Junius demurs on the point, maintaining that he does not agree with Aquinas.[21] Whatever the provenance, the emergence of such prelapsarianism was symptomatic of concern in the Dutch Reformed churches with the growing influence of Beza's supralapsarian notion of predestination during the late sixteenth century. Whether the attempts of the so-called Delft brethren, Reynier Donteklok and Arendt Cornelisz—two ministers of that city who were among the first Dutch theologians seeking to soften Beza's ideas during the late 1570s and the 1580s—are purely infralapsarian, as some secondary literature suggests, or whether they may also have incorporated elements of a prelapsarian approach to the problem of predestination, I have not as yet determined for want of access to original texts.[22] Yet it is certain that the Leiden professor, Franciscus Junius, of Tremellius-Junius Bible fame, sought to draw back from Beza in very much this way. Somewhere in the late 1590s, Arminius learned that Junius "was proposing some revisions" of Beza's supralapsarian position. Intrigued, he began a correspondence in which he set forth his views about Junius's thinking. Junius divided Arminius's epistle into twenty-seven "propositions," and to each he composed a reply. To every one of these replies, Arminius in turn added a rebuttal that concludes the discussion of each proposition.[23] Since the bulk of what is in essence a dialogue between Junius and Arminius (proposition 7 to the end) is devoted to the prelapsarian alternative that Junius propounded, it is relatively easy to determine some of the salient features that informed this notion of predestination.

The ends of the system (as described by Arminius but with Junius not objecting) entail the usual manifestation of "heerlycker ghenade" ("glorious grace") and the demonstration of divine justice, with the emphasis possibly on mercy more than justice.[24] In short, commonplace ends with which those specified in *Paradise Lost* and by both the supra- and infralapsarians are in line. However, Arminius, with Junius concurring, also speaks of the aim as being "ad declarandam libertatem bonitatis suae" ("to proclaim the freedom of his goodness")—a point in tune by implication perhaps with Milton's absolute election—while Junius demands that Arminius add the manifestation of the "perfectionem πολυποικίλου [sic] sapientiae suae" ("the perfection of his multivariegated wisdom") to the list of ends.[25] Obviously, the concern is with the divine virtues in general. One might at best say that *Paradise Lost* may incorporate these latter as implied ends, but they are not overtly stated as such.

Much more important, though, is the determinant matter of the order of the decrees. Arminius describes predestination in Junius's prelapsarianism as coming subsequent to the Creation but at the same time prior to the Fall.[26] Obviously, this arrangement is exactly the same as that which occurs in *Paradise Lost*. There is also fair harmony regarding the human object of the decree, of course. Both Junius (as described by Arminius) and Milton conceive of *homo creatus sed labilis*—man created but nonetheless capable of falling—as subject to the decree. However, in such "Junian" prelapsarianism, there is an additional wrinkle, for the dialogue speaks not just of *homo creatus* but of *homo* as created *in puris naturalibus*—man in his purely natural state and thence *labilis*, which correlates well with Adam's condition in *Paradise Lost*.[27] Regarding Milton's other object of predestination, though, *Paradise Lost* obviously differs from the prelapsarianism discussed in the dialogue between Arminius and Junius. For while Adam before the fall necessarily resembles the human object that Junius envisions, there are of course no fallen angels subject to the decree in Junian theory as set forth by Arminius. As for election and reprobation, the former is an act of supernal mercy, wisdom, and absolute freedom of divine good with respect to those creatures raised by grace above their natural state. The latter becomes an act of justice with respect to those passed by to be left in their natural state and thence foreseen as subsequently falling and ultimately being lost. Although the epic declines to present the fate of those who neglect or scorn the day of grace as reprobation, the phenomenon as vividly described in *Paradise Lost* bears an uncomfortable resemblance to the predicament of the reprobate in Junius's system. As we have said, Arminius opposed this sort of prelapsarianism as tantamount to supralapsarianism in its disregard of actual sin and merit in assigning election and reprobation.

In sum, *Paradise Lost* stems from endeavors hearkening back at least to the 1570s to render Beza's predestination palatable to the Reformed mainstream. Whereas *De doctrina Christiana* is flagrant in making its allegiance to supralapsarianism manifest, Milton is equally explicit in plotting his poem within a tradition that sought to undermine and shift the very base of the system that the treatise endeavors to uphold. Essentially he seeks a solution to the problem of God as author of sin quite different from that presented in *De doctrina Christiana*. Inasmuch as the poem and the treatise share a common urge to uphold fundamentally conservative systems and modify them in order to defend presumably against "proto Arminians" like Coornhert or later Remonstrant (that is, "Arminian") critics, it is not surprising that, at least with respect to predestination, the poem struck earlier readers as basically orthodox.[28] At the same time, one can very well understand that the revisionist impulse informing the treatise would interest a kindred modernizer like Milton enough to have the unpublished manuscript copied and kept at hand. Nevertheless, the systems that the respective documents attempt to justify are at core dissimilar, even with respect to matters of contingent grace and free will.

There are, then, but four hypotheses regarding authorship that can account for such differences on predestination in the treatise and *Paradise Lost:* (1) Milton authored neither work—an alternative absurd to everyone, presumably; (2) Milton authored both the treatise and *Paradise Lost,* but did not put down what he really thought in the one or the other of them; (3) Milton changed his mind between the times he wrote the two texts; (4) the author of *Paradise Lost* is not the author of the treatise, as William Hunter maintains.[29] The discrepancies between the treatise and the epic touching predestination indicate that Hunter has put his finger on a problem that is real. Unless we are willing to accept the second or the third alternative, it seems dubious that Milton authored *De doctrina Christiana.* Whatever the case, the treatise cannot be taken automatically as the authoritative gloss on *Paradise Lost* that Maurice Kelley envisioned.[30] Moreover, any attempt at such application must only proceed with extremely cautious, judicious discrimination and careful qualification, not to speak of exact and detailed knowledge of the Reformed schools and traditions within which Milton was operating. Finally, if it turns out that the English poet is not responsible for *De doctrina Christiana,* searches for the true author ought not to be confined solely to "liberal" theologians associated with progressive notions regarding free will or divorce. Given the Bezaesque hue of the kind of predestination on which the treatise builds, the hunt must include orthodox divines of even "extremist" colors too.

University of California, Los Angeles

NOTES

I am greatly indebted to Margriet Lacy, William B. Hunter, Jr., Barbara Packer, and others for reading, evaluating, and offering valuable suggestions for this essay. Needless to say, none of these scholars is responsible for the contents or to be taken as endorsing the thesis.

1. Hunter, "The Provenance of the *Christian Doctrine,*" *SEL* XXXII (1992): 129–42; Christopher Hill, "Professor William B. Hunter, Bishop Burgess, and John Milton," *SEL* XXXIV (1994): 168; compare Gordon Campbell, "The Authorship of *De Doctrina Christiana,*" *MQ* XXVI (1992): 129–30.

2. Barbara K. Lewalski, "Forum: Milton's *Christian Doctrine,*" *SEL* XXXII (1992): 150.

3. Liber I, caput iv, *De doctrina Christiana* in *The Works of John Milton,* ed. Frank Allen Patterson et al. (New York, 1931–38), vol. XIV, pp. 90–175. All quotations from Milton's prose and poetry are from this edition, and subsequent references will appear in the text as CM followed by volume, page and, where necessary, book and line numbers.

4. Klaas Dijk, *De strijd over infra- en supralapsarisme in de Gereformeerde Kerken van Nederland* (Kampen, 1912), pp. 45–46.

5. Ibid., pp. 46, 37–38.

6. Ibid., pp. 45–46, 38–43. Wollebius makes his infralapsarianism plain in book 1, chap. 3, sect. 3, prop. 11, and in all of chap. 4, and esp. chap. 4, sect. 2, prop. 6, of *Compendium Theologiae Christianae*, in *Reformed Dogmatics: J. Wollebius, G. Voetius, F. Turretin*, trans. John W. Beardslee III (New York, 1965), pp. 49, 50–53, and 56, respectively. In light of his express opposition to the position taken by *De doctrina Christiana* in denying reprobation (he says "those who teach the doctrine of election in such a way as to deny reprobation, are clearly wrong" [p. 54]), the treatise shows no indebtedness whatever to Wollebius on the matter of predestination.

7. The choice of these Latin terms may suggest a "narrow" conception of predestination informing the treatise as opposed to a "broad" one. See Dijk's description of Petrus van Mastricht's "vierderlei propositum Dei" (*De Strijd*, p. 48, item no. 3).

8. CM XIV, p. 90: "Decretum Dei speciale de hominibus praecipium praedestinatio nominatur."

9. Compare Dijk, *De strijd*, p. 40.

10. Compare CM XIV, p. 99: "Sed illam hic specialem electionem intelligimus, quae cum aeterna praedestinatione idem fere est. electio igitur pars praedestinationis non est multoque minus Reprobatio."

11. *Verklaring van Jacobus Arminius afgelegd in de vergadering van de Staten van Holland op 30 Oktober 1608*, ed. G. J. Hoenderdaal (Lochem, 1960), p. 102.

12. Compare ibid., p. 99.

13. Hill, "Professor William B. Hunter," 179.

14. Compare the section on Arminianism in Maurice Kelley's introduction to *De doctrina christiana* in *Complete Prose Works of John Milton*, ed. Don M. Wolfe et al. (New York, 1973), vol. IV, pp. 79–86. On Arminius's language, see *Disputationes privatae*, "Thesis quadragesima, de praedestinatione fidelium," in *Jacobi Arminii Veteraquinatis Batavi S. S. Theologiae Doctoris eximii, Opera theologica* (Leiden, 1629), VI, p. 390; *Disputationes privatae*, "Thesis quadragesima prima, de praedestinatione mediorum ad fidem," V, in *Opera*, p. 391; and *Examen libelli perkinsiani de praedestinatione ordine & modo*, in ibid., pp. 636, 639.

15. *Articuli nonnulli diligenti examine perpendendi, . . . de scriptura, et traditionibus humanis*, "De creatione, et maxime hominis," I, *Opera*, p. 952; *Articuli nonnulli*, "De lapsu Adami," I–VIII, in *Opera*, p. 955; *Examen libelli perkinsiani*, in ibid., p. 643; *Examination of the Theses of Dr. Francis Gomarus Respecting Predestination*, "Arminius's Consideration on Thesis XIII," in *The Works of James Arminius*, trans. William Nichols; rpt. (Grand Rapids, Mich., 1986), vol. III, p. 565.

16. *Verklaring*, pp. 104–05. Compare *Declaratio sententiae*, in *Opera*, p. 119.

17. *Verklaring*, p. 106. Also stated in *Articuli nonnulli*, "De decretis Dei salutem hominum peccatorum concernentibus ex proprio sensu," in *Opera*, p. 957. Compare Carl Bangs, *Arminius: A Study in the Dutch Reformation*, 2nd ed. (Grand Rapids, Mich., 1985), pp. 312–13.

18. The references to Arminius and Arminianism in the index to CM, whether early or late (for example, *Areopagitica; Of True Religion, Heresie, Schism, and Toleration*) always treat Arminius and his followers as either perverted from the truth (IV, p. 313) or involved in well-intentioned error that nonetheless ought to be tolerated (VI, pp. 168–69, 78, 366; see also III, pp. 330, 440).

19. *Disputationes publicae*, "Thesis decimaquinta, de divina praedestinatione. Resp. Wilhelmo Bastingio," IX–XV, in *Opera*, p. 285; *Examen libelli perkinsiani*, in ibid., pp. 650–51;

Disputationes privatae, "Thesis quadragesima prima, de praedestinatione mediorum ad fidem," III–X, in ibid., pp. 391–92.

20. *Verklaring,* pp. 62–103; *Amica cum D. Francisco Junio de praedestinatione per litteras habita collatio,* props. 1, 2, 4, 5, 7, in *Opera,* pp. 459, 463, 473, 475, and 506, respectively.

21. *Amica collatio,* "Responsio Junii ad 4. propositionem" and "Responsio Junii ad 7. propositionem," in *Opera,* pp. 472–73, 506, respectively. Compare Dijk, *De strijd,* p. 75.

22. Hendrik Johan Jaanus, *Hervormd Delft ten tijde van Arent Cornelisz (1573–1605)* (Amsterdam, 1950), pp. 188–94. I am indebted to Willem Heijting, head of the Department of Manuscripts and Rare Books, Free University Library, Amsterdam, for this reference. In their "Responsio ad argumenta quaedam Bezae et Calvini ex tractatu de praedestinatione, in caput IX ad Romanos," 1589, not until 1611 published (Leiden) by Donteklok under the title *Een grondich onderrecht uit Godts Heilighe Woort van de Predestinatie* (according to Dijk, *De strijd,* pp. 60–61n4). *Areopagitica* (CM IV, p. 313) shows that Milton was aware of the story of this tractate and its effect on Arminius when Lydius asked the latter to defend Beza against Donteklok and Cornelisz.

23. See Dijk, *De strijd,* pp. 71–75; Bangs, *Arminius,* pp. 199–201.

24. *Verklaring,* p. 97. Compare *Amica collatio,* "4. propositio Arminii," in *Opera,* p. 472.

25. *Amica collatio,* "Responsio Junii ad 4. propositionem," in *Opera,* pp. 472–73.

26. *Verklaring,* p. 101. Compare Dijk, *De strijd,* p. 80.

27. *Amica collatio,* "Propositio 9. Arminii," in *Opera,* p. 508; see Bangs, *Arminius,* p. 201. Compare *Articuli nonnulli,* "De praedestinatione in statu primaevo considerata," in *Opera,* p. 954, as well as "De peccato originis" and "De pradestinatione hominis, partim in statu primaevo, partim in lapsu considerati," in ibid., pp. 954–55.

28. For an overview, see Dijk, *De strijd,* pp. 57–115.

29. On point 2, compare William B. Hunter, "Animadversions Upon the Remonstrants' Defenses Against Burgess and Hunter," *SEL* XXXIV (1994): 196; on point 3, Barbara Packer observes tellingly that when Emerson was writing *Nature,* "the very act of codifying" his theology led him to understand what was wrong with it, "so that the last two chapters are a refutation of the first six. And this massive reorientation took place between June and September of one year" (Packer, letter to Paul R. Sellin, Los Angeles, April 22, 1995).

30. Kelley, introduction to *CD,* pp. 110–15.

THE ENVIRONMENTAL ETHICS OF *PARADISE LOST:* MILTON'S EXEGESIS OF GENESIS I–III

Jeffrey S. Theis

All ethics so far evolved rest upon a single premise: that the individual is a member of a community of interdependent parts. . . . That man is, in fact, only a member of a biotic team is shown by an ecological interpretation of history. Many historical events, hitherto explained solely in terms of human enterprise, were actually biotic interactions between people and land.

—Aldo Leopold, A *Sand County Almanac*

During the second half of the twentieth century, literary scholarship has witnessed a tremendous increase in ecological theory and criticism. Works as diverse as those by Leo Marx and Robert Pogue Harrison have analyzed literary representations of humankind's interactions with their natural environment and the complex, pervasive realities which are constructed through this sometimes ambivalent, tension-filled relationship. Within the larger field of ecological criticism lies a section devoted to analyzing what may be called "environmental ethics." The term's roots come, in part, from the environmentalist Aldo Leopold's writings which broaden the scope of ethics beyond the human community and argue that human survival depends upon the ethical treatment of nature.[1] In this light, environmental ethics parallels human ethics, for both ensure the preservation of human life through moderation and restraint of an individual's actions within larger communities, be they solely human or natural ecosystems. An environmental ethic focuses on the interaction between people and nature and contains a dialectic between action and reflection. Action involves our physical interactions with nature's flora and fauna. Reflection, often hidden in the action, asks, "what do these actions mean?" Reflection is the component which contextualizes these actions within a larger understanding of nature's ecological systems, hierarchies, and worth.[2] The implications of this larger understanding may pertain to many realms, be they political, gender related, scientific, or, as we will see with *Paradise Lost*, religious.

Though not overtly articulated in such terms, interest in environmental ethics during the English Renaissance is implied and pervasive. In tracing the sources of America's governing myths regarding humanity's relationship with nature, Leo Marx repeatedly returns to the literature of sixteenth- and seventeenth-century England and its depictions of nature. He explores pastoral ideals revealed in Shakespeare's *The Tempest*, and, more interestingly for this essay, he briefly notes Milton's representation of agricultural technology in *Paradise Lost* as antithetical to the perfection of Eden's landscape. From John Manwood's legal treatise to Henry Vaughan's poetry, Renaissance writers seek to understand nature and define what types of human behavior are appropriate within nature. As Alan Rudrum illustrates, the way an author envisions nature often reveals elaborate debates of the author's time, telling us more about such matters as Renaissance theology than about nature's ecosystems.[3] As seen within this milieu and through the lens of ecological criticism, Milton's *Paradise Lost* illustrates an elaborately constructed, religiously based environmental ethic. This ethic is created through his interpretation of the Genesis accounts of humanity's relation to God and nature. *Paradise Lost* can be read as a poetic explication of the tensions and ambiguities of the biblical text and its various exegeses. Milton explicates these sources by providing and developing multiple models of, and perspectives on, environmental ethics. Each model, illustrated by various characters in the poem, embodies one possible interpretation of how human beings should or should not interact with and conceptualize nature. When these various perspectives are woven together, *Paradise Lost* becomes a unified poetic treatise on a divine environmental ethic in which nature is the medium through which people worship and struggle to know God.

As will be illustrated through *Paradise Lost*, two of the most important dimensions of Renaissance environmental ethics have their source in exegeses: the call in Genesis, chapter i, for man to subdue and hold dominion over the land and the directive in chapter ii for Adam to till and dress the land. Of Genesis, ii–iii (and I would assert chapter i applies as well), Phyllis Trible says, "If the story is simple, it is not, at the same time, neat and tidy. Abrupt, terse, elliptic, tentative, its language carries a plurality of meanings. From beginning to end the narrative is riddled with ambiguity. Embodying tension, connotations, hints and guesses, it compels multiple interpretations, as centuries of exegesis amply demonstrate." Within the two biblical Creation stories exists a problematic relationship between human beings and nature that can be expressed as a dialectic between domination over and harmony with nature. After man and woman are created in chapter i, God commands them to "Be fruitful, and multiply, and replenish the earth, and subdue it: and have dominion over the fish of the sea, and over the fowl of the air, and over every living thing that moveth upon the earth" (Gen. i, 28). Ecological criticism of this text focuses upon "subdue" and "have dominion" and the original Hebrew words *kbš* and *rdh* from which they are derived. Of these verbs, Jeremy Cohen writes:

In the Hebrew Bible, *kbš* usually denotes the enslavement of people or the physical conquest of territory. *Rdh*, often reinforced by terms of harshness, refers in general to the rule over slaves, subjects, or enemies, at times to the vanquishing of an opponent in battle, and perhaps even to the trampling upon grapes in a winepress. As one might expect, the attempt to relate these terms to modern ecological concerns has produced a broad spectrum of opinion.

In this context, these words portray nature as a potential adversary which must be subjected to the rule of humanity. In terms of an environmental ethic, "subdue" is the call to action, and "dominion" is reflective in that it lets human beings know their relationship to nature (that is, human beings are rulers and nature is their subject). "Dominion" and "subdue" place human beings at the top of a natural hierarchy where they are like God in their role as rulers. Humankind may misinterpret the instruction to rule if it only focuses upon the negative connotations of "dominion" and "subdue." Humanity must balance the harsh tenor of the two words with the knowledge that God blesses every act of Creation. Thus, human beings, as one part of creation, must see all creation as harmonious and their rule over the creatures must reflect this harmony.[4]

Genesis ii–iii modifies and expands on chapter i by turning the Creation account into a dramatic narrative. While this second account is, in many ways, as brief and suggestively rich as the first account, it provides more information regarding how people should interact with nature. Trible's reading of this story often relies on the Hebrew text to demonstrate that the original meaning of Genesis has been subtly and not so subtly changed through the act of translation. Though the King James Version is consistent with the Hebrew text when it portrays humankind being formed out of the earth's dust, it loses the wordplay found in the original where the word for earth is *hā-ᵃdāmâ* and the word for person (really "earth creature") is *hā-'ādām*. Of these Hebrew words, Trible writes, "a play on words already establishes relationship between earth creature *(hā-'ādām)* and the earth *(hā-ᵃdāmâ)*. This pun is accessible to sight and sound. While uniting creature and soil, it also separates them."[5] The creation of the earth creature in ii, 7, makes an important addition to the first account of humankind's creation in i, 27. Both accounts signify God as the Creator, but the second account lets us know that the earth creature is created out of a substance, in particular, from the earth itself. The second account creates a link between humankind and nature and suggests that while humankind may be more perfect than the rest of nature, our ancestry from the earth places us in harmony with it, not in opposition to it.

After the first person is created, God puts "him into the garden of Eden to dress it and keep it" (ii, 15). Like i, 28, this passage implies that there is a natural hierarchy for which humanity is at the top. The tone and attitude of "to dress" and "to keep" are vastly different from "to subdue" and "have dominion," and reveal a different or altered understanding and work ethic toward nature. Of ii, 15, Trible writes: "The Hebrew verb 'bd, conventionally translated 'to till,' ['to dress' in the Authorized Version] means to serve. It connotes respect, indeed, reverence and worship. To till the garden is to serve the garden; to exercise power over it is to reverence it. Similarly, to keep (šmr) the garden is an act of protection (cf. 3:24), not of possession" (p. 85). The environmental ethic expressed in Genesis ii, 15, does not call for man "to subdue" violently but proposes a two-step call to action. First, man is meant "to dress" nature as a gardener would trim a plant so that it yields forth its bounty. "To keep" nature involves a second step which requires man to protect nature from any sort of danger. Protection of the garden, while a call to action, also serves as the reflective component of an environmental ethic. The garden that needs protecting is the garden that has intrinsic worth which man must understand and appreciate. Humanity's interactions with nature must be worshipful, indicating that God wants people to reflect on humankind's and nature's relationships to God the Creator. Genesis ii, 15, with its interaction between human beings and nature and their reflection on the importance of nature, reveals the twofold requirement of an environmental ethic.

Though the tone of this second account is very different from the first account, the second account also contains its own hierarchical dialectic. This dialectic is actually a modification of the first where dominion and harmony are in possible opposition. The second version asserts that there is a hierarchy in nature but that 'ādām, instead of standing outside of nature and subduing it, stands within it, and 'ādām's task of tilling and keeping the land helps complete the natural world. This modified dialectic, between hierarchy and harmony, lets human beings know their task and relationship to the environment.

Chapter iii of Genesis alters the dominion/harmony dialectic yet again with the first act of environmental degradation. After Adam and Eve disobey God, God says to them, "cursed is the ground for thy sake" (iii, 17). With this curse, nature is now filled with "thorns also and thistles" (18). God says to Adam "in the sweat of thy face shalt thou eat bread, till thou return unto the ground; for out of it wast thou taken: for dust thou art, and unto dust shalt thou return" (19). The divine harmony between human beings and their environment is radically altered by these pronouncements yet, in many ways, is also reinforced. Tilling and keeping the garden, once benign and loving work, become burdensome and laborious. Instead of freely yielding its bounty to Adam and Eve, nature now resists them and brings them pain. Nature is not in opposition to humanity, though; God indicates that its resistance to humanity is caused by Adam and Eve's disobedience. God's curse that man will return to the dust from whence he came completes an interconnected cycle between the earth and humanity. This pronouncement implies that Adam can never separate himself from nature and that the environmental degradation he brings to it (thorns and thistles) he has brought to himself as well. Thus the dialectic of hierarchy and harmony changes in that it is no longer only infused with divine happiness but is also now infused with sorrow.

Between Genesis i–iii and Milton's epic poem lies an equally complex tradition of exegesis and environmental ethics. Milton's reading of Genesis cannot be considered without some acknowledgment of other interpretations that may have influenced him and the environmental ethic of *Paradise Lost*. William Leiss explores a Christian tradition of interpreting the biblical creation story as a text that legitimates human mastery over nature. This mastery is not harmonious but embodies "the idea that man stands apart from nature and rightfully exercises a kind of authority over the natural world." This tradition accentuates the dissonant tenor of the first chapter of Genesis over the harmonious aspects of chapter ii. Ellen Goodman places Thomas Aquinas's exegesis within the tradition of which Leiss writes. According to Goodman, Aquinas views nature as hierarchical in structure, with nature's imperfect forms (vegetation) at the bottom and perfect forms of God's creation (human beings) at the top. The imperfect is to be governed by and used for the benefit of the perfect "in the fashion of slaves," says Goodman. Seen within this tradition, Adam and Eve's disobedience of God leads to the animals' disobedience of their human rulers. Goodman writes: "Viewing the Fall as a hierarchical disturbance between human beings as masters and their natural subjects, Aquinas presents the state of innocence as an ideal in which mastership would have enabled humans to use nature's provisions while protecting them from its hardships." As we will see, Milton uses the ideas of mastership and a natural hierarchy but alters the tone of Aquinas's model. In Milton's hierarchy, the lower creatures are not seen as unruly inferiors that need to be subdued, but, as Goodman argues, he injects contemporary, Protestant views of prelapsarian nature that create a more benign representation of mastership.[6]

Milton is not alone in interpreting Genesis i–iii as a call for humanity to live harmoniously with nature. Many sixteenth- and seventeenth-century writers move away from the violent and controlling language of Aquinas toward a temperate view of the call to subdue, till, and keep nature. In fact, John Calvin argues that the manner in which God calls for man to subdue and have dominion over nature is not a license for human beings to exercise power, but a reminder of the greater power of God and that the object of humanity's power is *limited* in its scope. As Calvin interprets it, dressing and keeping Eden were divine labor and "this labour, truly, was pleasant, and full of delight, entirely exempt from all trouble and weariness; since, however, God ordained that man should be exercised in the culture of the ground, he condemned, in his person, all indolent repose." "Frugal" and "moderate" dressing of nature is called for so that the person who "possesses a field" will not "suffer the ground to be injured by his negligence; but let him endeavour to hand it down to posterity as he received it, or even better cultivated." For Calvin, work in Eden is a way for Adam and Eve to improve themselves through interaction with nature. Even after Adam and Eve sin, Calvin interprets their punishment as congruous with their cultivation of nature before the Fall. According to Calvin, dressing and keeping the land, even if they are now arduous tasks, improve and discipline a person and demonstrate obedience to God through reverence for God's creation.[7]

Writers as diverse as John Donne and Walter Blith echo Calvin's impression that the care of one's soul and respect for God are both cultivated and revealed through dressing and keeping the earth. Donne writes that the book of life and the book of creatures are books "that all men may know, and cultivate, and manure their own part" and thus improve their souls.[8] Donne shifts from the metaphor of the human soul as a garden that needs dressing to nature itself and Genesis' call for us "to keep the world in reparation and leave it as well as we found it . . . since we have here two employments, one to conserve this world, another to increase God's kingdom" (p. 177). Donne sees conservation of the earth and being fruitful as harmonious and compatible commandments which simultaneously urge restraint and growth.

Blith's treatise proposes several technological methods for improving the land made barren by Adam and Eve's sin. Blith's invocation of Genesis i–iii is an attempt to link his practical advice to the divine by reminding his audience that "God himself" is the "great husbandman" for making the world (p. 3). Adam and Eve and their descendants come close to God when they parallel God's actions through their cultivation of the land. Though the Genesis account contains no such language, Blith argues that not only is Adam sent forth from Eden to till the earth, he is also required to "improve" it through human ingenuity. Though today's environmental movement often regards technological "improvement" of nature to be suspect at best and a sign of hubris at its worst, Blith's commentary shares Donne's and Calvin's tone of reparation or healing of a landscape first scarred and defiled by human sin. These authors, as well as Thomas Burnet, envision a prelapsarian place and time where "fruits . . . were spontaneous, and the ground without being torn and tormented satisfied the wants or desires of man. When nature was fresh and full, all things flow'd from her more easily and more pure, like the first running of the grape, or the honeycomb; but now she must be pressed and squeez'd, and her productions taste more of the earth and of bitterness."[9] For these authors, improving, keeping, and repairing nature are efforts to bring the landscape back to its original divinely created productivity. As the bitter land is an outward reflection of the inward fallen person, attempts to restore it through husbandry are "no less than the maintenance of our lives."[10]

Donne and Calvin, and, as we will see later, Milton, interpret dressing and keeping the land to be holy acts which require thoughtful restraint and temperance as much as worshipful devotion. They envision that this work improves each individual and helps him or her to know God aright. But, whereas Donne, Calvin, and Blith emphasize the postlapsarian sixteenth- and seventeenth-century person's relation to the biblical story, Milton almost exclusively centers *Paradise Lost* upon prelapsarian life in Eden.

Within the tradition of questioning how one should subdue, have dominion over, dress and keep nature, Milton's *Paradise Lost* constitutes an ingenious approach to the argument. The biblical creation story only relates the commandment to dress and keep the land and does not tell us whether, before their sin, Adam and Eve indeed obeyed this command (it is only after Cain and Abel are born that mention is made of human beings tilling or keeping the earth). In fact, Genesis only relates two prelapsarian actions by human beings. The first is Adam's naming the creatures; the second is the marriage of Adam and Eve. Beyond that, the reader has no knowledge as to how the two lived in Paradise or whether they even tilled, kept, or governed the garden. We do not know whether Adam and Eve successfully understood or practiced a divinely inspired environmental ethic. Diane Kelsey McColley focuses on this question by juxtaposing Milton's epic poem against a pictorial sequence of images that depict the creation story. Within this sequence, one image shows Eve being formed and the very next image shows Adam and Eve's fall; such iconography suggests that God's instructions to man and woman were not heeded.[11] McColley argues that by portraying a detailed and lengthy narrative between the creation of Eve and the disobedience, Milton creates a powerful and rich space. Within this space, Milton demonstrates what life might have been like before the Fall and that the Fall should not necessarily be seen as a felix culpa. Within this temporal and natural space, Adam and Eve are depicted at work tilling and keeping Eden as well as learning from Raphael's account of the War in Heaven how an environmental ethic can be a method for gaining knowledge or losing sight of God.

Milton, in order to construct and illustrate a divine environmental ethic, must create a Paradise which comes alive as a region worthy to be considered repository and proof of God's powers as well as a setting that is deserving of Adam and Eve's action in and reflection on it. This natural space, this life in Paradise, is sacred; thus, every act is imbued with added resonance and importance. Joseph Duncan, writing about how Milton uses classical myth for spiritual purposes, says: "One of the most important functions of classical myth in Milton's Paradise is to fix, intensify, and sustain an image, to slow the tempo while the imagination seeks the unimaginable beauty of an unfallen world."[12] Within this intensified space, nature takes on added importance and meaning. Duncan argues that "Milton's Nature is so strongly personified that she is almost another character as well as an endless source of creative energy bodying forth the omnipotence and love of God" (p. 238). Chaos is "the Womb of nature and perhaps her Grave" (II, 911). And, when Eve sinned, "Earth felt the wound, and Nature from her seat / Sighing through all her Works gave signs of woe, / That all was lost" (IX, 782–84). The personification of nature as a part of creation that is born, feels wounds and sighs, and may die serves to animate Paradise in such a way that it goes beyond the role of landscape backdrop and comes to the forefront of the poem.[13]

Nature's signs indicate another dimension of the character of nature; it is metaphorically a book which invites reflection. In the act of a person's observing and interpreting nature's signs through dressing and keeping, nature can be read and can impart knowledge. Nature yields such information because it is infused with divine wisdom.[14] Milton's source for this aspect of nature is Psalm civ, which injects wisdom into the natural world in a reworking of the Genesis story saying "how manifold are thy works! in wisdom hast thou made them all" (24). Nature is created through the Word of God and is a physical manifestation or product of the Word. As the Creator looks upon his creation, "In prospect from his Throne, how good, how fair, / Answering his great Idea" (VII, 556–57), we see that nature is conceived of as an answer. It is not a self-evident answer to Adam, though. Adam, in recounting his first experiences in the world to Raphael, looks at nature, names its creatures, and, through these actions, has intimations that he was made "by some great Maker" (VIII, 278). He asks of nature to "Tell me, how may I know him [the Creator], how adore, / From whom I have that thus I move and live, / And feel that I am happier than I know" (VIII, 280–82). Only when God reveals himself to Adam as a "Guide" (VIII, 312) and as "Author of all this thou seest" (VIII, 317) does Adam learn how to read nature clearly. To read nature's signs correctly requires that the Word of God, the original author of the natural text, serves as a supplement or a divine hermeneutic. Thus, nature and Word are sacred and work in tandem to inform a reflective Adam and Eve about the infinite capacities of God.

In Milton's "earthly Paradise," all of nature is sacred and can inform Adam and Eve about their creator's infinite power. In *Christian Doctrine*, Milton writes,

We may understand from other passages of Scripture, that when God infused the breath of life into man, what man thereby received was not a portion of God's essence, or a participation of the divine nature, but that measure of the divine virtue or influence, which was commensurate to the capabilities of the recipient. For it appears from Psal. civ. 29, 30. that he infused the breath of life into other living beings also;—"thou takest away their breath, they die . . . thou sendest forth thy spirit, they are created."[15]

Milton's use of Psalm civ counters the tradition that Leiss writes of where man and nature are split and nature is held in low regard. Instead, Milton provides an alternative hierarchy within which all living creatures have some amount of spirit "commensurate to the capabilities of the recipient." This hierarchy is articulated by Raphael to Adam in Book V:

> one Almighty is, from whom
> All things proceed, and up to him return,
> If not deprav'd from good, created all
> Such to perfection, one first matter all,
> Indu'd with various forms, various degrees
> Of substance, and in things that live, of life;
> But more refin'd, more spiritous, and pure,
> As nearer to him plac't or nearer tending
> Each in thir several active Spheres assign'd,
> Till body up to spirit work, in bounds
> Proportion'd to each kind.   (469–79)

Raphael illustrates this hierarchy by using the apt metaphor of a tree, whose earthy roots bring nourishment to more and more "aery" parts until the tree yields its sublime flower and fruit for the nourishment of Adam (479–83). This metaphor links the human intellect to the processes of the universe through the physical acts of growth and digestion. From the tree metaphor, Adam learns of his place in God's creation and that there are proper substances to nourish him until one day he may eat like the angels and have their level of knowledge. This elaborate metaphor serves several purposes. First, it establishes an ontological hierarchy where all is good and interconnected. Second, it places Adam within that hierarchy but not at its top. He may be at the top of the hierarchy in Eden but Eden is part of a larger hierarchy; this teaches Adam to act with humility. Third, within this hierarchy, Adam is not fixed but may rise if he takes nature's nourishing fruits and recognizes their true origin. Fourth, this description illustrates how nature and metaphor transcend their inherent limitations and reveal God to Adam. Raphael's metaphor portrays a hierarchy within which Adam must have knowledge both of what is beneath him and above him. This hierarchy lessens the severity of Aquinas's model and infuses it with Protestant theories regarding the beauty of all prelapsarian creation.

Raphael's discussion with Adam and Raphael's metaphor of creation as a tree illustrate one component of an environmental ethic. Raphael indicates that nature is the object worthy of Adam and Eve's intellectual reflection. Through this dialogue, Adam formulates an overarching understanding of the structures and purposes of nature. When Adam's questions no longer ask for information that will help him develop a worshipful environmental ethic, Raphael cuts him off and says he was sent to Adam for a specific purpose:

> to answer thy desire
> Of knowledge within bounds; beyond abstain
> To ask, nor let thine own inventions hope
> Things not reveal'd, which th' invisible King,
> Only Omniscient, hath supprest in Night,
> To none communicable in Earth or Heaven:
> Anough is left besides to search and know.   (VII, 119–25)

The angel's response to Adam's curiosity indicates that human knowledge of the Creator must be derived from reflection on a specific object; visible nature is that object.

Within the unique position that Paradise fills in God's creation, Adam and Eve are told to fulfill the other half of the environmental ethic's dialectic—to interact with nature. This action both informs and focuses their reflective minds and culminates in the worship and praise of God. In developing a call to action, Milton freely mixes the two Creation stories in Genesis and attempts to achieve a synthesis of the two through Raphael's and Adam's accounts of Creation. Raphael's account of the creation of Paradise to Adam interweaves and splices together parts of Genesis, chapters i and ii. In Raphael's account, man is created after the animals, and, almost simultaneously, woman is also created (VII, 529–30). Raphael slips into the

second version to relate how Adam was made out of the ground (VII, 524–25). Though Raphael tries to blend the two accounts together in a seamless fashion, it is crucial to note that much of the language is taken from Genesis, chapter i, not ii. Man is to "rule" (VII, 520) all the creatures of the earth, and, in this version, God blesses mankind, saying, "Be fruitful, multiply, and fill the Earth, / *Subdue* it, and throughout *Dominion* hold / Over Fish of the sea" (VII, 531–33; emphasis mine). This language is echoed by Michael in Book XI when he reminds Adam that Eden is not the only place on earth where people can follow God's command to interact with nature. Michael says, "All th' Earth he gave thee to possess and rule" (XI, 339).

Adam's account of his first moments on earth picks up from where Raphael leaves off. The two accounts differ in several places, primarily in how Adam must view nature. Adam uses the Genesis, chapter ii, terminology "to Till and keep" Paradise (VIII, 320) instead of Raphael's "subdue" and "dominion."[16] Later, Adam briefly uses Genesis, chapter i, terminology when he says that God told him to "possess" (VIII, 340) the whole earth and its creatures (not just the plants of Paradise referred to in line 320). J. M. Evans writes that "Raphael's disquisition has portrayed the Creation from above; Adam's now reveals how it appeared from below."[17] In this light, the dialogue is an interesting reconciliation of the differences in language and detail between Genesis i and ii by Milton, with chapter i considered as the divine overview and chapter ii as the more explicit and concrete information that Adam needs for implementing God's commands. For example, the word "subdue" could be understood in the context of God's subduing Chaos in order to create the universe. It is a word more appropriate to God than to Adam. "Tilling" and "keeping" the land are less abstract words than "subdue" and "dominion," and are well suited for practical implementation. Nonetheless, there is still a dialectical tension between the different language of the two accounts that is further complicated when Adam slips into "divine" language by mentioning that he is to "possess" (as opposed to coexist with mutually) the earth and its creatures. Though Adam primarily uses language found in Genesis, chapter ii, his use of "possess" blurs the boundaries between chapters i and ii.

The tension between these words ("possess" versus "till" and "keep") is abstract until we see Adam and Eve choose their own interpretation and make these abstract ideas tangible through physical actions that culminate in an environmental practice which fuses work in Eden with worship. God's georgic demand to tend nature is not an idle one. Nature is so fertile and abundant as a manifestation of God's own fertility that it has the potential to grow out of control. Satan's view of plant life outside Eden reveals "a steep wilderness, whose hairy sides / With thicket overgrown, grotesque

and wild, / Access deni'd" (IV, 135–37). It is "A Wilderness of sweets; for Nature here / Wanton'd as in her prime, and play'd at will / Her Virgin Fancies, pouring forth more sweet, / Wild above Rule or Art, enormous bliss" (V, 294–97) whose abundance appears as a threat to order. This does not mean that nature is flawed. Rather, it is not self-sufficient. Adam and Eve's gardening checks this growth and channels it toward an even higher level of productivity:

> On to thir morning's rural work they haste
> Among sweet dews and flow'rs; where any row
> Of Fruit-trees overwoody reach'd too far
> Thir pamper'd boughs, and needed hands to check
> Fruitless imbraces: or they led the Vine
> To wed her Elm.   (V, 211–16)

Michael Lieb associates the sexual overtones of nature's wantonness with Eve's sexually symbolic "wanton ringlets" (IV, 306) and tendril-like hair. He argues that both sexuality and nature represent an energy that has the potential to get out of control unless used for the "higher and more creative purpose of the submission of disorder or wantonness to the temperance of a higher or superior order." The marriage metaphor in the preceding passage, then, links the controlling act of gardening with the loving and productive act of marriage. Eve, though, is not merely associated with nature's potentially troubling growth; she is a gardener like Adam. Through their gardening, both exercise a form of governance. Goodman points out that "in exercising active governance, however, Adam and Eve do not simply rule in enlightened self-interest but actively serve their subjects." Their work improves both nature and themselves. This creates a complete whole within which nature and human beings are (in modern environmental terms) an interrelated ecosystem. With their work, Milton's Adam and Eve fulfill the spirit and tone of the Hebrew text of Genesis, chapter ii.[18]

The depiction of prelapsarian work, according to McColley, is one of many ways in which Milton redefines Christian interpretations of the first three books of Genesis. By creating a detailed life in prelapsarian Paradise, McColley argues, Milton reconstitutes work, nature, and sexuality as potential methods for worshiping God and his creation instead of conceiving them in terms of punishment, adversary, and cause of the Fall. Adam and Eve successfully read the book of nature through their labor and transform this knowledge into art.[19] Their knowledge rings out in songful praise as they sing "In these thy lowest works, yet these declare / Thy goodness beyond thought" (V, 158–59) for a morning prayer. McColley says,

In *Paradise Lost* work is a form of love. It prompts awareness of the needs and natures of other beings and concern for them, exercises mind and body, and provides understanding of the workings of nature and of the mind, limitless conversation, and the abounding interest of cooperating with nature. Eden is profuse; but it needs human work to guard its beauty and keep it fruitful. The same is true of human souls. (P. 188)

The interaction between Adam and Eve with and within nature is an earth-bound ethic that develops the human soul, and gives them the paradoxical possibility of rising and fulfilling their potential as replacements in heaven for Satan's rebels.

Adam and Eve's worshipful gardening is not the only model of an environmental ethic in *Paradise Lost*. In fact, their model tells us very little about how they should fulfill the second half of God's environmental command. How are they meant to keep nature? "To keep" implies an act of preservation, but preservation from what? This question is answered when Milton constructs two other distinct ethical models. These models are developed in Raphael's account of the War in Heaven and the subsequent creation of the universe. The first is Satan's ethic which embodies his dangerous rebelliousness. The second is the ethic of God and his Son. These environmental ethics, or models, reflect different possible readings of the Genesis Creation stories and highlight the problematic tensions between the two accounts that could lead either to misinterpretations or blessedness. These two models are educational for Adam and Eve and let them know what is at stake in their treatment of nature and obedience to God's rules. These models come in the middle books of *Paradise Lost*, indicating that though Adam and Eve's ethic seemingly has been correct, the dialectical tensions within it that heretofore have been hidden will soon be brought to the surface by Satan. The models given in Books V and VI are preemptive attempts to inform Adam and Eve as to the danger in misreading or mistreating nature and God.

As a prefatory note to the account of the War in Heaven, Raphael tells Adam that he can not give a literal account that will be intelligible to Adam. Instead,

> what surmounts the reach
> Of human sense, I shall delineate so,
> By lik'ning spiritual to corporal forms,
> As may express them best, though what if Earth
> Be but the shadow of Heav'n, and things therein
> Each to other like more than of Earth is thought?   (V, 571–76)

Raphael bridges the gap between heaven and earth by adjusting his metaphors and illustrations to a context that Adam understands; that context is
the nature and landscape of Eden. The corporeal substance that makes up
nature, though considered less pure than that substance which makes up
heaven, is equated with spiritual forms, which invest nature with a primacy
that reminds Adam of its significant value.

Sometimes the best way to understand the rules of a game is to break
them. This transgression reveals where the boundaries are, what they are
made of, and what they are meant to do. Raphael's account of Satan's complex fall from grace is educational for Adam, who is given the benefit of
hearing what can be learned from Satan's actions so that he will not repeat
Satan's pride-driven error. The first part of God's ethic that Satan breaks is
the reflective component. He does this by questioning the hierarchical
structure that places God and Son above the created beings. Whereas Milton's Adam learns from Raphael that every living thing has some element of
the divine within it that is proportionate to its nature, Satan openly defies
this wisdom by arguing, "We know no time when we were not as now; /
Know none before us, self-begot, self-rais'd" (V, 859–60). Satan flattens the
hierarchy of creator over creation by raising himself and lowering God. His
claim denies both God as the Creator and nature as repository or sign of
various levels of divinity. Once Satan convinces his followers of this alternative perspective,

> Who can in reason then or right assume
> Monarchy over such as live by right
> His equals, if in power and splendor less,
> In freedom equal?   (V, 794–97)

Thoughts like these lead to Satan's creative act of giving birth to Sin. Lieb
calls this a dialectical act of "uncreation" which serves as an antithesis to
God's own creative acts.[20]

Satan's reflection upon and questioning of the hierarchical order are
infused with language from Genesis, chapter i. As he attempts to persuade
the other angels to rebel, his opening words are "Thrones, Dominations,
Princedoms, Virtues, Powers" (V, 772). In this speech, Satan puts the history
of heaven in the biblical terms of dominion and rule. He interprets the
begetting of the Son as a tyrannical act by God over his creation. Because
Satan sees himself as a slave under the "yoke" of God (V, 786), one might
think that Satan would overturn the Genesis, chapter i, model of dominion
and subduing creation. Instead, Milton's Satan illustrates a possible literal
interpretation (and thus, a misinterpretation) of i, 26–28, by seeking to de-
pose God and insert himself in the role of ruler of heaven. Considering the

environmental ethic Milton has established for Adam and Eve, we already know that Satan is doomed to failure. He is doomed because, while his words "dominion" and "subdue" incorporate the dialectic of reflection (the questioning of a hierarchical order) and action (ruling over others), the ethic that results from this dialectic focuses not on God the Creator but Satan the usurper. Satan's ethic focuses only on possession without any greater sense of what it is that he possesses and where it comes from. Satanic possession, according to Lieb, constitutes a lust that "becomes an integral part of Satan's desire to accumulate wealth in defiance of God. And that desire . . . approximates the urge to 'create' in artifice what God has created in spiritual glory. Consequently, 'possession' is not only an uncreating act for Satan but, in the exercise of its materiality, an act of defilement" (p. 99).

This defilement which begins in Satan's mind (the reflective component of his ethic) is physically realized when he goes to battle (the active component of the ethic). After losing the first day's battle, Satan retreats and invents the "engine." Of the engine and where it comes from Satan says,

> Not uninvented that, which thou aright
> Believ'st so main to our success, I bring;
> Which of us who beholds the bright surface
> Of this Ethereous mould whereon we stand,
> This continent of spacious Heav'n adorn'd
> With Plant, Fruit, Flow'r Ambrosial, Gems and Gold,
> Whose Eye so superficially surveys
> These things, as not to mind from whence they grow
> Deep under ground, materials dark and crude,
> Of spiritous and fiery spume, till toucht
> With Heav'n's ray and temper'd they shoot forth
> So beauteous, op'ning to the ambient light.   (VI, 470–81)

The way in which Satan reads this environment is very informative of his ethic. Unlike Adam and Eve, who focus on plants and animals when they read the book of nature, Satan's focus briefly views the beauty of heaven's refined vegetation. His focus then moves to the elemental "originals of Nature in thir crude / Conception" (VI, 511–12). His shifting focus immediately calls into question whether his environmental ethic is environmental at all, for it is focused not on nature but, as Lieb points out, on that substance out of which nature is made (p. 115). Satan's error is one that Adam nearly commits when he asks Raphael misdirected questions that regard "things not reveal'd." Satan's ethic is misdirected because it is no longer concentrated on the correct object of study, visible nature.

With the creation of the engine, Milton introduces a satanic version of

Genesis, chapter ii. Here, Satan provides his own method of tilling the ground. His tilling and dressing do not add to or redefine nature in the way that Adam and Eve's gardening does. Rather, as Lieb demonstrates, his tilling (really mining and technology) of the most base part of nature is more like an act of "sexual violation" (p. 118); a violation in which the "originals of Nature" are the reproductive organs of Chaos that lie right beneath the ground of heaven. Satan's perverted tilling embodies a violent perspective of the "to subdue" of Genesis, chapter i, and has no sense of the harmony that is conveyed in chapter ii.

The ironic origin of the engines is revealed through Raphael's metaphoric description of them as "hollow'd bodies made of Oak or Fir / With branches lopt, in Wood or Mountain fell'd" (VI, 574–75). This language, while making the unimaginable intelligible to Adam, adds another dimension to the story. The engines are Satan's perverted attempt to mimic God's creation. While God's trees bring beauty and knowledge of Creation—as demonstrated by Raphael's hierarchical and metaphorical tree (Book V)—Satan's trees bring destruction. Where God's trees are solid, Satan's are hollow shells of the true Creation. The result of Satan's invention is modern warfare. According to Raphael, the engines' fire was effective against the good angels until the latter, "Thir Arms away they threw, and to the Hills / . . . From thir foundations loos'ning to and fro / They pluckt the seated Hills . . . / . . . [and] bore them in thir hands" (VI, 639–46) and threw the mountains on Satan's engines. The result of Satan's creation is an environmental ethic that manifests itself in environmental warfare. This ethic, or antiethic, turns the natural order of heaven to "confusion heapt / Upon confusion" (VI, 668–69) and threatens to return heaven to Chaos.

The implications of Satan's engines are many, but the destruction they create gives Adam a context within which he can understand what "to keep" means. In Paradise, Adam has not seen any ways in which nature (except for its potential to overrun itself if not pruned) is threatened and needs to be protected. Satan's act of defilement and Raphael's comment that the "Sons of men" might also one day create like weapons of mass destruction, illustrate that nature is a fragile system. Satan's defilement demonstrates that, if misinterpreted or abused, dressing nature can directly conflict with keeping nature. The result of Satan's warfare suggests that a correct embodiment of Genesis, chapter ii, involves restraint as a mode of action to complement tilling and dressing nature.[21]

The model of environmental ethic that Satan embodies demonstrates the many ways in which an ethic can be perverted. The perversion begins when the reflective component is misdirected because the ethic is no longer a method through which one tries to know and worship God. Satan's misdirected actions pit the tensions and ambiguities of Genesis i and ii against each other, for he fails to recognize the dominion/harmony dialectic. Instead, his character illustrates the dominion and violent subjugation of creation that one could read into chapter i and ignores the harmonious language of chapter ii. Satan's error is manifested in the second half of the environmental ethic. His actions are neither respectful nor worshipful. Adam learns that, when properly focused on God, an environmental ethic reveals harmonic order and not satanic confusion.

The second model of an environmental ethic presented by Raphael to Adam is embodied by God and the Son. Their providential actions serve to remind the created beings from whence comes nature and reestablish the intimate, visible bond between God and nature. The bond is revealed, during the war, by the first command that the Son issues from the "Chariot of Paternal Deity" (VI, 750), which concerns heaven's landscape, and not the conquering of Satan:

> At his command the uprooted Hills retir'd
> Each to his place, they heard his voice and went
> Obsequious, Heav'n his wonted face renew'd
> And with fresh Flow'rets Hill and Valley smil'd.   (VI, 781–84)

This event is less an act of creation than an act of restoration. Here is a model for Adam of how one must keep and preserve the natural order of creation.

The restoration of heaven's landscape precedes the destruction directed at Satan's rebels. Of the relationship between renewing and destroying, Lieb writes,

It is important to recognize the symbolical overtones of these antithetical motions, for such a recognition allows us to see what God's uncreating of the angels through the agency of the Son really implies. Paradoxically, the Son's uncreating of Satan and his crew is not an uncreative act. Unlike Satan, who destroys for the sake of destroying, the Son destroys in order to create.[22]

The paradoxical nature of his actions is revealed through the words used to describe how the Son conquers his foes. The Son does not unleash his full power "for he meant / Not to destroy, but *root* them out of Heav'n" (VI, 854–55; emphasis mine). The verb "root" directly echoes the "uprooted Hills," demonstrating that the two are related. Satan's band, like a bunch of weeds, has supplanted the proper vegetation (the hills) of heaven. The manner in which the Son restores order is similar to the allegorical garden scene in Shakespeare's *Richard II* where "the whole land [England], / Is full of weeds, her fairest flowers chok'd up" (III, iv, 43–44). In this play the gardener says, "O, what pity is it / That he [Richard II] had not so trimm'd and dress'd his land / As we this garden!" (III, iv, 55–57). As this drama points out, dressing nature is a metaphor for the process of rulership. The Son's action illustrates for Adam that tilling and dressing, as an act of maintaining nature, are positive embodiments of Genesis i, 26, 28. The Son's actions also demonstrate that dressing and keeping nature are often identical acts.

The models that Raphael presents to Adam culminate in Adam's own interpretation of his creation and ethic, but, finally, are not enough to save Adam and Eve. The moment that they decide to partake of the fruit of the forbidden tree, they have repeated Satan's error. They lose sight of God's goodness in nature and misuse nature by seeking a Godlike mastery over it through the acquisition of prohibited knowledge. Satan's temptation that seduces Eve is reminiscent of Raphael's account of the treelike hierarchy of creation. Satan says, "That ye should be as Gods, since I as Man, / Internal Man, is but proportion meet, / I of brute human, yee of human Gods" (IX, 710–12). This speech perverts God's hierarchy because it provides false methods for human advancement that do not include worshipful use of the land. By falsely representing the structures and purposes of nature, the reflective component of the ethic is perverted.

After Satan's oration, the narrator writes, "in her [Eve's] ears the sound / Yet rung of his persuasive words, impregn'd / With Reason" (IX, 736–38). "Impregn'd" echoes Satan's perverted generative sexuality from the War in Heaven. The offspring of this sexuality, in both cases, is violence toward nature. The moment Eve ate the fruit, "Earth felt the wound, and Nature from her seat / Sighing through all her Works gave signs of woe, / That all was lost" (IX, 782–84). When Adam followed Eve's lead, "Nature gave a second groan, / Sky low'r'd, and muttering Thunder, some sad drops / Wept at completing of the mortal Sin / Original" (IX, 1001–04). The importance of Milton's description of nature here is twofold. First, Adam and Eve's disobedience, when put in terms of nature, is an act of defilement that wounds the sacredness of nature much as Satan's defilement wounds Heaven (thus both actions are antithetical to the keeping of nature). Second, though wounded, nature is still one of the books of wisdom that, if Adam and Eve cared to read it, would indicate the failure of their ethic.

Adam and Eve's disobedience inexorably changes the dynamics of nature. The harmony that prevailed throughout nature and that issued from their interaction with it is now obscured. Earth's postlapsarian nature is infected by Sin and Death so that,

> Beast now with Beast gan war, and Fowl with Fowl,
> And Fish with Fish; to graze the Herb all leaving,

Devour'd each other; nor stood much in awe
Of Man, but fled him, or with count'nance grim
Glar'd on him passing: these were from without
The growing miseries, which Adam saw
Already in part, though hid in gloomiest shade.   (X, 710–16)

One of the results of Adam and Eve's failed environmental ethic is the clouding of nature. No longer is it a clear face of God. Nature still gives signs of God's will, but the signs are no longer always good. Of Adam and Eve's new condition, John Reichert says, "They must replace the knowledge of things seen with faith in things unseen, acquiring new skills in the reading of the book of the creatures and, more crucial still, an understanding of and a reliance on Scripture."[23] The expulsion is not the end of the environmental ethic. Michael reminds Adam that God is present throughout his creation and that "All th' Earth he gave thee to possess and rule" (XI, 339), and not simply Eden alone. A postlapsarian ethic, in many ways, will be more difficult to follow because its signs are more ambiguous, but it is not entirely different from the ethic Adam and Eve followed in Eden.

What are the readers of *Paradise Lost* to make of Milton's reading of Genesis i and ii as an environmental ethic? Perhaps Milton's *Of Education* provides the most insightful answer to this question:

The end then of learning is to repair the ruins of our first parents by regaining to know God aright, and out of that knowledge to love him, to imitate him, to be like him, as we may the nearest by possessing our souls of true virtue, which being united to the heavenly grace of faith makes up the highest perfection. But because our understanding cannot in this body found itself but on sensible things, nor arrive so clearly to the knowledge of God and things invisible as by orderly conning over the visible and inferior creature, the same method is necessarily to be followed in all discreet teaching. (P. 631)

Education and learning embody both components of an environmental ethic. They are reflective pursuits that focus upon nature and attempt to find through visible nature "knowledge of God and things invisible." Education and learning also metaphorically fulfill and update the active component of an environmental ethic for a postlapsarian world. The figurative reparation for the ruins is an act of keeping nature through the restoration of knowing God "aright."

Viewed from such a perspective, Milton himself embodies an environmental ethic that overarches the multiple ethics in *Paradise Lost*. His ethic, filled with Calvin's and Donne's spirit of repairing a damaged earth, is suitable for a postlapsarian world. As Michael Lieb writes, the poet is a creator who must create out of his fallenness. He argues: "a consideration of the poet as fallen individual reveals that the positive or glorious aspects of creativity manifest themselves only after the negative aspects have been overcome. That is, the poet must confront the uncreative aspects of the fall in order to create positively."[24] The poetic act parallels God's own creation of something new after something else has been uncreated (for example, the creation of the universe follows the defilement of heaven). As a poet, Milton confronts the uncreativity of the Fall by writing about how Paradise was lost. To parallel the creativity of God even further, Milton, in literary form, creates or re-creates God's creation, Paradise. In this divine light, *Paradise Lost* becomes a literary work of environmental reclamation that reinvigorates the Genesis accounts of how one should know God by living in the natural world. In the end, it is not only Adam and Eve who learn about the multiple incarnations of Genesis and the possibility of its environmental ethic; Milton and his readers are also exposed to this challenging text. In the process of developing a Miltonic environmental ethic, we learn that, according to Diane McColley, "we cannot return to Eden, but we can make Edenic choices."[25]

University of Illinois, Chicago

NOTES

I owe a major debt of thanks to Michael Lieb for his commentary and deft guidance throughout this project—from its beginning as a paper for his seminar on Milton and the Bible to its present state. Thanks also to Clark Hulse, Diane McColley, and Albert Labriola for their ideas regarding how to improve this essay both substantively and rhetorically.

1. Marx, *The Machine in the Garden: Technology and the Pastoral Ideal in America* (London, 1964); Harrison, *Forests: The Shadow of Civilization* (Chicago, 1992); Leopold, *A Sand County Almanac* (1949; rpt. New York, 1970). See pp. 239–41 for epigraph.

2. *Ecology* is a fairly recent word that only can be traced back to the nineteenth century. Interestingly, the root of the word is from the Greek *oikos*, meaning "house" or "dwelling." Thus ecology is the management or economy of our living house, the earth and the animals and plants that live within it.

3. Manwood, *A Treatise and Discourse of the Laws of the Forrest* (London, 1598); Rudrum, "Henry Vaughan, the Liberation of the Creatures, and Seventeenth-Century English Calvinism," *Seventeenth Century* IV (Spring 1989): 33–54. This article provides an excellent background to the theological milieu within which both Milton and Vaughan wrote their poetry.

4. Trible, *God and the Rhetoric of Sexuality* (Philadelphia, 1978), p. 72; biblical citations are from the King James Version; Cohen, *"Be Fertile and Increase, Fill the Earth and Master It": The Ancient and Medieval Career of a Biblical Text* (Ithaca, 1989), p. 16. Cohen's book provides an excellent and thorough account of Genesis i, 28's various exegeses from biblical times through the Middle Ages.

5. Trible, *God and the Rhetoric of Sexuality*, p. 77.

6. Leiss, *The Domination of Nature* (New York, 1972), p. 32; Goodman, "Human Mastership of Nature: Aquinas and Milton's *Paradise Lost*," *MQ* XXVI (1992): 9–15. Goodman's essay provides an opening to the question of Milton's concept of the mastery of nature as a harmonious environmental ethic.

7. Calvin, *Commentaries on the First Book of Moses Called Genesis*, vol. 1, trans. Rev. John King (Edinburgh, 1847), pp. 97, 125, 174–75.

8. Donne, *Essays in Divinity*, ed. Augustus Jessopp (London, 1855), pp. 12–13; Blith, *The English Improver Improved* (London, 1652).

9. Burnet, *The Theory of the Earth*, vol. 1 (London, 1684), pp. 181–82.

10. Blith, *The English Improver Improved*, p. 4.

11. McColley, *A Gust for Paradise: Milton's Eden and the Visual Arts* (Urbana, 1993), p. 38.

12. Duncan, *Milton's Earthly Paradise: A Historical Study of Eden* (Minneapolis, 1972), p. 30.

13. All references to Milton's works come from *John Milton: Complete Poems and Major Prose*, ed. Merritt Y. Hughes (New York, 1957), and are hereafter cited in the text. For more on Milton's personification of nature as well as the tension between the material and spiritual that results from this process, see William Madsen, "The Idea of Nature in Milton's Poetry," in *Three Studies in the Renaissance: Sidney, Jonson, Milton* (New Haven, 1958), pp. 231–33.

14. For a detailed study of the relationship between the books of nature and Scripture in relation to wisdom, see John Reichert, *Milton's Wisdom: Nature and Scripture in "Paradise Lost"* (Ann Arbor, 1992).

15. *CD*, p. 979. Though Milton's authorship of *Christian Doctrine* has been called into question, for the purposes of this essay I am working under the assumption that Milton wrote this work.

16. Although the King James Version does not use "to till" but "to keep," the tone that these words convey, as I take it from Trible's translation, is roughly synonymous with the Hebrew verb *'bd*.

17. Evans, *"Paradise Lost" and the Genesis Tradition* (Oxford, 1968), p. 256.

18. Lieb, *The Dialectics of Creation: Patterns of Birth and Regeneration in "Paradise Lost"* (Amherst, 1970), p. 72; Goodman, "Human Mastership of Nature," p. 13.

19. Art, in my formulation of a Miltonic environmental ethic, is observable evidence of the reflective mind's synthesis and interpretation of the relationship between people, nature, and God. This is largely derived from McColley's beautifully expressed reading of the "arts of Eden" in *A Gust for Paradise*.

20. Lieb, *Dialectics of Creation*, p. 85.

21. To consider Satan's engines in a broader perspective, see Leo Marx's very engaging account of the implications of the tensions between nature and technology in *The Machine in the Garden*.

22. Lieb, *Dialectics of Creation*, pp. 121–22.

23. Reichert, *Milton's Wisdom*, pp. 229–30.

24. Lieb, *Dialectics of Creation*, p. 37.

25. McColley, *A Gust for Paradise*, p. 190.

"LEST WILFULLY TRANSGRESSING": RAPHAEL'S NARRATION AND KNOWLEDGE IN *PARADISE LOST*

Charles Eric Reeves

A T A R E V E A L I N G juncture in God's charge to Raphael in Book V of *Paradise Lost*, there occurs a troubling, if subtle, verbal ambiguity. Raphael, readers will recall, has been instructed to let Adam know a good deal about his perilous state in Paradise, "Lest wilfully transgressing he pretend / Surprisal, unadmonisht, unforewarn'd" (V, 244–45).[1] In various discussions of this passage what has gone insufficiently remarked is that the conjunction "Lest" here can charge the clause that follows in two ways, though larger rhetorical pressures may obscure this. For, on a strict grammatical construal, God may be saying to Raphael: "tell Adam this so that *if* he falls, he won't later be able to claim that he did so because he wasn't warned." Or God may be saying: "tell Adam this so that *when* he falls, he won't later be able to blame anyone but himself."

Both the tone and the substance of the latter formulation have seemed distasteful to many, but a consideration of what has preceded in Book III, and the evidence of Milton's theological thinking in other contexts, would seem to make it the only logically possible reading. For of course an earlier colloquy between the Father and the Son (III, 80–216) has been conducted in such a way that all of heaven becomes party to the revelation of future spiritual history: how the "ingrate" man will "easily transgress the sole Command," though because he "falls deceiv'd" he shall ultimately find grace, if only someone can be found to "pay / The rigid satisfaction, death for death" (III, 211–12). When asked where such love can be found, "*all* the Heav'nly Choir stood mute" (italics mine). We may, in fact, wonder just when the heavenly host becomes party to a colloquy that seems initially to be between God and the Son ("Thus to his only Son foreseeing spake," III, 79). But clearly the entire heavenly population has heard enough for the culminating question to make sense; the "Heav'nly Choir" stands "mute" precisely because they have no answer to the question God has "ask'd" them: "Dwells in all Heaven charity so dear?" (III, 216). The angelic host is clearly and directly addressed: "Say Heav'nly Powers, where shall we find such love, /

Which of ye will be mortal to redeem / Man's mortal crime" (III, 213–15). Man's disobedience and its consequences are referred to explicitly in the lines immediately preceding, with no evidence of an intervening rhetorical shift from a "personal" to a "public" address, certainly not between the reference to "Man disobeying" (III, 203) and the concluding question of the verse paragraph. Thus Raphael, though absent at the "time" of worldly creation, must certainly be present for this crucial test; indeed, the scene fails theologically if any angel is exempted from the moment of supreme spiritual trial or fails to understand the nature and necessity of heavenly intercession:

> on man's behalf
> Patron or Intercessor none appear'd,
> Much less that durst upon his own head draw
> The deadly forfeiture, and ransom set.   (III, 218–21)

But if this is true, and Raphael is not suffering from angelic amnesia, then it is difficult to escape the conclusion that he must know the meaning of that "lest" in Book V. And if he does know that man will fall, then his entire discourse of warning, the central four books of the poem, are, it might plausibly be argued, a charade—a servile dignifying of God's creation of a creature who, if not "destined" to fall, will *certainly* fall—a certainty that becomes common knowledge as of the first two hundred lines of Book III. Raphael's graciousness, solicitousness, his circumspect wondering whether he has the authority to narrate all he does, his regard for Adam and Eve's well-being—all become, on this harsh reading, tawdry expedience, a covering of the "legal" bases. And his beautiful final words, apparently so resonant with a passionate angelic wisdom, must be read instead as a pro forma clearing of divine responsibility:

> Be strong, live happy, and love, but first of all
> Him whom to love is to obey, and keep
> His great command; take heed *lest* Passion sway
> Thy Judgment to do aught, which else free Will
> Would not admit.   (VIII, 633–37; italics mine)

Such a reading would force us to see in Raphael's use of "lest" here a brutally ironic recapitulation of God's charge to his angelic messenger, and evidence of the heavenly "distance and distaste" (IX, 9) that the poem's epic voice would have us believe is connected with the actual events of the Fall. The drama and narrative tension of the poem, and most especially of Book

IX, are seriously undercut, producing in their place a shabby denouement to the telling of a tale of spiritual inevitability.

I do not mean to argue for such an unpalatable reading, though some elements of it have certainly found their way into modern critical commentary on the poem, but rather to insist that there are legitimate and difficult questions about judgment, honesty, and knowledge in Raphael's great narration of warning. Moreover, I do want to ask about the logical implications of such a narration. For we can't blink the fact that Raphael *should* know, at the very least, what Book III reveals the entire heavenly host to know. The "lest" of Book V—meaning "for fear that," or "to avoid the possibility that"—can not be arbitrarily shorn of its larger context: what exactly does God "fear" or "wish to avoid," and what does Raphael "fear" or "wish to avoid," in turn, at Book VIII, line 635? Man will fall; this is known as certainly as anything can be known before it happens, because God says it will happen: "and [man] shall pervert" (III, 92). So it can't be fear *that* man will fall because no reasonable creature, whether "discursive" or "intuitive" by nature, can fear what will certainly occur. After all, we should remember that as a conjunction "lest" implies a cautionary attitude, a concern to *avoid* a certain state of affairs: "she whispered lest she should be overheard." But how can Raphael know what he knows and be rescued from performing in the thoroughly unappealing role I have described? And to push the question to its largest significance, how can God be rescued from the charge of having sent Raphael on a disingenuous and gratuitous mission? In other words, how does Raphael's difficulty become suggestive of the poem's largest theological difficulties?

The answer is likely to emerge only if the nature of Raphael's apparent narrative dilemma is fully appreciated, and despite considerable critical attention to God's charge to his archangel, this issue has not been addressed. The archangel's narrative and rhetorical *character* in Books V through VIII require a more persuasive account than either cynics or apologists have so far provided, notwithstanding the number of thoughtful, useful, and wide-ranging studies of Milton's angels, his angelology, classical parallels to the angelic embassies of *Paradise Lost,* and the surprisingly numerous studies of Raphael individually.[2] The problem lies in sharply divergent assumptions, whether explicit or implicit in larger arguments—assumptions which have not been made to confront one another directly enough. For those who discuss Raphael's extended discourse have assumed either that (1) he does know that the human couple will fall, but that despite this, his is not a speech disingenuous, unconcerned, or unloving (moments of apparent tactlessness or disingenuousness are folded within larger, more powerfully benign motives and tactics, or are explained away on the grounds of sheer necessity); or (2) Milton's God, by virtue of his charge to Raphael, has done an unfortunate, indeed disingenuous job of it, putting Raphael in an impossible position—and for all too human reasons of self-exculpation.

The particular crux I am trying to suggest concerning Raphael's knowledge and his narration, far from being a staple of critical or interpretive commentary—like the "double time" plot of *Othello* or the question about whether the narrating voice of *The Canterbury Tales* is or is not omniscient—has typically not been seen or construed as a problem in its own right. What I wish to argue is that this state of affairs ultimately says more about Milton's skill and intuitive sense of his poem's requirements than it does about any critical failing among his readers. For to pose the problem in its starkest form is already to glimpse a solution, a way of reading that accommodates both the demand for logical consistency and our sense of the deep compassion that guides Raphael's narration of warning in the central books of the poem. For much as Shakespeare in *Othello* finds that the exigencies of his drama oblige two time schemes (one accommodating the rapid transformation of Othello into jealous tyrant, the other a more expansive time scheme creating the *possibility* of Desdemona's "infidelity"), so also Milton in his epic discerns, consciously or unconsciously, the need for two "Raphaels."

On the one hand, Raphael is fully part of the timeless order of heaven, namelessly present at the exaltation of the Son, another warrior in the ranks of God's loyal angels (VI, 363) during the war in heaven. Intensely and benignly hierarchical, the order to which Raphael belongs is defined by the peculiarities of its ontology rather than by its temporality or a larger narrative logic. Indeed, so completely determined are the essentially static features of Milton's heaven that the only truly temporal "event" (in the sense of a state of affairs not fully continuous with that which precedes) is the emergence of sin in the unfallen Satan and the consequent war.[3] And precisely because this "event" occurs as a rupture in the harmonious hierarchy of heaven, it is radically inexplicable: despite the ostensible explanation ("he felt himself impair'd") we can neither know nor surmise why Satan should feel pride, feel impaired, on the occasion of the Son's exaltation (short of importing an irrelevant fallen human psychology), nor why God should have created creatures who he knew at the very moment of creation would disobey and suffer an eternity of torment in hell. This first, heavenly Raphael—insofar as we discern him at all—is simply one more ontic stipulation.

On the other hand, Raphael as "health of God," the "sociable spirit," the emissary bearing to earth heavenly knowledge along with God's warning and demand for obedience, conjoins, both physically and narratively, things

divine and human. His flight to Eden links heaven and earth by means of
extraordinarily suggestive visual imagery:

> Down thither prone in flight
> He speeds, and through the vast Ethereal Sky
> Sails between worlds and worlds, with steady wing
> Now on the polar winds, then with quick Fan
> Winnows the buxom Air; till within soar
> Of Tow'ring Eagles, to all the Fowls he seems
> A *Phoenix*, gaz'd by all.   (V, 266–72)

Moreover, the flight of Raphael marks in *Paradise Lost* the occasion for what
Thomas Greene has persuasively argued constitutes in epic poetry "a crucial
nexus of the narrative; it represents the intersection of time and the timeless; it points to the human realm of paramount concern to the gods; and it
brings divine authority to the unfolding heroic action."[4] In this centrally
important role, Raphael is no longer a mere ontic stipulation; he has entered
a realm distinguished—theologically and dramatically—by the looming possibility of a singular human "event." And to make this event fully intelligible
to his fallen audience, Milton will of course bring to bear his most extraordinary poetic and narrative resources.

   In other words, much as the time evoked dramatically in *Othello* is not
single, is not a uniform and continuous plane of sequenced perceptions, so
too the "character" of Raphael is not singular, but splits along the lines of his
heavenly being and his role as heavenly emissary to the realm of a massive
impending temporality. It may seem too convenient to rescue Milton from
the conflict I've remarked by simply saying there are two Raphaels, the
Raphael of heaven and the Raphael of earth. But convenient or not, it makes
sense of many modern readers' dramatic experience of the poem, preeminently the extended exchange between Raphael and Adam.

   One guide to this reading experience is again Greene, who remarks in
passing that God's generosity in dispatching Raphael "turns out to be not at
all a true magnanimity but a petty legalistic self-righteousness. Adam must
not be allowed to 'pretend surprisal, unadmonisht, unforewarned.' The majesty of Raphael's descent can only be appreciated if the awkwardness of
its motive remains half-forgotten" (p. 409). But how does Milton manage,
narratively, to make us "half-forget," to create what in a somewhat different
context Stanley Fish has called a "split reader": "one who is continually
responding to two distinct sets of stimuli—the experience of individual poetic moments and the ever present pressure of the Christian doctrine"?[5]
The answer lies not in claiming, as Fish goes on to do, that Raphael is
"struggling as we are with the burden of foreknowledge" (p. 230), at least

not unless such a struggle is clearly in evidence. The same must be said of Thomas Copeland's even stronger, more specific claims about Raphael's angelic and narrative "virtue"—that he must "combat a sense of the futility of his embassy," that he must "disguise the urgency of his errand," that he must cast about for "conversationally safe idea[s]," and that he must accept "his own frustration ungrudgingly as a necessary part of the divine plan."[6] But the poem reveals no such struggle on Raphael's part with foreknowledge; nor, I would argue, is there any compelling evidence of his "combatting," "disguising," or "frustration."

Indeed, the emotional (and intellectual) responses that the poem reveals on Raphael's part—from his doubt about what it is "lawful to reveal" (V, 570), to the gently expressed concern that Adam not seek to "scan" God's secrets, to the "contracted brow" with which he responds to Adam's confession of weakness before the "charm of Beauty's powerful glance," to the passionate enjoining of Adam to an obedience in which the entire heavenly host will be able to rejoice—all are entirely consistent with the loving, obedient virtue of a being genuinely seeking to warn another of God's creatures crucially at risk. Though perhaps surprising, it is the utter absence of evidence of foreknowledge, or rhetorical behavior clearly or decisively influenced by foreknowledge, that seems to me the striking quality of Raphael's narration.[7]

I am suggesting, then, that God's speech charging Raphael to warn Adam is distinct rhetorically, though not theologically, from the emphatic and avowedly omniscient declaration of Book III, marked as the later speech is by a refusal to say directly that the human creatures will fall:

> and such discourse bring on,
> As may advise him of his happy state,
> Happiness in his power left free to will,
> Left to his own free Will, his Will though free,
> Yet mutable; whence warn him to beware
> He swerve not too secure: tell him withal
> His danger, and from whom, what enemy
> Late fall'n himself from Heaven, is plotting now
> The fall of others from like state of bliss;
> By violence, no, for that shall be withstood,
> But by deceit and lies; this let him know,
> Lest wilfully transgressing he pretend
> Surprisal, unadmonisht, unforewarned.   (V, 233–45)

Without knowledge from other sources, we could hardly disambiguate the "Lest" of line 244, or point to any one moment in this passage indicating that the Fall will definitely occur: three lines declare or imply man's free will, though without a reiteration of how the exercise of that "freedom" will eventuate. And the controlling verb from line 240 on is "plotting," which is Satan's action, not that of an omnipotent, omniscient being. Insofar as "free" human will and action are further characterized, they are "mutable," distinctly not the features of an "ingrate" (III, 97). The urging that Adam be told to "beware / He swerve not too secure" has the feel as well as the readily construable sense of true warning, a cautioning about something that might genuinely be avoided.

I am arguing that this passage marks a significant rhetorical and narrative shift from Book III, though the poetic narrator's phrase at the beginning of the next verse paragraph ("and fulfilled / All Justice") certainly resonates decisively with the language of the earlier book. And with this shift comes the rhetorical possibility for an openness of human opportunity in Raphael's narration: there emerges in his exchange with Adam the possibility for a true drama of the Fall, one that would be impossible if the omniscient declaration of Book III were invoked to govern fully here.[8]

I should acknowledge that a recognition of what is logically at stake in my argument has led at least one critic in a very different direction: Philip Gallagher, in asking whether Raphael (and Milton) should have "preferred a blameless silence before the futile office of hopeless admonition," answers "Yes, assuredly—*if* one endorses the parsimonious assumption that the reiterated warnings of *Paradise Lost* ought to have been motivated by the hope (if not the certainty) that they would be heeded."[9] Dismissing such parsimony as "illogical," as of a piece with the "fallacy that to be adequately forewarned is ipso facto to be insuperably forearmed," Gallagher moves to a very different account of the motivation for Raphael's embassy: "Raphael descends, in short, to soften Adam's stony heart before it has hardened, to initiate his postlapsarian regeneration before he lapses" (p. 270). Adam's repentance will be hastened by virtue of his seeing with utter clarity that God "made him just and right, / Sufficient to have stood" (III, 98–99).

The problem here is that Gallagher (along with several other critics) has confused one very significant effect of Raphael's embassy, one that Gallagher articulates with real acuity, with its intent, an intent of warning that could not be more clearly stated, by God, or Raphael, or even Adam himself: "advise him of his happy state" (V, 234); "warn him to beware" (237); "tell him withal / His danger" (238–39); "this let him know, / Lest" (243–44); "Son of Heav'n and Earth, / Attend" (519–20); "Say Goddess, what ensu'd when *Raphaël*, / The affable Arch-angel, had forewarn'd / Adam" (VII, 40–42);

> Divine Interpreter, by favor sent
> Down from the Empyrean to forewarn
> Us timely of what might else have been our loss,
> Unknown, which human knowledge could not reach
> (VII, 72–75)

> take heed lest Passion sway
> Thy Judgment to do aught, which else free Will
> Would not admit; thine and of all thy Sons
> The weal or woe in thee is plac't; beware.   (VIII, 634–37)

Though the effect of these warnings, it may be argued, is subsequently to help bring Adam in Book X to a spiritually necessary self-conviction—"all my evasions vain / And reasonings, though through Mazes, lead me still / But to my own conviction" (X, 829–31)—this is not their clearly stated purpose. To argue, as Gallagher does, in such a theologically singular vein about "prelapsarian softening" risks justifying in yet another form the charge of disingenuousness on God's part, though perhaps not Raphael's. But more importantly, it cannot make sense of the rhetorical urgency that pervades Raphael's warnings, and works to undermine the drama of the Fall (whatever *our* "foreknowledge") that is sustained by that urgency.

Thus when Raphael replies to Adam's troubled "But say, / What meant that caution join'd, *if ye be found / Obedient?*" in Book V, we are obliged as readers to recall the divine certainty of Book III, but also to respond to the emphatic present tense, and the explicitly undetermined future:

> That thou art happy, owe to God;
> That thou continu'st such, owe to thyself,
> That is, to thy obedience; therein stand.
> This was that caution giv'n thee; be advis'd.
> God made thee perfet, not immutable;
> And good he made thee, but to persevere
> He left it in thy power, ordain'd thy will
> By nature free, not over-rul'd by Fate
> Inextricable, or strict necessity.   (V, 520–28)

Precisely how to make the two—present and future, freedom and fore-knowledge—cohere, given what we know from our reading of the poem as a whole, is a task that can not be managed on purely logical/theological grounds or on purely rhetorical grounds. What we require is an understanding that is, on Fish's terms, "split": responding to both "the ever present pressure of Christian doctrine" and "the experience of individual poetic moments." We must see Raphael simultaneously under the aspect of heavenly timelessness and earthly, if unfallen, temporality. It is entirely appropriate that at the end of Book VII, when Milton wishes to conclude the rapturous description of earthly creation, the comment on the new "Race of Worshippers" comes not directly from Raphael but through his "quoting" of the angelic chorus: "thrice happy if they know / Thir happiness, and persevere upright" (VII, 631–32). Crucial to the mystery of the Fall, as Joseph Summers has observed, is the question of how the human couple could come to deny, or forget, or not recognize their happiness; and at just the moment when the poem tenders the paradoxical, though humanly recognizable notion that our unfallen forebears might not "know" their happiness, Milton the poet recognizes the narrative necessity of having that paradox emblematized by the incommensurable perspectives of the divine and the earthly: the heavenly choir—timeless, perfected in obedience and consequent happiness—made present by the archangel speaking from within the confines of poetic narrative order and unfallen human temporality.[10]

The disjuncture of heavenly and earthly, the source of paradox in what I am arguing is Raphael's double presence in the poem, is of course completed only in Book IX with the Fall, prefaced by the poetic narrator's anticipatory words: "On the part of Heav'n / Now alienated, distance and distaste" (IX, 8–9). But Milton certainly intends that we also bear in mind here the contrast with the remarkable ontological possibility that Raphael has suggested in Book V:

> time may come when men
> With Angels may participate, and find
> No inconvenient Diet, nor too light Fare:
> And from these corporal nutriments perhaps
> Your bodies may at last turn all to spirit,
> Improv'd by tract of time, and wing'd ascend
> Ethereal, as wee. (V, 493–99)

It is precisely the contrast between what "may" be and what foreknowably *will* be that marks this passage as one in which the narrative character of Raphael is most discernibly at issue. For even on Gallagher's terms—that Raphael's task is essentially one of "initiat[ing Adam's] postlapsarian regeneration before he lapses"—it seems purposeless for a foreknowing Raphael to suggest what the course of spiritual history might be were there no Fall. Rather, the justification for this and related passages must be dramatic and rhetorical: if human freedom is to be experienced by the poetic reader in the most intense terms possible, then we require more than the assertions, however emphatic, of Book III; Raphael cannot be understood as tendering gratuitous or misleading suggestions about God's plans, or the course of his creation. He must speak, and be accepted by the reader as speaking, of what is truly, openly possible. Rather than reflecting Raphael's "struggle with the burden of foreknowledge," the narrative and rhetorical efficacy of Books V through VIII requires a Raphael who does *not* foreknow the Fall.

Even as I make this argument, entailing as it does two Raphaels, I think it important to note how carefully Milton manages at the end of Book VIII, at the point of Raphael's departure, to reestablish the ambiguity of language I noted in God's initial instructions. Raphael's instructing of Adam has been completed; indeed, in responding to Adam's confession of weakness before the "charm of Beauty's powerful glance," Raphael offers a final and crucial correction, which, though fully accepted by Adam of Book VIII, will tragically lose its force in the exchange between the human couple in Book IX. For Adam has offered an ironically revealing self-assessment:

> yet when I approach
> Her loveliness, so absolute she seems
> And in herself complete, so well to know
> Her own, that what she wills to do or say,
> Seems wisest, virtuousest, discreetest, best.   (VIII, 546–50)

With "contracted brow" Raphael urges that Adam "be not diffident / Of Wisdom, she deserts thee not, if thou / Dismiss not her" (VIII, 562–64). And yet it is just such a dismissal of wisdom, and a reliance on appearance (what "seems"), that defines the moment in which Adam relinquishes Eve to solitary labor (IX, 351–72). At the point of narrative climax, in which human choice, and thus freedom, becomes committed to a course of self-destruction, Raphael's words loom as deeply prescient. But this needn't entail foreknowledge, only the poet's obligation to make good on the promised completeness of warning. That completeness achieved, Raphael's words on departing from Adam recapture exactly the quality in God's instructions of "theological" accuracy without commitment to what will be, or any suggestion of predetermination:

> Be strong, live happy, and love, but first of all
> Him whom to love is to obey, and keep
> His great command; take heed lest Passion sway
> Thy Judgment to do aught, which else free Will
> Would not admit; thine and of all thy Sons
> The weal or woe in thee is plac'd; beware.
> I in thy persevering shall rejoice,
> And all the Blest: stand fast; to stand or fall
> Free in thine own Arbitrement it lies.
> Perfet within, no outward aid require;
> And all temptation to transgress repel.   (VIII, 633–43)

But not only does Raphael's final utterance not require foreknowledge: as a closural declaration, with its echo of God's "Lest" from Book V, it becomes most vulnerable to the charge of disingenuousness were we to assume his foreknowledge. For again, the issue I am posing for the poem is not the logical compatibility of human freedom and God's knowledge of what will certainly occur, but whether such a moment in the narrative, beyond its function as warning, could be rhetorically convincing in the context of angelic foreknowledge. "I in thy persevering shall rejoice, / And all the Blest": this, for example, seems especially gratuitous if it were to come from one who knows precisely that Adam and Eve will not "persevere." But more generally, I am arguing, a foreknowing Raphael can hardly speak so variously in the imperative mood ("Be strong, live happy, and love," "take heed lest Passion sway / Thy judgment," "beware," "stand fast") without an awkward rhetorical incongruity: if it makes sense to *warn* Adam emphatically, it would hardly do so to *exhort* him to be "happy" in light of a certain knowledge of his impending fall and unhappiness. Strength, happiness, and love: all depend upon a knowledge of which the human couple has been fully possessed by God, and by the Raphael of Books V through VIII; all will be lost by virtue of their eating of the Tree of Knowledge. Milton's epic and its residual aspirations to drama depend upon this vast irony, an irony which must be a function of the reader's retrospective perceptions, not a belated recognition of angelic equivocation.

Does an argument for two Raphaels, for the apparent incompatibility of his ontological and narrative presence, constitute a narrative "deconstruction" of *Paradise Lost?* Is such an argument another way of proclaiming a de Manian "undecidability" about Raphael's knowledge and rhetoric? To be sure, there is some similarity between de Man's characteristic textual "critique," in which epistemological questions are subsumed within rhetorical exploration, and my claim that the knowledge Raphael possesses by way of his heavenly nature is at odds with the rhetorical exigencies of his conversation with Adam. But rhetoric and knowledge are not pointlessly at odds; this is, finally, no textual aporia. On the contrary, there is a clear poetic purpose, indeed necessity to the incompatibility of what Raphael knows by virtue of his presence before the divine colloquy of Book III and what he must *not* know in the conversation with Adam, as Milton attempts to make as dramatic as possible the narration precedent to the Fall. Because this incompatibility is implicit, perhaps unconscious on Milton's part, there is no corresponding necessity to say that it is the sheer contradiction that is grist for deconstructive mills.

The more instructive question that literary criticism and history might pose about the apparent contradiction within the poem is whether it was perceived, or might be expected to have been perceived, by Milton's seventeenth-century Christian audience. For any treatment, theological or poetic, of biblical history reaching to the New Testament would seem to presume an ability to reconcile contradictory elements of the gospels. Most central, any representation of the Son must account for the mysterious mixture of human and divine, must work to explain divine knowledge and anointing ("And lo a voice from heaven, saying, This is my beloved Son") and the utterly human agony of the Passion ("My God, my God, why has thou forsaken me?").[11] The complexities of Milton's own Christology aside (as well as the relation of his views on the Son in *Paradise Lost* and in *De doctrina Christiana*), we may wonder how the first readers of his epic would have reconciled the divine and human natures of Christ in any context, and to what extent that process lends itself, in the reading of epic poetry, to critical or psychological analysis.[12] Perhaps, then, the largest question posed by what I perceive as a narrative incompatibility within the poem is whether there has been a shift in sensibilities between Milton's time and our own—a shift so deep-rooted as to be very difficult to produce evidence for, much less analyze in detail. For, given the theological tradition extending from Boethius to the seventeenth century, it might well be that the first readers of *Paradise Lost* would not have understood my argument or seen its relevance: convinced deeply and intuitively of the compatibility of foreknowledge and free will, they would have experienced no narrative conflict or rhetorical shift within the poem. As a problem in literary history, or more precisely the history of literary reading, this shift in theological sensibility seems both difficult and elusive. Moreover, since our own canons of narrative coherence are so largely a function of the eighteenth- and nineteenth-century novel, we can't presume to understand the very different narrative ethos of the Renaissance epic without a significant leap of critical imagination.[13]

More suggestive of what is at stake thematically and rhetorically in this narrative peculiarity of *Paradise Lost* are the radical Protestant impulses characteristically represented in our own century by Karl Barth's theology. For if there is a central, insistent concern in Barth's work, running from the early *Der Römerbrief* through the massive *Church Dogmatics*, it is that theology—how we speak about God—must rigorously and consistently resist becoming merely the reflection or embodiment of human culture, whether understood metaphysically, ideologically, or rhetorically. Rather, theology must be guided by God's manifestation of his reality: the Incarnation, to which we have access only by means of Scripture. For Barth, theology founders when it becomes dependent upon analogies between the divine and the natural realms, or upon other forms of human intellectual conclusion.[14] My argument here is that Milton, the supreme Protestant poet of Europe, intuited in his epic (and for that matter, in his theological treatise) a similar necessity and danger. Though his own bold attempt to speak directly about God, indeed to have God speak in Book III, was a matter of extraordinary narrative and poetic daring, it was tempered by an implicit understanding of how difficult it is to speak about God's omniscience and human freedom without contradiction—or at least without recourse to logic and philosophy, those two most powerful temptations of human culture.[15]

To be sure many readers of *Paradise Lost* feel that in Book III Milton was not only tempted but overcome, producing a harsh and defensive God without compelling scriptural justification, as well as adducing peremptory, insufficiently defended claims about the relation of human freedom and divine foreknowledge. But Raphael's narration in Books V through VIII is, ironically, theologically "pure"—informed only, on my "parsimonious" reading, by God's direct, if crucially ambiguous, instructions. Though Raphael may wonder, for example, whether it is "lawful to reveal" the matter of the war in heaven, and though his ontological account is remarkably extended, narrative justification for what he says to Adam derives always from his understanding of, and unwavering (because unfallen) faith in, God's word. There is no version of the theologically problematic, anticipatory self-exculpation of Book III; and as a consequence Raphael may simply declare the absoluteness of human freedom ("not over-rul'd by Fate," V, 527) without any commitment to theological (or philosophical) defense of the sort that Milton evidently feels when he has God using human, nonscriptural words, even engaging in various of the conventions of human conversational behavior.

Freed from the obligations of theological defense, the figure of Raphael may assume the particular narrative character that best serves Milton's poetic and rhetorical needs in the great middle of his poem. Crucial to that character is a full knowledge of the conditions for human love, happiness, and obedience; equally important, however, is that this knowledge not vitiate the drama of the Fall—that Raphael's "lest" of Book VIII, line 635 not merely "fulfill all Justice," but suggest persuasively and unironically the openness, the radical freedom of the tragic "Arbitrement" of Book IX. It is a tragedy whose irony can survive divine omniscience, human retrospection, but not, given the narrative organization of *Paradise Lost*, angelic foreknowing.

Smith College

NOTES

I would like to thank Douglas Patey, Ron Macdonald, and Harold Skulsky for their invaluable help and insight in the development of this essay; and I am especially grateful for the editorial care and intelligence of Albert C. Labriola of *Milton Studies*.

1. Quotations of Milton's prose and poetry are from *John Milton: Complete Poems and Major Prose*, ed. Merritt Y. Hughes (New York, 1957).

2. See especially Thomas Copeland, "Raphael, the Angelic Virtue," *MQ* XXIV (1990): 128–36; Marc Cyr, "The Archangel Raphael: Narrative Authority in Milton's War in Heaven," *Journal of Narrative Technique* XVII (1987): 309–16; Philip Gallagher, "The Role of Raphael in *Samson Agonistes*," in *Milton Studies* XVIII, ed. James D. Simmonds (Pittsburgh, 1983), pp. 255–94; Barbara Lewalski, *"Paradise Lost" and the Rhetoric of Literary Forms* (Princeton, 1985); Jason Rosenblatt, "Angelic Tact: Raphael on Creation," in *Milton and the Middle Ages*, ed. John Mulryan (Lewisburg, 1982), pp. 21–31; Beverly Sherry, "Not by Bread Alone: The Communication of Adam and Raphael," *MQ* XIII (1979): 111–14; Hideyuki Shitaka, " 'Them Thus Employed Beheld / With Pity Heaven's High King': God's Dispatch of Raphael in *Paradise Lost*," *MQ* XXIV (1990): 128–36; Kathleen Swaim, *Before and After the Fall: Contrasting Modes in "Paradise Lost"* (Amherst, Mass., 1986); Robert West, *Milton and the Angels* (Athens, Ga., 1955); Mark Wollaeger, "Raphael and the Book of Tobit," in *Milton Studies* XXI, ed. James D. Simmonds (Pittsburgh, 1985), pp. 137–56. All argue for or assume angelic foreknowledge, or pass over the issue; I, on the other hand, argue explicitly for a reading of Raphael's narration and character that makes such foreknowledge interpretively untenable, at least in terms of the poem's drama and rhetoric.

3. The exaltation of the Son is the other possible "event," though it is in fact fully continuous with God's knowledge and being—an event in name only, one is tempted to say.

4. Greene, *The Descent from Heaven: A Study in Epic Continuity* (New Haven, 1963), p. 7.

5. Fish, *Surprised by Sin: The Reader in "Paradise Lost"* (Berkeley, 1967), p. 42.

6. Copeland, "Raphael, the Angelic Virtue," 119, 120, 126.

7. Shitaka, " 'Them Thus Employed,' " p. 131, problematically assumes that without "foreknowledge, Raphael could not predict that 'Some one [of Adam's race] . . . might devise / Like instrument [cannon] to plague the sons of men / For sin, on war and mutual slaughter bent' (VI, 503–06)." This selective quotation obscures the nature of Raphael's full utterance:

> yet *haply* of thy Race
> In future days, *if* Malice should abound,
> Some one intent on mischief, or inspir'd
> With dev'lish machination *might* devise
> Like instrument to plague the Sons of men
> For sin, on war and mutual slaughter bent.   (VI, 501–06; italics mine)

Not only does this fuller quotation of the passage at issue reveal a highly conditional speculation, obscured by Shitaka's elision of "haply" and "if," but that speculation is quite possible as an extrapolation from Raphael's knowledge of the war in heaven; foreknowledge is simply not logically implicated. Moreover, speculation about the development of military technology hardly seems the most likely way for an epic poet to reveal something as crucial as angelic foreknowledge. Perhaps even more significant for my larger argument is the gratuitous disingenuousness we would have to assume of a foreknowing Raphael speaking in such a highly conditional fashion. Indeed, the strains and overreaching conclusions within Shitaka's analysis here are ultimately revealing of the weakness of an argument for angelic foreknowledge.

8. I must of necessity here merely acknowledge several rich, suggestive, and exceedingly complex discussions that have addressed the question of whether free will and foreknowledge can logically coexist. Though the issue is of obvious importance to my general topic, and the larger theological questions it raises, it does not bear directly on my claim about Raphael's narration, and hence I must address it in a subsequent essay. I should note in passing my view that while there is certainly medieval and Renaissance precedent for the claim that divine foreknowledge and human freedom are compatible (e.g., in Ockham's *De praedestinatione* or Molina's *On Divine Foreknowledge*), and while Milton may have known a good deal about these theological developments, there is not in *Paradise Lost* what might be understood as a justification, logically and philosophically perspicuous, for the claim of compatibility, but rather a complex set of *stipulations* that make up God's "argument" in Book III. Two of the best discussions of the topic are Dennis Danielson, *Milton's Good God: A Study in Literary Theodicy* (Cambridge, 1982), esp. chapt. 5; and Linda Zagzebski, *The Dilemma of Freedom and Foreknowledge* (Oxford, 1991).

9. Gallagher, "The Role of Raphael in *Samson Agonistes*," p. 263.

10. Summers, *The Muse's Method: An Introduction to "Paradise Lost"* (Cambridge, Mass., 1962), p. 150.

11. For a comprehensive modern discussion of the acute difficulties posed in reconciling Jesus' final words in the Passion narrations of Matthew and Mark with the larger narrative context of the New Testament, see Raymond Brown, *The Death of the Messiah: From Gethsemane to the Grave* (New York, 1994), pp. 1043–58, 1085–88. The issue is, to be sure, as old as Patristic exegetical commentary.

12. Of course, the classical epics posed a similar sort of difficulty in reconciling various instances of belief and "knowledge." In the *Iliad*, for example, Hector tells Andromache (VI, 447–49) that he "knows well" that Troy will fall; yet at XIII, 823–32 he rejects Ajax's prophecy of Trojan defeat, and at XV, 486–99, he envisions the Trojans repulsing the Greeks. Indeed, at XVI, 830–61, he suggests that he may kill Achilles and survive himself. Though unfreighted by the logical problems posed by the Christian doctrine of divine omniscience, the reading of classical epics has also required a reconciling of different, and contradictory, moments of knowing.

13. The question at issue here seems to exist however widespread were various explicit theological and doctrinal commitments on the part of Milton's contemporaries. For what I am asking about is how these commitments work to create a habit of mind, a distinctive quality of reading attention: how were theologically consequential poetic parts made by readers to cohere into the whole of a poem? Evidence here is likely to be inferential and circumstantial, and again I must defer further discussion to a subsequent essay.

14. I am not, of course, arguing that there is anything inappropriate in Milton's having Raphael speak by means of analogy between heaven and earth, or that the perfections of the earthly Paradise can not legitimately be compared to the rather different perfections of heaven. Rather, I am saying that Milton the Protestant poet, fully aware of humanity's fallen condition, reveals an awareness in *Paradise Lost* of the necessity for scriptural justification where possible, and divine poetic inspiration where not, when speaking of God. Certainly Milton is not averse to traditional arguments about God's nature as evidenced by worldly beauty and purposiveness: "There can be no doubt but that every thing in the world, by the beauty of its order, and the evidence of a determinate and beneficial purpose which pervades it, testifies that some supreme efficient Power must have pre-existed, by which the whole was

ordained for a specific end" (*Christian Doctrine*, p. 904). And as Swaim, *Before and After the Fall*, p. 173, observes, "from beginning to end Raphael's mission and communication are governed by the need to reinforce and expand Adam's unified consciousness and unified cosmos by presenting comparative alignments between Heaven and earth."

15. This seems the cautionary purpose of Milton's description in Book II of a few intellectually inclined fallen angels:

> Others apart sat on a Hill retir'd
> In thoughts more elevate, and reason'd high
> Of Providence, Foreknowledge, Will, and Fate,
> Fixt Fate, Free Will, Foreknowledge absolute
> And found no end, in wand'ring mazes lost.   (II, 557–61)

PARADISE LOST, BOOKS XI AND XII, AND THE HOMILETIC TRADITION

Jameela Lares

THE LAST TWO books of *Paradise Lost* have occupied Miltonists for centuries. After the epic and engaging difficulties of Satan, Adam, and Eve, the action gives way to a sacred history lesson presented by Michael to Adam. Joseph Addison was unhappy with the disjunction between the final books, and they may have caused Samuel Johnson to pronounce that none ever wished *Paradise Lost* longer. Even C. S. Lewis thought that the historical section was an artistic failure.[1]

This critical view held until 1958, when F. T. Prince showed that the two last books were integral to the design of the epic because a vision of futurity was necessary in order to justify the ways of God to men. Since then, Miltonists have generally agreed that the final two books of *Paradise Lost* are necessary to the epic, although not always stylistically pleasing, especially since Michael's visionary presentation of Book XI gives way to a straight verbal narration in Book XII.[2]

At the moment, the dominant model for understanding the last two books is pedagogical, that is, that Milton is modeling the archangel Michael after his own theories of pedagogy, mostly enunciated in his 1644 tractate *Of Education.* This approach compares Michael's pedagogy with Raphael's, and sometimes with the Father's. But this approach is not always satisfactory. For one thing, pedagogical responsibility should not displace Adam and Eve's moral responsibility for the Fall.[3] A focus on the methods and temperaments of the two angels can also obscure the rhetorical considerations of time, place, and person by which the angels must adjust their messages. True, Raphael is the "sociable Spirit" (V, 221) whereas Michael is a warrior, come with his powers "to seize / Possession of the Garden" (XI, 221–22), but it is also true that Raphael delivers his mild admonishment as an after-dinner chat to the lord of the world, whereas Michael is speaking to a felon on probation.[4]

In any case, considering the angels preeminently as pedagogues confuses intellect with will. Adam and Eve's sin is not a failure of information, but a failure of volition. The Father sent Raphael less to instruct Adam than to warn him: "Lest wilfully transgressing he pretend / Surprisal, unadmonisht, unforewarn'd" (V, 244–45). Raphael in fact warns repeatedly about the fall, which God has already foreseen. It is not that Raphael fails to instruct, but rather that Adam and Eve fail to obey.

Some recent critics have also focused on what they claim is the frustration of typology in the last two books. For instance, Regina Schwartz finds so much deferral of closure in the final two books ("Summary conclusions that continue, and so do not summarize or conclude; moments of enlightenment that turn out to be veiled after all") that she suggests Milton is actually talking about death because of his disappointment in the deferred millennium.[5]

I propose, instead of such pedagogical or typological readings, that Milton followed a structuring of the final two books which has virtually been overlooked: the sermon. I will argue that Books XI and XII of *Paradise Lost* are heavily informed by those methods of sermon construction which were pervasive in the England of the seventeenth century, and particularly by the two sermon types of correction and consolation. In fact, these sermon types are announced in the first five lines of *Paradise Lost* and structure the epic throughout. Moreover, Michael himself is a type of preacher and his discourse to Adam is sermonic in form. He expounds a text, enunciates a "use" or "application" for it, and takes care that his auditor's will and emotions are engaged. Understanding the homiletic nature of the final two books can help us see their structural continuities with the rest of the epic and also the extent to which their style is consonant with their subject matter, including the switch in Michael's presentation from vision to narration.[6]

The subject of *Paradise Lost,* Milton tells us in the first line of the epic, is "disobedience." The word is an odd one upon which to build an epic, although we lose sight of this fact after three hundred years of familiarity. We might as well expect Homer to talk about Achilles's lack of contentment or for Virgil to write about Aeneas's peacelessness. Miltonists have long had difficulty with Milton's use of the term. For instance, John T. Shawcross has recast the theme of *Paradise Lost* as "the need for and means of obedience."[7]

But any attempt to rephrase the subject without the contradictive grammatical construction ("dis-") obscures an important clue as to Milton's rhetorical strategies. By announcing his subject as *dis*-obedience, Milton is operating in the recognizably homiletic mode of correction. This type of sermon called for the preacher to identify deviations from the standard of virtue and to dissuade his hearers from continuing in such deviations. As Richard Bernard (1607) puts it, "Use of Doctrine is corrective . . . when the lesson is used against corruption in maners, vice and wickednesse." The sermon type was derived, as Bernard says, "by the contrarie" (p. 67), and frequently discussed in terms which were, grammatically speaking, contradictives, that is, terms which reflected the mere contrary of another term. Thus William Perkins (1592) uses grammatical contradictives to define correction, calling it "that, whereby the doctrine is applied to reforme the life from ungodlinesse and unrighteous dealing." Milton's tutor William Chappell (1648) advises, if somewhat opaquely, that the names of virtues may be used both for instruction in virtue as well as for correction of vice: "[The presence of the evil] may be taken chiefly from the proper adjuncts, and opposites without a medium; because that from these we may always argue, both affirmatively and negatively."[8]

Interestingly enough, Milton's concern for correction demonstrates itself even in his tractate *Of Education*. When Milton says that the end of learning is "to repair the ruins of our first parents" (YP II, pp. 366–67), that statement is at odds with many other works of pedagogy in which the primary architectural metaphor is new construction, not repair. In fact, Samuel Hartlib, to whom Milton directs *Of Education*, proposes his model for Latin instruction in terms of such new construction: "it is not possible to build a new House where an old is standing, till the old one be pulled down. . . . we finde after long experience, that it will be impossible to raise a Firme and Commodious Building upon the Old Foundation." The metaphor of pedagogy as new construction was employed before and after Milton's *Paradise Lost*. Abraham Fleming (1581) stresses the importance of grammatical instruction as the foundation of a new building, "For hee that determineth to erect and build a dwelling house, beginneth not at the roofe, but at the foundation." William Walker (1669) talks about the paramount importance of "the very First Grounding of the Schollar, and laying the Foundation of all his future attainments." To insist on repairing ruins rather than building afresh is a remedial emphasis allied more with the sermon type of correction than with the concerns of pedagogy.[9]

Milton is also operating, in the first few lines of *Paradise Lost*, in the homiletic mode of consolation. Sin, the contrary of virtue, brings "Death into the World, and all our woe," but only until "one greater Man / Restore us, and regain the blissful Seat" (I, 3–5). This consolatory mode is present in *Paradise Lost*, even from the beginning, as a counterpoint to correction, and the epic ends on at least a provisional note of consolation. The human pair leaves Eden "not disconsolate": "Some natural tears they dropp'd, but wip'd them soon" (XII, 645).[10]

The consolatory sermon is often understood to balance the corrective one. Richard Bernard even phrases his definition by means of the very term which Milton will later employ: obedience and its absence. "[The type is] Consolatorie . . . when the doctrine is used to raise up the spirit with comfort, which is humbled and cast downe, and to encourage such as be obedient." In fact, when Bernard discusses consolation, he places it directly after correction. He also includes in his discussion the suggestion that man suffers specific privations which are remedied by God's general providence:

The reasons of Comforts and Encouragements, particularly must be framed, according to the discomforts and discouragements: being divers, inward, outward, publike, private, in bodie, in good name, goods, &c. But generally from Gods providence; his promises of helpe and blessings, his minaces against the enemies of the godly, his power, his constancie.[11]

The presence of correction and consolation in *Paradise Lost* is no coincidence; Milton would have known about these two sermon types from his first tutor at Cambridge, William Chappell. Of all the English sermon theorists of the sixteenth and seventeenth centuries, Chappell most insisted on combining correction (which he calls "reprehension") with consolation. He discusses these sermon types even before the others. He also discusses them in *The Use of Holy Scripture* (1653), which is his account of the scriptural authority underlying his preaching system. Chappell never actually finished this text; it was published posthumously from his draft manuscript. Significantly, the sections on reprehension and consolation are the only sections which are finished.[12]

Chappell's twofold model is particularly appropriate for an Adam who is prone to excesses of both despair and hope, as when he laments the fate of man in the Lazar house ("Why is life giv'n / To be thus wrested from us?" XI, 502–03) or when he misinterprets the "sons of God" sequence ("Here Nature seems fulfill'd in all her ends," XI, 602). Chappell explains that the Greek word which the King James Version translates as "correction," ἐπανόρθωσιν *(epanórthosin)*, represents a "rectifying" of the extremes of either complacency or sorrow.[13] Thus, when Michael announces as the purpose of his discourse that Adam "learn / True patience, and to temper joy with fear / And pious sorrow, equally inur'd / By moderation either state to bear" (XI, 360–63), we need not read this passage as an expression of pagan stoicism; this moderate state could also be the result of such twofold rectifying. When the Father sends Michael to speak to Adam, it is with the directive that Adam experience "joy, but with fear yet linkt" (XI, 139).

The two sermon types of correction and consolation structure *Paradise Lost* from beginning to end. Before Adam and Eve's actual act of disobedience, Satan plans their fall, God foresees it, and they remind one another that the fruit is forbidden. The action of the poem culminates in their eating the fruit and the immediate consequences of so doing. The long dénouement further stresses the effects or "fruit" of their disobedience. The interdictions against eating the fruit, and against disobedience in general, are mentioned not once but again and again throughout the poem, both before and after the fall. These admonishments ("Lest wilfully transgressing he pretend / Surprisal," V, 244–45) have their parallels in the advice of sermon manuals, advice which enjoins the preacher to clarify the nature of a sin to be avoided and forbids him to correct an "uncertain" sin.[14]

Some modern critics have complained that the consolation of *Paradise Lost* is not very comforting. But the term *consolation* was understood differently by the sermon theorists. According to William Ames, consolation

is not properly a rejoicing of the soule (as some thinke) but rather a repression, or a mitigation, or an allaying of griefe, feare, or sadnesse. For that man is said to receive comfort and consolation, when he hath in some sort put away griefe, although joy be not yet come in the place, or if his sadnesse, and sorrow, be at least in some sort mitigated, and lessend. For sometimes there may be a mixture of sorrow and consolation together.

Ames's model of consolation reflects the practical requirement that a sinner not be comforted before he or she had fully come to terms with sin. Thomas Wilson (the divine) cites such a pattern of correction and consolation as a hermeneutic rule:

It is the manner of the Propheticall writing, first to use reprehensions and threatenings of judgement, and after to joyne the promises of mercy by Christ to come. Because men are not to receive comforts before their naturall pride (being humbled and tamed with feare,) they can see a neede, and have a desire after the promises of grace. . . . This rule may be a directory for preachers to governe their teaching, for the manner of it in respect of their hearers unhumbled.

Martin Luther had proposed a similar model of consolation in his commentary on Isaiah XL, 1 ("Comfort ye, comfort ye, my people"):

God's people are those who need comfort because they have been wounded and terrified by the Law and they are an empty vessel capable of receiving comfort. Only those who are afflicted have comfort and are capable of it, because comfort means nothing unless there is a malady.

Such a carefully qualified consolation balances the correction of *Paradise Lost*. As Michael is commanded, he gives the human pair counsel which will enable them to leave Eden "not disconsolate" (XI, 113).[15]

Not only do the Father and his angels console Adam and Eve, but the fallen humans seek to console each other. Adam urges "let us . . . strive / In offices of Love, how we may light'n / Each other's burden in our share of woe" (X, 958–61). In fact, only hell offers no consolation, and the villain of this poem about correction and consolation is one who can know neither repentance nor comfort. Satan realizes, as does God, that "feign'd submission" would only produce a more profound fall and punishment later on, "So farewell Hope . . . / Farewell Remorse" (IV, 108–09).

The movement from correction to consolation reflects a redemptive paradox common to the seventeenth century. As John Donne says, "Be this my Text, my Sermon to mine owne, / Therefore that he may raise the Lord throws down." I am not suggesting that Milton is espousing some facile idea that humankind has benefited from a "fortunate fall," as proposed by Arthur Lovejoy. Rather, Milton is tempering the homiletic mode of correction with the subdued consolation recommended by his own age.[16]

In the foregoing I have argued only that the sermon types of correction and consolation structure and inform *Paradise Lost*. But they do more than that; they also inform the two angelic discourses which come at the middle (Books V–VI) and end (Books XI–XII) of the epic. This is not to deny that these discourses are also conversations which are freighted with significant cultural and thematic material, as has already been demonstrated by various critics. Yet one can also demonstrate that these discourses are sermons.

The fact that the speakers in *Paradise Lost* are angels rather than human preachers does not disqualify them from their role. In the second and third chapters of the Apocalypse, the human leaders of the seven churches are referred to as "angels," as in the verse beginning "Unto the angel of the church of Ephesus write" (ii, 1). These seven "angels" were routinely understood throughout the Reformation to be ministers (that is, preachers). Reformation England produced an extensive commentary on these angels, always identifying them as ministers. For instance, Arthur Dent's 1607 commentary on Revelation has this explanation: "By this word Angel, [the author] meaneth not the invisible spirits which we call the Angels of heaven . . . But by the word Angell, he meaneth the Minister or Pastor of every Church." The specific identity of the angel in Ephesians was also an important issue in the prelatical debate. Milton himself identifies the angel in the Ephesians passage as a collective term referring to ministers in general (YP I, pp. 712–13).[17]

The seventeenth-century mind not only accepted angels as types of preachers, but they could also extend preaching to small, informal auditories, even to one individual. Parish visitation to and exhortation of individuals were enjoined upon ministers by both comforming and dissenting authors as a means of extending the impact of sermons. Although the Canons of 1604 themselves were noticeably nervous about any church activity outside of the church grounds, individual visitation was in fact widely advocated by other writers.[18]

Individual visitation was particularly urged during the later seventeenth century. The need for individual instruction is the burden of Richard Baxter's *Gildas Salvianus* (1656), which urges "personal Conference, and Examination, and Instruction." Jeremy Taylor also urges that preaching be extended by private visitation, "for by preaching, and catechising, and private entercourse, all the needs of Souls can best be serv'd; but by preaching alone they cannot." At the end of the century, Gilbert Burnet claims that the worst Protestant abuse is the neglect of such pastoral care, including "the Instructing, the Exhorting, the Admonishing and Reproving . . . the visiting and comforting the People of the Parish." Thus, neither the fact that the speakers are angels nor the fact that their auditory is a single person can disqualify them from preaching.[19]

Michael's discourse in Books XI and XII follows a sermonic format in a number of ways. For one, it has as its text—as has already been shown in Milton criticism—the *protevangelium* of Genesis iii, 15, "the seed of the woman will bruise the head of the serpent."[20] For another, it has an explicit and preacherly "use" or "application":

> know I am sent
> To show thee what shall come in future days
> To thee and to thy Offspring; good with bad
> Expect to hear, supernal Grace contending
> With sinfulness of Men; thereby to learn
> True patience, and to temper joy with fear
> And pious sorrow, equally inur'd
> By moderation either state to bear. (XI, 356–63)

Sermon theorists agreed that the preacher must urge the relevance of the doctrine taught to the individual's life, engaging not just the intellect but the will and passions as well. This focus was the familiar "use" of the Puritan sermon, sometimes separated into "use" and "application," but the Anglican John Wilkins put no less emphasis on its importance than did the exiled William Ames. Wilkins calls the use "the life and soule of a Sermon, whereby these sacred truthes are brought home to a mans particular conscience and occasions, and the affections ingaged to any truth or duty."[21] Milton himself underscores the importance of such application of doctrine when he complains in *Of Reformation* that the present church polity is hindering it:

for albeit in purity of Doctrine we agree [with other Reformed church overseas]; yet in Discipline, which is the execution and applying of Doctrine home, and laying the salve to the very Orifice of the wound; yea tenting and searching to the Core, without which Pulpit Preaching is but shooting at Rovers; in this we are no better then a Schisme. (YP I, p. 526)

At the end of Michael's sermon, Adam himself recounts its lesson in the passage beginning "Henceforth I learn, that to obey is best" (XII, 561–73). Michael is satisfied: "This having learnt, thou hast attain'd the sum / Of wisdom; hope no higher" (XII, 575–76).

In our secular age, we might question whether the mere hearing of a sermon could be a valid religious experience, but in the seventeenth century, hearing the word of God, even almost in terms of the auditory reception itself, was thought to be crucial to salvation. As Thomas Hall says, "The bare Reading of the Scriptures seldom conduces much to Conversion; the word preached by an Applicatory Voice hath some kinde of secret energy in it." Milton's own age did not necessarily consider private reading of the Bible to be sufficient. Rather, it often insisted on the agency of the preacher to unpack the meaning of Scripture. As Samuel Hieron says, "The text is the Word of God more abridged: Preaching is the Word of God more enlarged." The agency of the preacher in salvation was urged by Scripture itself: "For whosoever shall call upon the name of the Lord shall be saved. / How then shall they call on him in whom they have not believed? and how shall they believe in him of whom they have not heard? and how shall they hear without a preacher?" (Rom. X, 13–14). As William Perkins explains, the hearing of the word preached is the means of the new birth: "That we may be saved, we must have a special faith: speciall faith requires a speciall word: and the written word beeing otherwise generall, is made speciall by application: and this application is effectually made by the ministerie of the word." Milton cites Romans X, 14 when he discusses preaching in *Christian Doctrine* (YP VI, p. 568).[22]

For that matter, many of the exemplary Bible figures in Michael's discourse are preachers, who urge either correction of life (such as Enoch, Noah, and Moses) or the more visionary promises proclaimed by the preachers of the church age. The parallels have often been noted between the dramatis personae of Michael's discourse and the "heroes of faith" listed in Hebrews, chapter xi, but Milton makes these heroes of faith into preachers as well.[23] Richard Bernard identifies many of the same biblical characters as preachers:

It was from the beginning Preaching and Prophecying, before the fall and after. In Paradise God taught Adam and Eve both Law and Gospell. Before the floud, Enoch, Noah. After the floud, to Moses, Abraham, Isaac and Jacob, Joseph. From Moses, the Lord ceased not to send his servants the Prophets. And S. James witnesseth that Moses had his ordinarie teachers, continued to his daies. The Apostle S. Paul tels us, that as Christ sent out his Apostles, and gave them a charge at his Ascension, with a promise, so he gave gifts for the Ministerie and Preaching of the Word unto the worlds end.[24]

The plot of Milton's last two books is in many ways closer to Richard Bernard's discussion of preaching than it is to the narrative structure of the Hebrews chapter.

Another indication of the sermonic nature of Michael's discourse is the extent to which it "moves the passions," that is, appeals to various emotions in the hearer to assist the will to perform the right actions. The auditor's emotions were generally to be moved at the end of the sermon. According to John Wilkins, "The Conclusion should consist of some such matter as may engage the hearers to a serious remembrance and consideration of the truths delivered." Milder passions, τὰ ἤθη (*tà 'ê'thê*), are appropriate to the introduction, but τὰ πάθη (*tà páthê*), the "more eager and vehement affections, will best become the conclusion."[25] It should be noted that Michael does not rebuke Adam for his emotional display but for his lack of correct understanding. Michael approves, for instance, Adam's abhorrence of Nimrod's tyranny (XII, 79–80).

These last two books are far more informed by homiletics than they are by mere pedagogical theory. This is not to say that Milton says nothing about the passions in *Of Education*. He does advise the teacher to "lead and draw [his pupils] in willing obedience, enflam'd with the study of learning and the admiration of vertue; stirred up with high hopes," but he also advocates "mild and effectuall perswasions" to do so (YP II, pp. 384–85), and the tone of his discussion is calm and objective throughout. In marked contrast is his description of ministerial temperaments in *An Apology Against a Pamphlet* (1642). When he turns to the severe correction of those "false Doctors" who propose new heresies or old corruptions, Milton's discussion itself becomes passionate, with his picture of "Zeale whose substance is ethereal, arming in compleat diamond ascends his fiery Chariot drawn with two blazing Meteors figur'd like beasts" (YP I, p. 900). It would appear that for Milton, as for his age, the stirring of emotions was more a homiletic activity than a pedagogical one.

And Michael's visions and discourse do stir Adam's emotions. When Abel is slain, "Much at that sight was Adam in his heart / Dismay'd" (XI, 448–49) and Adam says, "Alas, both for the deed and for the cause!" (461). When Adam sees the various ways in which his offspring will die, he weeps (XI, 495–99); when he sees how the godly give themselves up to uxoriousness, he is of "short joy bereft" (XI, 628). When he sees how pervasive evil is in the time of Enoch, Adam is "all in tears" and "Lamenting . . . full sad" (XI, 674–75). Adam is particularly moved over the Flood, "as when a Father mourns / His Children, all in view destroy'd at once" (760–61).

Adam also experiences great relief and joy. When Michael tells Adam about God's redemptive dealings with Israel, Adam interrupts him with, "O sent from Heav'n, / Enlight'ner of my darkness, gracious things / Thou hast reveal'd . . . now first I find / Mine eyes true op'ning, and my heart much eas'd" (XII, 270–72, 273–74); when Adam hears about Christ, he is even more moved. He is "with such joy / Surcharg'd, as he had like grief been dew'd in tears" (XII, 372–73), and he calls Michael "Prophet of glad tidings, finisher / Of utmost hope!" (XII, 375–76). When he hears of the end of all time and the glorification of the saints, Adam, "Replete with joy and wonder," says, "O goodness infinite, goodness immense!" (XII, 468–69).

According to Debora K. Shuger, Renaissance theorists championed two rhetorical means for moving the passions. One of these was *magnitudo*, the importance of the subject itself, which could be assisted by *amplificatio*, that is, the repetition or elaboration of the message. The other means was *enargia* or *hypotyposis*, vividness of description.[26] Michael makes use of both of these means, *enargia* in Book XI and *magnitudo* in Book XII. In Book XI, the correction represents the Old Testament Law and is visual, iconic. Adam is exhorted by Michael, "ope thine eyes, and first behold / Th'effects which thy original crime hath wrought" (XI, 423–24). In Book XII, however, words replace images, just as "strict laws" give way to "free / Acceptance of large Grace, from servile fear / To filial, works of Law to works of Faith" (XII, 304–06).

The shift in Michael's presentation from vision to narration is motivated by the difference between law and grace, between correction and consolation. It is the law and correction which operate in Book XI, where Michael moves Adam to sorrow over sin by means of vivid pictures. But when Michael has accomplished this end, when Adam has fully repented, it is time for consolation, it is time for grace, and according to the reformed understanding of Scripture, grace is verbal, not visual: "And the Word was made flesh, and dwelt among us . . . full of grace and truth" (John i, 14).[27]

Nor, according to Scripture, can consolation be visual: "hope that is seen is not hope: for what a man seeth, why doth he yet hope for?" (Rom. viii, 24). John Wilkins urges the preacher who wishes to console his auditor to move from sense to faith: "In all afflictions whether outward or inward, we should endevour to cheere up the faith of the dejected hearer, by proposing sutable comforts, by raising his thoughts from sense to faith, from present things to future" (p. 18). The *protevangelium* of Genesis iii, 15, the promise that the seed of the woman would crush the head of the serpent, is contained in a metaphor, not in an image. Its meaning must be construed verbally. When Satan explains the promise at face value to his followers in Book X, he does so to his own embarrassment:

> I am to bruise his heel;
> His Seed, when is not set, shall bruise my head:
> A World who would not purchase with a bruise,
> Or much more grievous pain? (X, 498–501)

The profoundly sensual Satan, however, does not work out the metaphor. He expects instead a literal, one-to-one correspondence between the word and physical reality. It is in that moment that he and his followers are turned into earthbound serpents. Michael advises Adam against a similar error of interpretation: "Dream not of thir fight / As of a Duel, or the local wounds / Of head or heel" (XII, 386–88).

Correction is assisted by vivid pictures, but the emotional states proper to consolation are produced by verbal promises. These emotional states, according to one sermon manual, are hope, joy, constancy, and patience.[28] In Book XII, Michael comforts Adam with the *magnitudo* of God's redemption. In fact, he had already prefigured this comfort in Book XI, when Adam "Greatly rejoic'd" to see the redemption of Noah (XI, 869). This mixing of correction and consolation is consonant with William Perkins's counsel to the preacher:

Let thy proceeding bee after this manner with those, that are humbled in part. Let the Law bee propounded, yet so discreetly tempered with the Gospell, that beeing terrified with their sinnes, and with the meditation of Gods judgement, they may together also at the same instant receive solace by the Gospel.[29]

Michael's final discourse actually includes a wide number of consolations, more than could be included in any one sermon. Richard Bernard lists the general categories of consolation as God's providence, his promises to help and bless, his threatenings against the enemies of the godly, his power, and his constancy. These lessons can be learned from trials, from earlier experiences of God's love, from examples of patience on the part of others and reports of their deliverances, and from the consideration of the shortness of this life compared with the duration of happy life after death.[30]

In an actual pulpit, these individual lessons and promises would have to be individually handled in different sermons; Milton combines them all in this one archetypal sermon of consolation. They all find their analogues in Adam's conclusion as he departs "greatly in peace of thought":

> How soon hath thy prediction, Seer blest,
> Measur'd this transient World
> . . . .

Henceforth I learn, that to obey is best,
And love with fear the only God, to walk
As in his presence, ever to observe,
His providence, and on him sole depend,
Merciful over all his works

· · · · · · · ·

that suffering for Truth's sake
Is fortitude to highest victory
And to the faithful Death the Gate of Life.

(XII, 553–54, 561–65, 569–71)

Michael's discourse thus represents not a single sermon, but a multitude of them.

Multiplicity of sermon material may explain why Regina Schwartz found in the last two books of *Paradise Lost* so many "summary conclusions that continue, and so do not summarize or conclude." But what we have at the end of *Paradise Lost* is not deferral of closure but enjambment of closure, not one lesson, but many lessons, all sermons, produced as it were from a single text, Genesis iii, 15, that the seed of the woman would bruise the head of the serpent. In fact, John Boys, a well-known divine of the earlier seventeenth century, said that this verse generated all sermons:

And in truth, all our Sermons are nothing else, but rehearsals of that old Spittle Sermon, (as it were) preached by God himselfe to decayed Adam and Eva, Gen. 3.15. For first, all that is said by Christ and his blessed Apostles in the New Testament, is summarily nothing else, but a repetition and explanation of that one prophecy, *Semen mulieris conteret caput serpentis*.

This verse also furnishes sermon material for Michael the heavenly preacher, as well as for Milton the preacherly poet, who structures *Paradise Lost* around the twin sermonic modes of correction and consolation.[31]

I have argued that the last two books of *Paradise Lost* are better understood in terms of homiletics than in terms of pedagogy or even of typology. If we understand Michael primarily as a teacher, we will find that his pedagogy strays unaccountably outside normal pedagogical expectations, whereas if Michael is understood as a preacher, his behavior becomes far more recognizable. He speaks from an explicit text (Gen. iii, 15), and in the course of his sermon moves Adam's will and rectifies his emotions, all with the aim of correcting and consoling him. The stylistic shift from vision to narration in these last two books, in fact, parallels the difference between correction and consolation, between law and grace. Similarly unsatisfactory is a reading of these books primarily in terms of frustrated typology. Milton may provide so many types that he appears to frustrate or interrogate typology rather than fulfill it, yet if Michael is meant to be a preacher, then the profusion of material parallels the way in which the *artes praedicandi* of Milton's own day insisted that a single verse can produce a number of different sermons.

In presenting this thesis, I have implicitly challenged the longstanding assumption among Miltonists that Milton's decision not to enter the ministry represented such a radical break with past habits of thought that homiletics had virtually no influence on his future writing.[32] Such a cognitive disjunction in any author's life would be remarkable; to find it in an author whose shaping of poetic matter parallels so closely the rhetorical patterns of the pulpit would be nothing short of a psychological miracle. As I have shown, the continued influence of the pulpit on *Paradise Lost* calls this particular miracle into serious question.

University of Southern Mississippi

NOTES

1. I will not be analyzing the slight structural differences between Milton's ten-book original (1667) and his twelve-book revision (1674), since these differences have no bearing on my argument.

Addison, *Spectator* no. 369, in Joseph Addison, Richard Steele et al., *The Spectator*, 5 vols., ed. Donald F. Bond (Oxford, 1965), vol. 3, p. 386; Johnson, "Milton," in *Samuel Johnson*, ed. Donald Greene (Oxford, 1984), p. 711; Lewis, *A Preface to Paradise Lost* (1942; rpt. London, 1961), p. 129.

Prince, "On the Last Two Books of *Paradise Lost*," *Essays and Studies*, n.s. XI (1958): 38–52. For an account of the change in critical reception, see Stanley Fish, "Transmuting the Lump: *Paradise Lost*, 1942–1979," in *Doing What Comes Naturally: Change, Rhetoric, and the Practice of Theory in Literary and Legal Studies* (Durham, N.C., 1989), pp. 247–87.

3. Michael Allen may be overstating the case when he places the "onus for effective education" squarely on Raphael and Michael. "Divine Instruction: *Of Education* and the Pedagogy of Raphael, Michael, and the Father," *MQ* XXVI (1992): 113–21. See also Kathleen M. Swaim, *Before and After the Fall: Contrasting Modes in "Paradise Lost"* (Amherst, 1986), pp. 192–238; Ann Baynes Coiro, " 'To Repair the Ruins of our First Parents': *Of Education* and Fallen Adam," *SEL* XXVIII (1988): 133–47; and Vincent Paul di Benedetto, *Education, Poetic Restoration, and the Narrator of "Paradise Lost," Dissertation Abstracts International* XLIX, no. 9 (1989): 2666A. An earlier, and more tentative, investigation of Milton and pedagogy is Murray W. Bundy, "Milton's View of Education in *Paradise Lost*," *JEGP* XXI (1922): 127–52. Bundy does not blame Raphael for Adam's disobedience (140).

4. All citations from Milton's poetry are from Merritt Y. Hughes, *John Milton: Complete Poems and Major Prose* (Indianapolis, 1957); all prose citations are from the *Complete Prose Works of John Milton*, 8 vols., ed. Don M. Wolfe et al. (New Haven, 1953–82), hereafter cited as YP.

5. Schwartz, "From Shadowy Types to Shadowy Types: The Unendings of *Paradise*

Lost," Milton Studies, vol. XXIV, ed. James D. Simmonds (Pittsburgh, 1989), p. 137. In the first line of her article, Schwartz identifies Michael's activity as teaching (p. 123). For another recent discussion of typology in *Paradise Lost*, see William Walker, "Typology and *Paradise Lost*, Books XI and XII," *Milton Studies*, vol. XXV, ed. James D. Simmonds (Pittsburgh, 1990), pp. 245–64.

6. Various Miltonists have mentioned preaching in regard to the final books of *Paradise Lost*, but these mentions were in the course of other analyses. Balachandra Rajan, *Paradise Lost and the Seventeenth Century Reader* (London, 1947), for instance, says, "Michael makes the moral of his sermon plain" (p. 80), but Rajan is not investigating homiletics. Barbara Kiefer Lewalski's excellent discussion of Adam's movement from sight to faith, "Structure and the Symbolism of Vision in Michael's Prophecy, *Paradise Lost*, Books XI–XII," *PQ* XLII (1963): 25–35, also identifies part of Michael's discourse as "a sermon on temperance in food and drink" (27), but Lewalski does not show how Michael's discourse is, in fact, sermonic throughout. Robert L. Entzminger, "Milton's Options and Milton's Poetry, *Paradise Lost* XI and XII," *ELR* VIII (1978), tells us that the historical message of the last books is "available only in Scripture and expounded only from the pulpits of God's consecrated ministers" (198), but his discussion focuses on spiritual biography rather than preaching. The most extensive mention of homiletics in the last two books of *Paradise Lost* is that of J. B. Broadbent, *Some Graver Subject: An Essay on "Paradise Lost"* (London, 1960), pp. 276–77, who tells us that "Michael is in fact preaching a seventeenth-century sermon of the plain Puritan kind recommended in William Perkins's *Art of Prophesying*." He goes on accurately to describe the Puritan sermon, even naming William Chappell as the writer of an *ars praedicandi*, and tells us that such a sermon form accounts for the plain style. Broadbent, however, does not investigate the structural significance of the sermon form or the varieties of sermon types; his concern is with literary style.

I am indebted to Stella P. Revard for drawing my attention to how much correction and consolation are employed in the final books of *Paradise Lost*.

7. A.S.P. Woodhouse, "Milton," in *The Poet and His Faith: Religion and Poetry in England from Spenser to Eliot and Auden* (Chicago and London, 1965), p. 110, identifies the theme of the epic as the fall of man. Merritt Y. Hughes, "Beyond Disobedience," in *Approaches to "Paradise Lost,"* ed. C. A. Patrides (London, 1968), complains that the "use of the word and concept of disobedience is too vague to be very helpful to defenders of his architectonic power and of the unity of *Paradise Lost*" (p. 182); I intend here to demonstrate the opposite. In the same collection of essays as Hughes, Irene Samuel, "*Paradise Lost* as Mimesis," p. 17, downplays the first line of the epic in favor of the entire unfolding action. Martin Mueller, "*Paradise Lost* and the *Iliad*," *Comparative Literature Studies* VI (1969), seeks to reduce the difference between Achilles's anger and the term *disobedience*, calling the latter "an act of disobedience, just as *mênixs* means an action caused by wrath" (293). More recently, Balachandra Rajan, "*Paradise Lost*: The Uncertain Epic," in *Milton Studies*, vol. XVII, ed. Richard S. Ide and Joseph Wittreich (Pittsburgh, 1983), p. 112, in a perceptive reading of the "minidrama" which is played out in the first five lines of the epic by the individual nouns and adjectives, nevertheless fails to mention "disobedience." Gordon Teskey, "Milton's Choice of Subject in the Context of Renaissance Critical Theory," *ELH* LIII (1986): 53–55, says that a question about Milton's choice of subject is "too large, and too fundamental" to be asked, and he instead seeks to frame the context of that choice in terms of Renaissance critical theory.

Shawcross, "The Poet in the Poem: John Milton's Presence in "*Paradise Lost*," *CEA Critic* XLVIII–XLIX (1986): 39. In an earlier work, "The Thesis and the Theme," *With Mortal Voice: The Creation of "Paradise Lost"* (Lexington, Ky., 1982), pp. 22–24, Shawcross argues that the subject of the poem cannot be disobedience, since that would make Book IX the climax of the poem.

8. Bernard, *The Faithfull Shepheard: or the Shepheards Faithfulnesse: Wherein is . . . Set Forth the Excellencie and Necessitie of the Ministerie* (London, 1607), p. 67. Bernard recast this text twice, once in 1609 and again in 1621.

Hans Marchand, *The Categories and Types of Present-Day English Word-Formation: A Synchronic-Diachronic Approach*, 2nd ed. (Munich, 1969), p. 161, specifically lists "disobedience" as a grammatical contradictive. For a longer discussion of categories in English negation, see Ralph Stuart Carlson, *A Study of Some Lexical Negatives in English* (Ph.D. diss., University of Oregon, 1978).

Perkins, *The Arte of Prophecying. Or, a Treatise Concerning the Sacred and Onely True Manner and Methode of Preaching* (1607) in *Works*, 3 vols. (London, 1612; Cambridge, 1613), vol. II, pp. 668–69. Perkins's *Arte of Prophecying* is a translation of his earlier *Prophetica, sive de sacra et unica ratione concionandi tractatus* (Cambridge, 1592).

Chappell, *The Preacher, or The Art and Method of Preaching: Shewing the Most Ample Directions and Rules for Invention, Method, Expression* (London, 1656), p. 155. Chappell's text originally appeared in Latin as *Methodus concionandi* (London, 1648).

9. For further discussion of architectural metaphors in pedagogical treatises, see Linda C. Mitchell, *Controversies over Grammar: Contexts and Purposes in Seventeenth- and Eighteenth-Century England* (Ph.D. diss., University of Southern California, 1996), chap. 2. Hartlib, *The True and Readie Way to Learne the Latine Tongue* (London, [1654]), pp. A2r, A3r. Fleming, "The Schoole of Skill, Or the Rule of a Reformed Life," *The Diamond of Devotion* (London, 1608), p. I2r. Walker, "Preface," *Some Improvements to the Art of Teaching, Especially in the First Grounding of a Young Scholar in Grammar Learning* (London, 1669), p. A5v. Thomas Kranidas, "Milton on Teachers and Teaching," *MQ* XX (1986), claims to find descriptions of teaching within Milton's tracts which makes it "an honourable activity parallel, if not quite equal, to preaching and poesy" (26).

10. For other consolatory traditions, see Christopher Fitter, " 'Native Soil': Exile Lament and Exile Consolation in *Paradise Lost*," in *Milton Studies*, vol. XX, ed. James D. Simmonds (Pittsburgh, 1984), pp. 147–62, and Ann W. Astell, "The Medieval *Consolatio* and the Conclusion of *Paradise Lost*," *SP* LXXXII (1985): 477–92.

11. Bernard, *The Faithful Shepheard* (1607), pp. 69–70.

12. Chappell, *The Preacher* (1656), p. 153. For further discussion of Milton's debt to Chappell and English Reformation homiletics in general, see my "Milton and the 'Office of a Pulpit,' " *Ben Jonson Journal* (forthcoming). Chappell, *The Use of Holy Scripture Gravely and Methodically Discoursed* (London, 1653), pp. 103–45.

13. All citations from the Bible are from the King James Version. The text here cited is 2 Timothy iii, 16, from which Andreas Gerhard Hyperius, *De formandis concionibus sacris, seu de interpretatione scripturarum populari* (Marburg, 1553); *Of Framing of Divine Sermons, or Popular Interpretation of the Scriptures*, trans. John Ludham ([London?], 1577), ff. 18r–20v, first developed the sermon types of doctrine, reproof, instruction, and correction in 1553. He derived consolation from Romans xv, 4.

14. The Father foresees the Fall (III, 93–95); the narrator wishes for the "warning voice" of the Apocalypse (IV, 1–2); Eve dreams of "the Tree / Of interdicted Knowledge" (V, 51–52); the Father sends Raphael to warn Adam so as to give him no excuse for his impending disobedience (V, 243–45); Raphael exhorts Adam to obedience (V, 501–03) and warns him repeatedly about disobedience and its consequences (V, 611–15; VI, 395–97; VII, 542–47; VIII, 323–35, 633–43); the narrator begins Book IX on the tragic note of man's disobedience (IX, 5–8); Adam

warns Eve about their adversary (IX, 251–56), which she acknowledges (274–78). After the fall, the narrator recalls the injunction (X, 12–13), as does the Father (XI, 84–86).

An example from a sermon manual is "Nihil reprehendatur de quo non certô constat" ("Nothing is to be reprehended which cannot be certainly determined"), *Officium concionatoris in quo praecepta utilissima de invenienda habendaque concione* (Cambridge, 1676), p. 35.

15. Louis L. Martz, *"Paradise Lost:* The Journey of the Mind," in *The Paradise Within: Studies in Vaughan, Traherne, and Milton* (New Haven, 1964), says of the brutal vision of Babel, "Nothing could be further from the promised sympathy and consolation" (p. 158); see also William Empson, *Milton's God* (London, 1961). Balachandra Rajan, "The Uncertain Epic," asks, "How far does the tragic actuality frustrate and even nullify the epic promise?" (p. 113).

Ames, *Conscience with the Power and the Cases Thereof* ([London,] 1639), bk. II, p. 36. It may be of some importance that Ames was, like Milton, an editor of Ramus. Of even more importance might be the line of pedagogical succession from William Perkins to Ames, thence to Ames's student Chappell, and then to Chappell's student Milton. Perkins, Ames, and Chappell all wrote directions for preaching.

Wilson, *Theological Rules, to Guide Us in the Understanding and Practise of Holy Scriptures. Two Centuries* (London, 1615), pp. 79–80. This Thomas Wilson (the divine) should not be confused with the author of *The Arte of Rhetorique* (1553). Luther, *Lectures on Isaiah, Chapters 40–66,* in *Luther's Works,* vol. XVII, ed. Hilton C. Oswald (St. Louis, 1972), p. 3.

Jason Rosenblatt, "Adam's Pisgah Vision: *Paradise Lost,* Books XI and XII," *ELH* XXXIX (1972), linking Adam's vision of futurity to Moses' view of the promised land he could not enter, notes, "Reformation expositors recognized the mingling of pain and consolation in the Scriptural account of Moses' ascent to the Pisgah height" (74–75).

16. Donne, "Hymne to God My God, in My Sicknesse," in *The Complete Poetry of John Donne,* ed. John T. Shawcross (Garden City, N.Y., 1967), p. 392, lines 29–30.

Lovejoy, "Milton and the Paradox of the Fortunate Fall," *ELH* IV (1937): 161–79. Lovejoy's reading has been challenged successfully by Virginia R. Mollenkott, "Milton's Rejection of the Fortunate Fall," *MQ* VI (1972): 1–5, and by Dennis Richard Danielson, *"Paradise Lost* and the Unfortunate Fall," *Milton's Good God: A Study in Literary Theodicy* (Cambridge, 1982), pp. 202–27.

17. Dent, *The Ruine of Rome: or, An Exposition upon the Whole Revelation* (London, 1603), pp. 26–27. See also John Bale, *The Image of Both Churches After the Moste Wonderful and Heavenly Revelacion of Sainct John the Evangelist* (London, 1550), p. B7r: James Brocard [Giacopo Brocardo], *The Revelation of S. John Reveled,* trans. James Sanford (London, 1582), f. 40v; George Gyffard, *Sermons Upon the Whole Booke of the Revelation* (London, 1596), p. 36; William Perkins, *A Godly and Learned Exposition or Commentarie upon the Three First Chapters of the Revelation, Works* (1612–13), vol. III, p. 261; Hezekiah Holland, *An Exposition or, A Short, But Full, Plaine, and Perfect Epitome of the Most Choice Commentaries Upon the Revelation of Saint John* (London, 1650), p. 10; James Durham, *A Commentarie Upon the Book of the Revelation* (London, 1658), p. 66.

Milton's identification of the angel in Ephesians as ministers in general is, of course, consonant with Milton's denial of the apostolic authority of the prelates, whereas Bishop Joseph Hall and others like him claimed that the "angel" of Ephesus was its bishop, thereby giving episcopacy scriptural warrant.

18. The Canons of 1604 called for the catechizing of children every Sunday for at least one-half hour (LIX) and visitation of the sick (LXVII), but they forbade preaching or the administration of sacraments in private houses except in cases of physical extremity (LXXI). Edward Cardwell, *Synodalia: A Collection of Articles of Religion, Canons, and Proceedings of Convocations,* 2 vols. (Oxford, 1842), vol. 1, pp. 280, 284, 287. William Perkins, *The Second Treatise of*

the Duties and Dignities of the Ministerie, Works (1612–13), vol. III, urged that ministers must especially learn to follow St. Paul's counsel to be "instant in season and out of season, to preach and exhort, to comfort and rebuke, publikely and privately (p. 444). Perkins is partly paraphrasing 2 Timothy iv, 2; "publikely and privately" is his addition. See also George Herbert, *A Priest to the Temple*, 2nd ed. (London, 1671), pp. 25, 49; William Ames, *Conscience with the Power* (1639), bk. IV, pp. 80–81; Westminster Assembly of Divines, *A Directory for the Publique Worship of God* (London, 1644), p. 31.

19. Baxter, *Gildes Salvianus; The Reformed Pastor. Shewing the Nature of the Pastoral Work; Especially in Private Instruction and Catechizing*, 2nd ed. (London, 1657), sig. B5v. Taylor, *Rules and Advices to the Clergy of the Dioceses of Down and Conner, for Their Deportment in Their Personal and Publick Capacities*, 2nd ed. (London, 1663), p. 25. Burnet, *A Discourse of the Pastoral Care* (London, 1692), p. xvi.

20. See esp. John M. Steadman, "Adam and the Prophesied Redeemer (*Paradise Lost*, XII, 359–623)," *SP* LVI (1959): 214–25, and C. A. Patrides, "The 'Protevangelium' in Renaissance Theology and *Paradise Lost*," *SEL* III (1963): 19–30. See also *CD* I, xxvi: "The covenant of grace itself is first made public from God's point of view, Gen. iii.15" (YP VI, p. 515).

21. Wilkins, *Ecclesiastes, or, A Discourse Concerning the Gift of Preaching as It Fals Under the Rules of Art* (London, 1646), p. 14.

22. Hall, *An Apologie for the Ministry and Its Maintenance* (London, 1660), p. 93; Hieron, *The Dignitie of Preaching*, in *Workes* (London, 1634[?]), p. 583. Editions of Hieron's *Workes* vary; this citation is from the Huntington Library copy, accession no. 321541; Perkins, "An Instruction Touching Religious or Divine Worship," *Works*, (1612–13), vol. I, p. 708.

23. For parallels between *Paradise Lost* XI and XII and the eleventh chapter of Hebrews, see for instance Joseph H. Summers, "The Final Vision," *The Muse's Method: An Introduction to "Paradise Lost"* (London, 1962), p. 198; H. R. MacCallum, "Milton and Sacred History: Books XI and XII of *Paradise Lost*," *Essays in English Literature from the Renaissance to the Victorian Age Presented to A.S.P. Woodhouse*, ed. Millar MacLure and F. W. Watt (Toronto, 1964), p. 158; Balachandra Rajan, "*Paradise Lost*: The Hill of History," *The Lofty Rhyme: A Study of Milton's Major Poetry* (London, 1970), p. 84; Raymond B. Waddington, "The Death of Adam: Vision and Voice and Books XI and XII of *Paradise Lost*," *MP* LXX (1972): 9–21.

24. Bernard, *The Faithful Shepheard* (1607), pp. 1–2. I have omitted the numerous Bible citations in this passage.

25. John Wilkins, *Ecclesiastes* (1646), pp. 19–20.

26. Shuger, "God, Self, and Psyche: The Theological Bases of the Grand Style," *Sacred Rhetoric: The Christian Grand Style in the English Renaissance* (Princeton, 1988), pp. 193–240, esp. pp. 194–223.

27. On the Reformation move from the visual to the verbal, see Georgia B. Christopher, "Milton's 'Literary' Theology," *Milton and the Science of the Saints* (Princeton, 1982), pp. 3–29.

28. *Affectus praecipuê hîc movendi sunt; 1. spes; 2. gaudiam; 3. constantia; 4. patientia." Officium concionatoris*, p. 34.

29. Perkins, *The Arte of Prophesying, Works*, vol. II, p. 666.

30. Bernard, *The Faithful Shepheard*, pp. 69–70.

31. Schwartz, "From Shadowy Types," p. 133. I am not suggesting here that "multiplicity" means "superfluity," nor that the wealth of potential sermon material need cause anxiety in the preacher or the audience. For a discussion of interpretive anxiety earlier in *Paradise Lost*, see Dayton Haskin, *Milton's Burden of Interpretation* (Philadelphia, 1994). Boys, "Sermon for the Second Sunday in Lent," in *The Works of John Boys* (n.p., 1629 [1638]), p. 242.

32. See, for instance, Harris Francis Fletcher, *The Intellectual Development of John*

Milton, 2 vols. (Urbana, 1956–61), vol. II, p. 509, who puts the decision against the ministry as early as 1627–28; David Masson, *The Life of John Milton: Narrated in Connexion with the Political, Ecclesiastical, and Literary History of His Time*, 6 vols. (1859–94, rpt. New York, 1946), vol. I, p. 323, who puts the decision before 1632; Christopher Hill, *Milton and the English Revolution* (1977; rpt. New York, 1978), p. 39, who puts the decision "within three or four years" after 1629; and A.S.P. Woodhouse, "Notes on Milton's Early Development," *UTQ* XIII (1943–44): 68, who dates Milton's final decision during his period of postgraduate study. William Haller, *The Rise of Puritanism, or, The Way to the New Jerusalem as Set Forth in Pulpit and Press from Thomas Cartwright to John Lilburne and John Milton, 1570–1643* (New York, 1938), p. 289, on the other hand, insists that the decision to forego the ministry did not erase its impress upon Milton, and Haller puts this decision fairly late. Other Miltonists who have objected to a strict divorce of Milton's poetry from the pulpit are William Riley Parker, *Milton: A Biography*, 2 vols. (Oxford, 1968), vol. I, p. 153, and vol. II, p. 776; John Spencer Hill, "Poet-Priest: Vocational Tension in Milton's Early Development," in *Milton Studies*, vol. VIII, ed. James D. Simmonds (Pittsburgh, 1975), pp. 41–69, and "Ministerial Vocation, 1625–1640," *John Milton: Poet, Priest and Prophet. A Study of Divine Vocation in Milton's Poetry and Prose* (Totowa, N.J., 1979), pp. 27–49; Christopher Grose, " 'Unweapon'd Creature in the Word': A Revision of Milton's Letter to a Friend," *ELN* XXI (1983): 29–34, and *Milton and the Sense of Tradition* (New Haven, 1988), pp. 30–33.

"HIS VOLANT TOUCH": MILTON AND THE GOLDEN SECTION

J. Karl Franson

M ILTON'S LOVE of the orderly and mathematical produced in him
a fascination with the forms of architecture, music, and poetry. His
passionate interest in structure is reflected not only in allusions throughout
his works, but in the structures of the works themselves. This aspect of his
poetry has led one scholar to applaud his "majestic control over structure,"
another to consider him the greatest architect in English poetry, a third to
judge him the preeminent poet of cosmic order. In *Paradise Lost* we find
one of many examples of his interest in formal design in a reference to God
as "the sov'ran Architect" who lays out the universe with "golden Com-
passes," a visual representation of Sir Thomas Browne's assertion that God
must be a geometrician.[1] Both Milton and Browne reflect the popular view
of Creation as geometrically and mathematically ordered, an idea first expressed in Plato's *Timaeus,* namely that beauty, harmony, and balance in
the cosmos derive from geometric proportion.[2] The concept is later given
biblical authority in a passage from the Wisdom of Solomon, often cited in
the Renaissance, wherein God is said to have "ordered all things in measure
and number and weight" (xi, 20).[3]

When Neoplatonist Christoforo Landino writes, therefore, that "God is
the supreme poet, and the world is His poem," thus making implicit the
notion of poets as creators *in imitatio Dei,* we are at the door of the Renaissance poet's interest in numbers. A century later, the notion of the poet as
creator reappears in George Puttenham's *The Art of English Poesie* (1589),
wherein poets are enjoined to imitate the paradigms of the cosmos by utiliz-
ing geometry and mathematics, for as the author puts it, "All things stand
by proportion, and . . . without it nothing could stand to be good or beautiful." Sir Philip Sidney's *Defence of poesie* (1595) gives English prominence
to the concept when he presents poetry as "a mathematical system reflecting
celestial beauty," numerical elements such as metrics being quintessential,
the numbers encoding within the work a correspondence with divinity and
thus manifesting the poet's harmony with the celestial. Many uses of mathematics in poetry were explored during the period, including both mystical
and "temporal" numerology; and while some are primarily symbolic, others

117

are primarily structural. Heninger categorizes the latter under the term "subtext of form," differentiating them from symbolic numerology (*Subtext*, pp. 41, 90).[4]

Renaissance artists were expected, however, to conceal their methods, the techniques by which they achieved their effects. Plato cautions against revealing the secrets of a profession or craft, advice Sidney repeats for poets: "There are many mysteries contained in poetry which of purpose were written darkly lest by prophane wits it should be abused." Indeed, the scarcity of Renaissance commentary by poets explaining their methods suggests that secrecy was an acknowledged aspect of the poet's work, as it was in many professions.[5] A prime case in point is the intricate mathematical structure of Dante's *Commedia:* Hardt explains that even before Dante began to write, he conducted complicated, painstaking calculations that would control the structure of his work, yet his calculations are carefully concealed. Dante's use of numbers, Hardt concludes, is a textual strategy for creating an "inner sphere of the poem" addressed specifically to God. Unlike architectural works in which the perceptive observer usually recognizes the designer's geometrical plan, mathematical structuring in most other art forms disappears in the finished work, as it does in Dante's. Only its effects, such as unity, harmony, and proportion, remain.[6] While it was in the craftsman's best interests to guard the techniques of his or her artistry, such a practice resulted in the eventual loss of many principles and methods. Milton's longer poetical works must have been composed from detailed plans, even if never put to paper, embodying the principles upon which his creative imagination worked. Even his shorter works carry the imprint of precompositional pattern, form, or numerical design, but surviving manuscripts reveal little of his compositional method.

Milton's interest in poetical forms, as recent studies have begun to show, led him to consider the variety of structural and symbolic possibilities offered by numbers. He was well educated in the mathematics of his time, despite indifference toward the subject at Cambridge where he took his degrees.[7] Although he never refers directly to the Divine Proportion, today called the golden section (represented by the Greek letter ϕ), the frequent appearance of the proportion as a structuring device in his works leaves no doubt he knew of it, perhaps through Luca Pacioli's *La divina proportione* (1509) or Mario Equicola's *Libro di natura d'amore* (1531).[8] An irrational or incommensurate number (that is, a nonrepeating decimal), the golden section is a geometric proportion in which the smaller part is to the larger as the larger is to the whole. In mathematical notation, it is expressed as $1 + \sqrt{5} \div 2$, or $1.61803399\ldots$ If the whole is 1, the reciprocal of the section equals .61803399 . . . , so that any quantity approximately 62 percent of another (or its inverse, 38 percent) creates a golden section relationship.

The golden section was known in ancient Egypt, if not earlier, but the Greeks popularized it as a highly desirable ratio in architecture and art deriving from proportions of the human body. Only in modern times has it been observed in a multitude of organic forms, such as the arrangement of leaves around a stem, the pentamerous configuration of petals so common among flowers, the elegant logarithmic spiral of the chambered nautilus. During the Renaissance the proportion was revered by the astronomer Kepler as a "precious gem, one of the two treasures of geometry" and accorded an extravagant importance.[9] Because an infinite number of integers is required to specify an irrational number precisely, it can never be known exactly, and for this reason irrational numbers were considered mysterious by the Pythagoreans and their very existence kept secret. Even in the Renaissance they retained the glamour of secrecy and of the occult, but Galileo, among others, made a clear break with such number mysticism by refusing, as one writer puts it, "to endow mathematical forms with ontological dignity," even though he too believed the universe to be "written in the language of mathematics." Treatises by Pacioli and Equicola also did much to demystify the golden section by giving it wide exposure and a solid mathematical basis.[10]

Pacioli's *La divina proportione* proposes rules of proportion for all the arts and advances the golden section in particular as an elegant and dynamic proportion readily adapted to art, music, and poetry (Heninger, *Subtext*, p. 73*n12*). The unique qualities of the golden section are defined in this quatrain by Guy du Faur:

> *Vertue*, betweene the Two extremes that haunts;
> Betweene two-mickle and two-little sizes;
> Exceedes in nothing, and in nothing wants:
> Borrowes of none: but to it-selfe suffizes.[11]

In our own century, the supposed aesthetic superiority of the section is expressed in much the same fashion: in Wittkower's words, "It is indeed a proportion of extraordinaray beauty and perfection" because, unlike all other true proportions, it contains "only two magnitudes [in which] the two smaller members always equal the whole" (p. 204). Further, it represents the perfect balance between "two unequal asymmetrical parts, which means that the dominant is neither too big nor too small, so that this ratio appears at once clear and 'of just measure,'" hence its uncommon beauty.[12] As a consequence, the section communicates an "endless proportional consonance" and a "particular richness of resonance" (Coates, *Geometry, Proportion,* p. 17).

Modern attempts to demonstrate a clear preference for the golden section, most conducted in the visual domain, have proven inconclusive.[13] Precision with respect to the use of this proportion in an art form, therefore, may be more a matter of conformity to a mathematical ideal than a consciously discernible aesthetic discriminiation on the part of the artist.[14] Although a popular twentieth-century view suggests that beauty is entirely subjective and cannot be calculated mathematically, not until the eighteenth century did a break occur between the arts and mathematics. Previously, Platonic and Pythagorean dictums that certain ratios and proportions possessed intrinsic beauty went unquestioned.[15] At least in one field of art we have come full circle, for in computer graphics "artistic sensibilities and aesthetic judgements have, to a large extent, been replaced by precise mathematical formulas" (Field and Golubitsky, *Symmetry in Chaos,* p. 3).

Coates's recent study of early stringed instruments provides proof that Renaissance luthiers consciously employed numerical proportions, including the golden section, to give their instruments beauty, strength, and structural integrity. A 1666 violin by Antonio Stradivari, for instance, exhibits a "sustained and beautiful use of φ proportion" in the neck and body lengths, the placement of the f-holes, and in other features. Golden section proportioning is also used in musical composition, such as the Gregorian chant of the late Middle Ages, and has continued into the present century. A composer so organizes a work, or portion of a work, that its most critical point occurs at one of the golden means (38 percent or 62 percent of the work). This juncture may be an emotional peak, a moment of special significance, a change of form (often indicated by a major repeat), or simply the beginning or ending of a musical phrase. Such proportioning, however, cannot be sensed until the conclusion is reached, unless the length is known in advance, for only at the end does the aural memory sense the respective proportions between small segment and large, between large and the whole.[16]

The appearance of the golden section in music and its effects upon the listener are of paramount importance in a study of Milton's use of the proportion, for he had an intimate knowledge of music, including music theory, and undoubtedly was more influenced by musical composition than by other art forms.[17] In addition, the fundamental laws governing music are the same as those of poetry, excepting that the poetical experience is produced by a visual engagement with the text (unless the poem is being read aloud by another). This engagement invariably causes the eye to form an initial impression of the work's length, stanzaic form (if any), and line length. As a consequence, the literary experience, while primarily durational like that of music, has important spatial components as well, particularly regarding short verse printed on a single page that presents the reader an immediate spatial configuration. And when an important juncture is encountered, be the poem short or long, the eye senses, even before completing the work, the relative proportions created by this juncture.

While the effects of numerical structures in music are largely understood, those in literature are not.[18] Such structures, including golden section proportioning, are used in literature not primarily as numerical symbols, although they may function symbolically in representing divinity and the infinite, but to provide harmonic proportion. The major demand made of symbolic numerology in literature, that of deepening understanding and increasing thematic significance of the work (Reiss, "Number Symbolism," 168), can hardly be made of mathematical structuring. Perhaps this is one reason Heninger insists upon differentiating between the two, categorizing the latter as a subtext of form (*Subtext*, p. 6n7). Still, it seems only sensible to expect a unity of form and content, for aesthetic theory depends upon clear relationships between form and function.

Although the appearance of the famous proportion in literature has yet to receive the attention it deserves, modern studies reveal its appearance in Virgil, Spenser, and Jonson, poets known to have influenced Milton, and later in Wordsworth. The *Aeneid* exhibits an obsession with the section: Virgil employs it in over a thousand instances. Spenser, perhaps aware of Virgil's practice, employs it in his numerically intricate *Epithalamion*, and Jonson uses it in all the masques of the 1616 Folio.[19] Milton's use of the golden section, however, is much less pervasive than Virgil's, for while he employs the "bipartite pattern" evident throughout the *Aeneid*, he does not include complex forms such as Virgil's "recessed tripartite" framework. Nor does he place sections within sections as Virgil does, a layering technique called "nesting" or "embedding" in music.[20] A comprehensive study of this proportion in Milton's poetical works, as well as that of other Renaissance poets and dramatists, most likely will reveal that his use of the proportion lies within a well-established tradition.

It is certain Milton knew of the potentialities of the proportion long before his introduction to the academies of Florence and Rome in 1638–39, where mathematical principles of beauty were discussed (Ghyka, *Geometry*, p. 149), for he uses it in poetry as early as 1626, shortly after his admission to Christ's College. At least fifteen of his hundred poetical works contain evidence of golden section proportioning, including major works like "Lycidas" and *Paradise Lost*, some more obviously deliberate than others. These works fall into five categories based upon structural or thematic elements appearing at one of the golden means: a key event, a shift in address, a parenthetical expression, the shortest line, and the longest line. *Paradise Lost* is the sole representation of the first category. The creation of Eve, with its emphasis on beauty, is introduced at the major golden mean (VII, 1094; VIII, 457, in subsequent editions). Immediately preceding this line is a twenty-line address by God to Adam concerning Adam's "other self," followed by a twenty-line passage describing the creation of Eve from Adam's rib. First pointed out by John T. Shawcross, this use of the golden section is a consummate example of proportional beauty.[21] The second category, a shift in address, is represented by three works, "*Anno ætatis 17. In obitum Præsulis Eliensis*" ("On the Death of the Bishop of Ely"), "An Epitaph on the Marchioness of *Winchester*," and *Sonnet XVI* ("When I consider how my light is spent"), and constitutes the focus of the present study. The remaining groups are represented by poems divided at a mean by less arresting structural elements, suggesting that the presence of the section, in certain instances, is apt to be intuitive or coincidental.[22] The proportioning of the three poems discussed below, as well as *Paradise Lost*, approximates the section far more closely than mere chance would lead us to expect, proof of deliberate numerical calculation among Milton's compositional methods.[23]

In the poet's Cambridge elegy on the death of the Bishop of Ely, Nicholas Felton (1556–1626), we can observe an early but remarkably accurate example of his interest in golden section proportioning. This elegy, "*In obitum Præsulis Eliensis*" (*Poems*, 1645; *CPW* I, pp. 244–45), was composed in the late fall of 1626 when the poet was not quite eighteen. Its only structural and thematic shift, an immediately obvious one, occurs after line 26 (of sixty-eight lines) when a confrontation occurs. The initial twenty-six lines comprise the speaker-poet's lament. Thereafter he imagines the departed bishop delivering a Christian-Platonic monologue on death that continues forty-two lines to the poem's end. The break between lines 26 and 27, therefore, is dramatic, dividing the poem into two asymmetrical parts at an obvious discontinuity: "*Audisse tales videor attonitus sonos / Leni, sub aurâ, flamine*" ("Astonished, I seem to hear such sounds as these, / on the gentle breeze beneath the air," 25–26), followed by, "*Cæcos furores pone, pone vitream / Bilemque & irritas minas*" ("Put away your blind madness; put away your transparent / melancholy and your ineffectual threats," 27–28). Calculated by the number of lines, this juncture appears at the minor golden mean, or after .3824 of the work has transpired ($26 \div 68$). The respective ratios of the two partitions thus created are .6190 ($26 \div 42$) and .6176 ($42 \div 68$), with deviations of a mere .0010 ($.6190 - .6180$) and .0004 ($.6180 - .6176$) from the means. It should be obvious that the percent of deviation from the golden section at a structural reference point is of paramount importance in judging whether it is being used deliberately. In this case, the section could not have been used more accurately. Moving the beginning of the bishop's speech *by even a syllable either way* would move it farther from the mean, leading us to the inescapable conclusion that Milton structured "Eliensis" around the golden section deliberately.[24]

This and subsequent examples suggest that Milton used either lines, metrical feet, or syllables when positioning a natural juncture at a mean. It is obvious that only the latter two, which he would have counted routinely in composing metrical verse, accurately represent the duration of time. Probability of chance occurrence, that the juncture after line 26 corresponds to the minor mean because of coincidence, is one in sixty-eight, or 1.47 percent, if calculated by the number of lines. If calculated by syllables, it is 1 in 680, or a negligible .15 percent. Such precision leads us to conclude that in making structural computations Milton used the more accurate figures of .6180 and .3820 rather than .62 and .38. Most likely it is true of poets as well as composers that the more profound the artist, the more meticulous the technique.[25] Milton's precision with this proportion, a virtuosic demonstration of the young poet's desire to bestow upon his work an elegant structural integrity and an added proof of high seriousness, strikes the imagination with force.

Just how precise a deliberately fashioned numerical structure must be, however, to remove all suspicion of coincidence has not been established. Fortunately, Milton's use of this proportion, like Mozart's (for instance), displays a fine degree of accuracy, rendering the probability of coincidence statistically negligible.[26] The allowable deviation from the proportion in studies of music and literature ranges from one percent to five percent either way among scholars' attempts to identify a fair approximation of the proportion, but all are arbitrary.[27] A pragmatic approach like the following might be more meaningful. Because a poet, for convenience, might use a whole-number percentage when partitioning a work (for example, 62 percent), the slight deviation from the proportion this figure represents, $\pm.0020$, should be allowed as a matter of course when it cannot be determined which figure, .62 or .6180, the poet is using (so small a deviation would have no effect upon short works). Second, wherever the poet can be shown to have approximated the proportion as closely as possible without resorting to fractions of discrete units (such as lines), the resultant deviation should be allowed, since it is unavoidable.[28]

A comment about intuition might be in order. The title of the present study includes Milton's reference to an ancient musician (Gen. iii, 21), whose "volant" or skillful touch is "instinct through all proportions," or impelled by the music of the spheres, even while he brings to his composition a conscious attention to musical proportions "low and high" (*PL* X, 557–58; XI, 561–62 in subsequent editions). Milton's own compositional process with the golden section might also be imagined as impelled by an intuitive sense. Early in the writing process he must have sensed the approximate location of the major and minor means, later making adjustments to draw the key juncture into more precise conformity with the proportion. A similar view has been put forward for Mozart, centering on the Kantian ideal that the work of genius involves many intuitive judgments, that it is more natural than nurtural (Perry-Camp, "Time and Temporal Proportion," pp. 161–62).

Beauty involves delicate phenomena that are difficult, if not impossible, to define. As a consequence, when a geometrical relationship like that of the golden section is employed in a durational-spatial art form like *"Eliensis"* to enhance the aural and (to a lesser extent) spatial qualities by introducing proportional beauty, the effect upon the reader is not easily described nor verified. Because golden section proportioning in the elegy is invisible, most readers will be unaware of it. But it does not necessarily follow that they will fail to sense the harmonious relationship between parts. Proportioning brings to the poem a comfortable balance between conventional hyperboles of flowing tears and curses upon Death, and the rational, reassuring outlook upon Death presented by the amiable bishop, happy to exchange his "loathsome prison" for the "crystalline realm" above (46, 63). The respective lengths of the two parts of the elegy cannot be allowed to continue long without its exaggerated grief exposed for what it is. As the bishop firmly instructs him, "Cæcos furores pone" (27). Yet it would be fatuous to imagine that a syllable, a word, even a line or two, would alter in any perceptible sense our appreciation of this balance. So Milton's precision with the proportion must reflect a compulsion to place the juncture with extreme accuracy primarily to conform to a matrix established by earlier poets. Furthermore, it suggests he considered the poetical subject worthy of the effort to give it a geometrical, hence sacred, dimension.

While still at Cambridge, Milton composed an elegy in English on the death of a young noblewoman, Lady Jane (Savage) Paulet, Marchioness of Winchester, who died of infection from a facial abscess soon after the birth of a stillborn son. Her death occasioned an unusual outpouring of published sentiment, including Milton's "An Epitaph on the Marchioness of *Winchester*" (1645).[29] This work bears close structural similarity to *"Eliensis,"* and as we shall also see, to *Sonnet XVI*. It is partitioned into two unequal parts by a shift in the direction of address. The first portion of "Epitaph" is an address to the reader (1–46), the second an apostrophe to the Marchioness. Milton's structural reference point, therefore, is signaled by the first word of line 47, "Gentle," which initiates the apostrophe: "Gentle Lady may thy grave / Peace and quiet ever have" (47–48). As in *"Eliensis,"* this reference point approximates the golden section extremely closely. Calculated by lines (after forty-six of seventy-four), or feet (after 184 of 296), the juncture produces ratios of .6087 and .6216, with deviations of .0093 and .0036. Once again, the intersection is located as closely as possible to the mean; and the probability of chance occurrence, calculated by lines, is one in seventy-four, or 1.35 percent.[30]

A notable difference in the partitioning format between *"Eliensis"* and this poem is Milton's reversal of the earlier pattern, here selecting the major rather than the minor mean as the structural reference point. While both formats work well in their respective poems, the effects of the two are quite different. For one thing, the minor-major pattern of *"Eliensis"* seems more manipulative, redirecting reader response before midpoint, and the second portion is likely to become tedious after so early a climax. The major-minor pattern of "Epitaph," in contrast, allows for a more gradual involvement, followed by a shorter, subordinate consolation and disengagement. Lendvai's study of the two formats in music corroborates this general view. Not surprisingly, composers of Gregorian chants studied by Larson chose the major-minor format twice as often as its opposite, thus providing additional evidence of its superiority in a durational art form.[31]

The most apparent significance, then, to Milton's choice of the major-minor format in "Epitaph" is that of providing for a suitable introduction to lady, child, and their shared misfortune during which the reader's sympathy is engaged, then a shorter speech addressed to the lady and aimed at comforting her spirit, her grieving family and friends. In contrast to *"Eliensis,"* the resultant effect is appropriately contemplative and calming. As the work concludes, we have an evocation upon Lady Jane of eternal peace, quiet, and rest (48), a figurative presentation of tears, flowers, and bays (55–59), and a vision of her in heaven accompanied by Rachel, "much like to [her] in story" (62). Similarities between the women's situations are remarkable, as the poet himself notes: both endured years of barrenness, delivered a firstborn son, and died while giving birth to a second son (63–68; compare Gen. xxx, 1, 22–24; xxxv, 18–19). In addition, both are associated with a waiting period of seven years, Rachel because she was obliged to wait seven years to marry (Gen. xxix, 20, 27–28), Lady Jane because she waited seven years, after marriage, for her first child, a fact included in the earlier version of the poem mentioned previously (Parker, "Milton and the Marchioness," 548–49).

Milton's most well-known sonnet, "When I consider how my light is spent," composed about 1652 and numbered XVI in his 1673 *Poems* (but XIX in most modern editions), begins with a mood of depression caused by the onset of blindness and ends with quiet resignation. It contains an obvious turning point of the type found in *"Eliensis"* and "Epitaph," a confrontation between speaker-poet and a personage imagined to be present. This crux signals a change in the direction of address. We first have a monologue conveying grief over the loss of sight, with the implication that the speaker's days as a poet are finished, then a speech of consolation by Patience enabling the speaker-poet to rise out of self-pity and disillusionment. The break between speakers is thus clearly delineated: "But patience to prevent / That murmur, soon replies, God doth not need / Either man's work or his own gifts" (8–10). This intersection between "replies" and "God," as Anna K. Nardo explains, marks a radical redirection of mood, faith, and sentiment: "As [the speaker-poet] falls to the greatest recess of the Inferno within his heart, patience brings the light of true reason to dispel his folly." Nardo also observes that Milton's use of pronouns differentiates the two portions of the poem: "Not one first person pronoun trespasses the barrier between the octave and sestet to taint the new theocentric vision of the old egocentric blindness."[32]

But unlike the traditional break between octave and sestet, after 75 percent of the work has transpired (such as in *Sonnet VII,* "How soon hath time"), Milton here inserts an explanation of eleven words between octave and sestet, shifting the position of the juncture between them. A minor break occurs after "I fondly ask," a major break after "soon replies," initiating the speech by Patience. The latter juncture, after 8.60 of fourteen lines (the break occurs, in line 8, after twenty-one of thirty-five alphabet characters, or .60 of the line), is numerically significant. Calculated by metrical feet, of which there are seventy, it occurs after forty-three feet, or .6143 of the poem. Thus it corresponds as closely as possible to the major mean without involving fractions of feet, creating ratios of .6279 and .6143 (based on lines or feet), with insignificant deviations of .0099 and .0037.[33] In so short a poem, the higher probability of coincidence must be taken into account; but the probability of chance occurrence calculated by feet is one in seventy, or only 1.43 percent, leading us to believe the correspondence between the juncture and the golden section is deliberate.

Milton's use of the famous proportion as a compositional principle or rule of artistic arrangement thus spans most of his writing career, from "In obitum Præsulis Eliensis" to *Sonnet XVI* and *Paradise Lost.* He favors the major-minor format in proportioning a work, locating the structural reference point at approximately .6180 rather than at .3820 of a work. This allows for a gradual, extended crescendo, followed by a shorter resolution. He appears to have used the more accurate figure .6180 rather than 62 percent, perhaps in keeping with a natural inclination toward precision. He preferred lines as the unit of calculation for structuring longer poems, metrical feet for shorter poems.

The mathematical care evident in Milton's use of the golden section, accurate in certain cases to five decimal places, constitutes unquestionable evidence that in selected poems he consciously positioned an important structural element at one of the golden means. During early stages of composition he may have established proportions instinctively, but at a later stage he brought the juncture into close correlation with the mean by counting lines or metrical feet. His purpose, it seems safe to assume, was to provide the poetical work a proportional integrity and harmony, a subtext of form he believed derived from paradigms of the universe. Perhaps his imitation of cosmic mathematics was driven ultimately by a desire to please "the great Architect" himself (*PL* VII, 709), since his use of the section is not consciously perceived by readers. Still, sensitive as he was to the movement of sound in time, he must also have wished to enhance the aural appeal of his verse by structuring it around the most beautiful proportion he knew.

University of Maine at Farmington

NOTES

For their assistance with this study, the following have my sincere thanks: Janine L. Bonk, Raymond A. DeSandre, Lester R. Dickey, my wife Jeanine F. Franson, Gail L. Lange, Kathy McLaughlin, Mark McPherran, Russell H. Rainville, John T. Shawcross, and Shari L. Witham. It is affectionately dedicated to my granddaughter Leah K. Franson.

1. Milton's interest in the proportions of music and poetry is noted by Sigmund Spaeth, *Milton's Knowledge of Music: Its Sources and Its Significance in His Works* (1913; rpt. New York, 1973), pp. 58–59. Scholars cited are Marjorie Hope Nicolson, *John Milton: A Reader's Guide to His Poetry* (New York, 1963), p. 174; Isabel G. MacCaffrey, "*Lycidas:* The Poet in a Landscape," in *The Lyric and Dramatic Milton: Selected Papers from the English Institute,* ed. Joseph H. Summers (New York, 1965), p. 65; and C. A. Patrides, *Milton and the Christian Tradition* (Oxford, 1966), p. 156. Citations from Milton's verse come from their respective first editions unless otherwise noted, as reprinted in *John Milton's Complete Poetical Works, Reproduced in Photographic Facsimile,* 4 vols., comp. and ed. Harris Francis Fletcher (Urbana, Ill., 1943–48), hereafter cited as *CPW* in the text; citations from *Paradise Lost* come from V, 256, and VII, 225. Browne's statement comes from *Religio Medici* (1643), bk. I, sect. 16, in *The Prose of Sir Thomas Browne,* ed. Norman Endicott (Garden City, N.Y., 1967), p. 22.

2. Plato appears to be the first to have written of the mathematical ordering of Creation. See Ian Stewart and Martin Golubitsky, *Fearful Symmetry: Is God a Geometer?* (Oxford, 1992), p. 1; Plato, *Timaeus,* 31b–34b ("The body of the cosmos"), in *Dialogues of Plato,* 4th ed., trans. Benjamin Jowett (1891; rev., 1953), rpt. in *The Collected Dialogues of Plato, Including the Letters,* ed. Edith Hamilton and Hamilton Cairns (New York, 1961), pp. 1163–65, hereafter cited as *Collected Dialogues.* A passage in Plato's *Gorgias* also applies the laws of mathematical proportion to cosmic structure: see *Socratic Dialogues* (1953), ed. and trans. W. D. Woodhead,

rpt. in *Collected Dialogues*, 507e–508a, p. 290. Milton knew Plato's works well, even as a young man. See, for example, Milton's *Apology against a Pamphlet* (1642), in *Complete Prose Works of John Milton*, 8 vols., ed. Don M. Wolfe et al. (New Haven, 1953–82), vol. I, p. 891; hereafter cited as *YP*. See also Herbert Agar, *Milton and Plato* (1928; rpt. Gloucester, Mass., 1965); and Irene Samuel, *Plato and Milton* (1947; rpt. Ithaca, N.Y., 1965).

3. According to S. K. Heninger, Jr., *The Subtext of Form in the English Renaissance: Proportion Poetical* (University Park, Pa., 1994), p. 41, this passage is "repeated endlessly by the literati as well as theologians and natural scientists." Tayler suggests that the organizational principle delineated in the passage constitutes a key concept in Renaissance literary theory and practice, as evidenced, for example, by its appearance at the conclusion of Marvell's preface to the second edition of *Paradise Lost* ("Thy Verse created like thy Theme sublime, / In Number, Weight, and Measure, needs not Rhime," 53–54); see Edward W. Tayler, ed., *Literary Criticism of Seventeenth-Century England* (New York, 1967), p. 294n3. In an essay widely admired in the Renaissance, mathematician and astrologer John Dee, preface, *The Elements of Geometrie of the most auncient Philosopher Euclide of Megara*, trans. Henry Billingsley (London, 1570), sigs. *i^r, *i^v, writes that the "patterne of the minde of the Creator" is mathematical, that the "Creatyng of all thinges" was the numbering of the elements created.

4. Dante, *Divina commedia*, ed. Christoforo Landino (Florence, 1481), sig. [*]8^v, cited by S. K. Heninger, Jr., *Touches of Sweet Harmony: Pythagorean Cosmology and Renaissance Poetics* (San Marino, Calif., 1974), p. 395n27; George Puttenham, *The Arte of English Poesie*, in *Elizabethan Critical Essays*, 2 vols., ed. G. Gregory Smith (1914; rpt. London, 1964), vol. II, pp. 3, 67. Sidney's discussion of the poet as maker can be found in *Sir Philip Sidney's Defense of Poesy*, ed. Lewis Soens (Lincoln, Neb., 1970), p. 8; as he points out, the Greek etymology of *poesis* denotes "making" or "creating." That Sidney's *Defence* popularized the notion is the conclusion of Heninger, *Touches of Sweet Harmony*, pp. 289–90 (pp. 287–324 are devoted to the "Poet as Maker"). It is generally agreed that Dante's *Commedia* represents the supreme example of a poetical work deliberately fashioned "as an analogue of that great 'poem' which is the created universe"; see Charles S. Singleton, *Dante's Commedia: Elements of Structure* (1954; rpt. Baltimore, 1977), p. viii. Additional representative Renaissance works that discuss proportionality are noted by Heninger, *Subtext*, p. 73n12. Robert Lucas, "The Golden Section in the Structure of an Old French Poem," *Romance Notes* VIII (1967): 323, observes that the thirteenth-century French poet Guillermus de Oye imitated the Creation in his poetical work by filling it with all the mathematical elements and harmonies it could receive. "Temporal" numerology, that pertaining to vital statistics such as the age of a person, or birth and death dates, is a term first used by Christopher Butler and Alastair Fowler, "Time-Beguiling Sport: Number Symbolism in Shakespeare's *Venus and Adonis*," in *Shakespeare, 1564–1964: A Collection of Modern Essays by Various Hands*, ed. Edward A. Bloom (Providence, R.I., 1964), pp. 124–33, 217–18.

5. Plato's admonition, from *Epistle* VII (341e), is as follows: "I do not, however, think the attempt to tell mankind of these matters a good thing, except in the case of some few who are capable of discovering the truth for themselves with a little guidance. In the case of the rest, to do so would excite in some an unjustified contempt in a thoroughly offensive fashion, in others certain lofty and vain hopes, as if they had acquired some awesome lore." From *Thirteen Epistles of Plato*, trans. L. A. Post (1925), in *Collected Dialogues*, p. 1589. Sidney's statement comes from *Defence*, pp. 55–56. It seems apparent that the 'mysteries' of a successful poet's technique, if passed to apprentices, was done verbally with the understanding they would be divulged only to trusted and promising poets. The obvious fact that God himself did not reveal the principles and techniques of Creation is noted in *Paradise Lost*: "The great Architect / Did wisely to conceal, and not divulge / His secrets" (VII, 709–11; VIII, 72–74 in

subsequent editions). Edward E. Lowinsky, *Secret Chromatic Art in the Netherlands Motet*, trans. Carl Buchman (1946; rpt. New York, 1967), p. 164, observes that hidden meaning is often an essential element in Renaissance poetry. Alastair Fowler, *Spenser and the Numbers of Time* (London, 1964), p. 238, concurs: "Numerical composition was essentially an arcane practice in the Renaissance, so that the last thing we should expect to find is an unveiled authorial exposition. . . . Even in the Middle Ages it was usually the less serious poet who divulged the secrets of his creation." See also Maren-Sofie Röstvig, "*Elaborate Song:* Conceptual Structure in Milton's 'On the Morning of Christ's Nativity,' " in *Fair Forms: Essays in English Literature from Spenser to Jane Austen,* ed. Maren-Sofie Röstvig (Cambridge, 1975), p. 57; and Kevin Coates, *Geometry, Proportion and the Art of Lutherie* (1985; rpt. Oxford, 1986), pp. 168–70.

6. Manfred Hardt, "Dante and Arithmetic," in *The Divine Comedy and the Encyclopedia of Arts and Sciences,* ed. Giuseppe Di Scipio and Aldo Scaglione (Amsterdam, 1988), pp. 83, 89, 92–93; on the matter of audience, see also Charles S. Singleton's essay on Dante, "The Poet's Number at the Center," *MLN* LXXX (1965): 10. In his study of stringed instruments, Coates observes that in architecture the "geometrizing of the designer is usually apparent [because of] the usual retention of the rectilinear forms of the original geometry"; but this is much less so with painting and the construction of stringed instruments, for in viewing them we may be aware of beauty and harmony, but totally unaware of conscious proportional planning because the mathematical design is an invisible one (p. 166). This serves to remind us that being unaware of structures consciously incorporated into a work is no argument against their existence. See George E. Duckworth, *Structural Patterns and Porportions in Vergil's Aeneid: A Study in Mathematical Composition* (Ann Arbor, Mich., 1962), p. 37.

7. A useful survey of numerical studies of Milton is provided by Gerald H. Snare, "Numerology," *A Milton Encyclopedia,* 9 vols., ed. William B. Hunter et al. (Lewisburg, Pa., 1979), vol. V, pp. 201–03. Among the best studies of Milton in this field are the following: Arthur Barker, "The Pattern of Milton's 'Nativity Ode,' " *UTQ* X (1940–41): 167–81; Gunnar Qvarnström, *The Enchanted Palace: Some Structural Aspects of "Paradise Lost"* (Stockholm, 1967); Galbraith Miller Crump, *The Mystical Design of "Paradise Lost"* (Lewisburg, Pa., 1975); and Mary Wilson Carpenter, "Milton's Secret Garden: Structural Correspondences Between Michael's Prophecy and *Paradise Regained*," in *Milton Studies,* vol. XIV, ed. James D. Simmonds (Pittsburgh, 1980), pp. 153–82. Representative studies of literary numerology include Maren-Sofie Röstvig, "Renaissance Numerology: Acrostics or Criticism?" *Essays in Criticism* XVI (1966): 6–21; Christopher Butler, *Number Symbolism* (London, 1970); Alastair Fowler, *Triumphal Forms: Structural Patterns in Elizabethan Poetry* (Cambridge, 1970); Edmund Reiss, "Number Symbolism in Medieval Literature," *Medievalia et Humanistica,* n.s. I (1970): 161–74; and John MacQueen, *Numerology: Theory and Outline History of a Literary Mode* (Edinburgh, 1985). Still the best reference work on number symbolism is Vincent Foster Hopper, *Medieval Number Symbolism* (New York, 1938).

In *Defensio Secunda* (1645), Milton writes of having a keen interest in mathematical and musical discoveries during the Horton period (YP IV, 614); Lawrence Babb, *The Moral Cosmos of Paradise Lost* (East Lansing, Mich., 1970), pp. 22–23, believes Milton was well informed in the mathematics of his time, but not in other sciences. Mathematical textbooks he used in teaching his nephews are noted by Edward Phillips, "The Life of Milton," in *Complete Poems and Major Prose,* ed. Merritt Y. Hughes (Indianapolis, Ind., 1957), p. 1030. Although mathematics was studied seriously in Italy and Germany during this time, it was virtually ignored at Cambridge and Oxford. See William T. Costello, *The Scholastic Curriculum at Early Seventeenth-Century Cambridge* (Cambridge, Mass., 1958), pp. 102–03.

8. Neither treatise has been translated into English. Pacioli's work, illustrated by his friend Leonardo da Vinci, is available (in Italian and German) in *Quellenschriften für Kunstge-*

schichte und Kunsttechnik des Mittelalters und der Neuzeit, ed. and trans. Constantin Winterberg (1889; rpt. Hildesheim, W. Germ., 1974), pp. 17–163; Pacioli's earlier *Summa de arithmetica, geometria, proportioni et proportionalita* (Venice, 1494), rpt. in John B. Geijsbeek, *Ancient Double-Entry Bookkeeping* (1914; rpt. Houston, 1974), also gives prominent treatment to proportionality. A useful mathematical history of the proportion is provided by D. H. Fowler, "A Generalization of the Golden Section," *Fibonacci Quarterly* XX (1982): 146–58. The proportion is referred to as the "extreme and mean ratio" in Euclid's *Elements,* (300 B.C.), Book VI.30, in *The Thirteen Books of Euclid's Elements,* 3 vols., 2nd ed., trans. Sir Thomas Heath (1925; rpt. New York, 1956), vol. II, p. 267. The term "golden section" (that is, noteworthy section), which has come into general use, was coined by Martin Ohm in 1834 or 1835. See D. H. Fowler, *The Mathematics of Plato's Academy: A New Reconstruction* (Oxford, 1987), p. 105n3.5b.

9. Kepler is cited by P. H. Scholfield, *The Theory of Proportion in Architecture* (Cambridge, Eng., 1958), p. 54. Reference to the possible use of the section in Chaldea as far back as 3000 B.C. appears in Ernö Lendvai, *Béla Bartók: An Analysis of His Music,* trans. T. Ungar (London, 1971), pp. vii–viii; and in ancient Egypt, Samuel Colman, *Nature's Harmonic Unity: A Treatise on Its Relation to Proportional Form,* ed. C. Arthur Coan (1912; rpt. New York, 1971), pp. 43–48, and appendix E. Euclid's *Elements* contains the first written accounts of it (Heath trans., vol. I, p. 402 and vol. II, p. 267). Matila Ghyka, *The Geometry of Art and Life* (1946; rpt. New York, 1977), pp. xi, 102–09, asserts (as others do) that the golden section was first discovered in the human figure and became the primary proportion in Greek and Gothic architecture; the idea can be traced to Protagoras (ca. 485–451 B.C.), cited in Plato's *Theaetetus* (Coates, *Geometry, Proportion,* p. 164). The Roman architect Vitruvius (fl. first cent. B.C.) first gave popularity to the idea that proportions of the human form, including the golden section, should be the model for architecture; see his *Ten Books on Architecture,* trans. Morris Hicky Morgan (1914; rpt. New York, 1960), pp. 72–74. Various depictions of the "Vitruvius man" appeared in the Renaissance, most notably Leonardo's, a copy of which appears in György Doczi, *The Power of Limits: Proportional Harmonies in Nature, Art and Architecture* (Boulder, Colo., 1981), p. 93. On the anthropomorphism of stringed instrument design and terminology, which also involves the section, see Coates, *Geometry, Proportion,* p. 164. For a study of the golden section in Greek temple architecture, see Jay Hambidge, *The Parthenon and Other Greek Temples* (New Haven, 1924); and in the design of Greek vases, Lacey D. Caskey, *Geometry of Greek Vases* (Boston, 1922). See also Tons Brunés, *The Secrets of Ancient Geometry and Its Use,* 2 vols., trans. Charles M. Napier (Copenhagen, 1967), vol. II, p. 59; Dan Pedoe, *Geometry and the Liberal Arts* (New York, 1976), p. 107; and Heninger, *Subtext,* pp. 55, 98. Studies of the proportion in biological growth that might be cited include D'Arcy Wentworth Thompson, *On Growth and Form* (1917; abridged ed., Cambridge, Mass., 1977); Ghyka, *Geometry;* Peter S. Stevens, *Patterns in Nature* (Boston, 1974); and Doczi, *Power of Limits.* It has been discovered in such diverse elements as atomic and subatomic particles, and the distances of the moons of Jupiter, Saturn, and Uranus from their parent planets. See Jonathan Kramer, "The Fibonacci Series in Twentieth-Century Music," *Journal of Music Theory* XVII (1973): 112–13.

10. For an account of Pythagorean consternation over irrational numbers, see Michael Field and Martin Golubitsky, *Symmetry in Chaos: A Search for Pattern in Mathematics, Art and Nature* (Oxford, 1992), p. 125. Coates, *Geometry, Proportion,* p. 7, believes these numbers were thought to belong to "a primitive and incomprehensible chaos . . . involving, as they do, the terrifying concept of the infinite." Something of their mystique is conveyed by Doczi's description: "Irrational numbers are not unreasonable; they are only *beyond* reason, in the sense that they are beyond the grasp of whole numbers. They are infinite and intangible. In

patterns of organic growth the irrational φ ratio of the golden section reveals that there is indeed an infinite and intangible side to our world" (*Power of Limits*, p. 5). Galileo's break with mysticism is discussed by P. M. Rattanski, "The Scientific Background," in *The Age of Milton: Backgrounds to Seventeenth Century Literature*, ed. C. A. Patrides and Raymond B. Waddington (Manchester, Eng., 1980), p. 229. Galileo's statement comes from his *Assayer* (1623), in *Discoveries and Opinions of Galileo*, trans. Stillman Drake (New York, 1957), p. 238. Demystification of the section is discussed by Charles Bouleau, *The Painters' Secret Geometry: A Study of Composition in Art*, trans. Jonathan Griffin (1963; rpt. New York, 1980), p. 77.

11. For this passage I am indebted to Heninger, *Touches of Sweet Harmony*, p. 278n11; it is appended to a copy of Guillaume du Bartas, *His devine weekes and workes*, trans. Joshua Sylvester (London, 1605), p. 681.

12. Miloutine Borissavlièvitch, *The Golden Number and the Scientific Aesthetics of Architecture* (1952; rpt. New York, 1958), pp. 37–38. Adolf Zeising was the first to present a formal definition of the superiority of the section, in *Neue Lehre von den Proportionen des menschlichen Körpers* (Leipzig, 1854); in his opinion, paraphrased by Rudolf Wittkower, "The Changing Concept of Proportion," *Daedalus* LXXXIX (1960): 205, it is "the perfect mean between absolute unity and absolute variety, between mere repetition and disorder."

13. Architectural theorist Borissavlièvitch claims that the section pleases the eye more than any other ratio (*The Golden Number*, p. 3), but his assertion is based upon an inductive experiment now considered unreliable, that of Gustave T. Fechner, *Vorschule der Aesthetik* (Leipzig, 1854). On the inconclusive results of aesthetic studies of the proportion, see, for example, Scholfield, *Theory of Proportion*, pp. 100–01; Wittkower, "Changing Concept," pp. 206, 209–10; and Butler, *Number Symbolism*, pp. 173–75. Mathematician George D. Birkhoff, *Aesthetic Measure* (Cambridge, Mass., 1933), p. 72, believes the eye cannot discriminate between the section and similar proportions; compare Borissavlièvitch, *The Golden Number*, p. 9. According to Michael R. Rogers, "Rehearings: Chopin, Prelude in A Minor, Op. 28, No. 2," *Nineteenth Century Music* IV (1981): 246n7, in music if the difference between the section and another proportion is less than 10 percent, the listener cannot discriminate. Whether the calculus of variations, a field of mathematics dealing with optimal forms in geometry and nature, and with problems of maxima and minima, might be turned to account in the study of geometrical aesthetics remains unexplored. See Stefan Hildebrandt and Anthony Tromba, *Mathematics and Optimal Form* (New York, 1985), p. ix. On probability theory, see A. Kent Hieatt, "Numerical Structures in Verse: Second-Generation Studies Needed (Exemplified in *Sir Gawain* and the *Chanson de Roland*)," in *Essays in Numerical Criticism of Medieval Literature*, ed. Caroline D. Eckhardt (Lewisburg, Pa., 1980), p. 76.

14. Additional aesthetic considerations include the following: what appears spatially balanced to the eye may not seem so to the ear in a musical composition or poem because the proportions of a building or painting are experienced visually all at once, those of music and poetry aurally in a fixed order, and at a given rate. See Jonathan D. Kramer, *The Time of Music: New Meanings, New Temporalities, New Listening Strategies* (New York, 1988), p. 317. As pointed out by Jane Perry-Camp, "Time and Temporal Proportion: The Golden Section Metaphor in Mozart, Music, and History," *Journal of Musicological Research* III (1979): 152, "In music there is the practical question of how accurately the memory can proportion a temporal duration of any great length."

15. Wittkower, "Changing Concept," 200–02. The modern notion that beauty is entirely subjective and cannot be quantified hearkens back at least to Aristoxenus (fl. 380 B.C.), a disciple of Aristotle, who was derided in the Middle Ages as a man who trusted the senses more than reason because he maintained that notes of a scale should be determined by ear, not by mathematics. See Edward E. Lowinsky, "The Musical Avant-Garde of the Renaissance or: The

Peril and Profit of Foresight," in *Art, Science, and History in the Renaissance,* ed. Charles S. Singleton (Baltimore, 1968), pp. 120, 123.

16. Coates, *Geometry, Proportion,* p. 76; the Stradivari violin is described on pp. 73–76, a useful diagram of its golden section proportions appearing on p. 75. Coates examines thirty-three instruments from the sixteenth, seventeenth, and eighteenth centuries, among which 21 percent exhibit the section as a primary proportion (p. 158). He believes the study presently provides "irrefutable evidence and undeniable proof that geometry and numerical proportioning were constant, conscious considerations of the luthier" (p. 163). Although Coates suspects that acoustics depend more upon thickness, type, and quality of wood than upon predetermined proportions (p. 2), a practicing luthier informs me that one approach to acoustics involves the establishment of a 60 percent weight-ratio between front and back plates, thus approximating the golden section.

Paul Larson, "The Golden Section in the Earliest Notated Western Music," *The Fibonacci Quarterly* XVI (1976): 513–15, reveals the use of the section in 72 percent of 146 discrete portions of thirty Gregorian chants spanning more than six hundred years. M. Van Crevel, *Sub Tuum Presidium,* in *Opera Omnia,* 7 vols., ed. M. Van Crevel (Amsterdam, 1959), vol. VI, p. xxiv, finds the section used in a Mass by Jacobus Obrecht (1425–1505). Later composers who employ the proportion extensively include J. S. Bach, Haydn, Mozart, Beethoven, Chopin, Debussy, and Bartók. For allusions to harmonic proportion in Renaissance music, although not specifically to the golden section, see Thomas Morley, *A Plain and Easy Introduction to Practical Music* (1597), 2nd ed., ed. R. Alec Harman (1963; rpt. New York, 1973), pp. 41, 46–61, 127–31. For information on Elizabethan composers' predilection for strict mathematical rules, see Spaeth, *Milton's Knowledge of Music,* pp. 7, 11, 59.

The first movement of Mozart's *Piano Sonata in B♭* Major (K.333) presents an appealing and easily discerned example of golden section proportioning. The single internal repeat (another appears at the movement's end), which signals a distinct shift in mood and harmony, creates discrete portions of 63 and 102 measures, with ratios of .6176 and .6182. This approximates the proportion as closely as possible, or within .0004 and .0002, respectively. In Mozart's nineteen piano sonatas, 23 percent of the ratios tend toward the golden section (Perry-Camp, "Time and Temporal Proportion," 150–51).

17. Ida Langdon, *Milton's Theory of Poetry and Fine Art: An Essay* (New York, 1965), pp. 32, 37; see also Spaeth, *Milton's Knowledge of Music,* p. 79.

18. MacQueen, *Numerology,* p. 68. An acknowledged effect of the golden section in modern music, for instance, is the creation of irrational rhythms, that is, rhythms that suggest no regular beat: "From the outset, composers found that generating such rhythms from little numerical 'games' stimulated their imaginations, assured a measure of consistency, and taught them to free their minds from old and ingrained habits . . . , providing an alternative both to the old techniques and to randomness." See Edward L. Lowman, "An Example of Fibonacci Numbers Used to Generate Rhythmic Values in Modern Music," *The Fibonacci Quarterly* IX (1971): 423, 436.

19. Apparently the first to write about this proportion in Virgil is Guy Le Grelle, "Le Premier Livre des *Géorgiques,* Poème Pythagoricien," *Les Etudes Classiques* XVII (1949): 139–235. He was followed by Duckworth, *Structural Patterns,* who presents abundant evidence Virgil deliberately introduced the Golden Mean ratios into every part of his narrative (p. 47). Virgil's method was to compose "the smaller units of each book in the approximate Golden Mean ratio and then [combine] them into larger sections, also in proportion, until he created the main divisions of each book" (p. 45). Virgil also uses the proportion in his *Eclogues* and *Georgics.* So many Roman poets of the first century B.C. use it, including Catullus, Lucretius, and Horace, that its role in Roman poetic theory is of great importance (pp. 73, 76–77). It

may be worth noting that two sixteenth-century critics believed the *Aeneid* to be numerically structured: see R. M. Cummings, "Two Sixteenth-Century Notices of Numerical Composition in Virgil's 'Aeneid,'" *N&Q*, n.s. XVI (1969): 26. Spenser's use of the proportion is described by David Chinitz, "The Poem as Sacrament: Spenser's *Epithalamion* and the Golden Section," *Journal of Medieval and Renaissance Studies* XXI (1991): 251–68; see also J. M. Richardson, "More Symbolic Numbers in Spenser's 'Aprill,'" *N&Q*, n.s. XXIX (1982): 411–12. For a study of the section in Jonson's masques, see A. W. Johnson, *Ben Jonson: Poetry and Architecture* (Oxford, 1994), pp. 203–08, 213–17. Wordsworth's use of the proportion, in his day called "continuous division," is discussed by Lee M. Johnson, *Wordsworth's Metaphysical Verse: Geometry, Nature, and Form* (Toronto, 1982), p. 11 and *passim*.

20. These terms describing Virgil's structures come from Duckworth, *Structural Patterns*, pp. 121, 46–47. Sections within sections are noted on p. 75; musical terms describing such a pattern come, respectively, from Kramer, *Time*, p. 11, and Rogers, "Rehearings," 248.

21. John T. Shawcross, *With Mortal Voice: The Creation of Paradise Lost* (Lexington, Ky., 1982), pp. 62–63 (as the author has pointed out to me, his reference to VIII, 477, should read VIII, 457). I am indebted to Professor Shawcross for delineating the printer's errors in the marginal numbering of the 1667 edition of *Paradise Lost*, noted as well in *CPW*, which must be considered in locating the major mean of the epic (letter, 21 Sept. 1994).

22. The category of parenthetical expressions is represented solely by Psalm ii (*CPW* I, p. 80), wherein the only such expression in the work ("though ye rebell") falls at the minor mean, line 12 of twenty-eight lines. The category of longest lines (based upon the number of alphabet characters) is represented by the unfinished "Passion" (I, pp. 164–66), in which the longest line among its fifty-six lines, line 35, falls at the major mean; by "Lycidas" (I, pp. 185–89), in which the longest line among its 193 lines, line 119 ("Blind mouthes!"), falls at the major mean (1645 ed.; the 1638 ed. has 192 lines, line 177 ["In the blest Kingdoms"] having been dropped by the printer); and by *Sonnet X* ("Daughter of that good Earl," I, p. 182), wherein the longest line among fourteen lines, line 9, falls at the major mean. Finally, the category of shortest lines (again based upon the number of alphabet characters) is represented by the following: *"In eandem"* (*"Purgatorem animæ derisit"* I, p. 236), line 6 of 14 (minor mean); *"Song: On May Morning"* (I, pp. 169–70), line 6 of 10 (major mean); *"Canzone"* (*"Ridonsi donne e giovani amorosi,"* I, pp. 179–80), line 9 of 15 (major mean); Psalm cxiv (Greek version, I, p. 250), line 14 of 22 (major mean); *Sonnet XII* ("I did but prompt the age," I, pp. 42–43), line 6 of 14 (major mean, which is also emphasized by the appearance in the line of the only word in italic type, *Latona's*); *Sonnet* (*"Fairfax*, whose name in armes," I, p. 372), line 9 of 14 (major mean); and *Sonnet* (*"Vane*, young in yeares," I, p. 373), line 9 of 14 (major mean).

23. In evaluating Milton's use of this proportion, I attempt to follow a strict procedural method, as suggested in guidelines for numerical studies of literature: I confine my attention to internal passages clearly defined by discontinuities such as the termination of sentences, lines, or speeches, taking no license in setting the termination of the count; I maintain a consistency of method, even though the poet himself may not have been consistent (for example, if in one tabulation I omit titles, subtitles, and headnotes, I omit them in subsequent tabulations); finally, I propose no theories nor structures based upon data about which I am doubtful. For guidelines on numerical studies in literature, see Fowler, *Spenser*, pp. 251–52; William Nelson, review of Fowler, *Spenser*, in *Renaissance News* XVIII (1965): 52–57; Butler, *Number Symbolism*, p. 176; A. Kent Hieatt, review of Fowler, *Triumphal Forms*, in *Renaissance Quarterly* XXIV (1971): 557–60; and Hieatt, "Numerical Structures," pp. 70–76.

24. The translation of Milton cited here is by John T. Shawcross, *The Complete Poetry of John Milton*, rev. ed. (Garden City, N.Y., 1971), pp. 22–23. Throughout the study I follow a consistent format in presenting calculations, giving first the minor golden mean (the "extreme"

ratio), or the small portion divided by the large portion, then the major golden mean (the "mean" ratio), or the large portion divided by the whole. I then provide deviations from the respective golden section ratios, .3820 . . . and .6180 . . . , to four decimal places.

Because of the precise metrical regularity of "*Eliensis*," calculating the juncture by syllables (after 260 of 680) or feet (after 104 of 272) obviously produces the same ratios as those calculated by lines. In this poem, but not in the subsequent examples I cite, calculations based upon the number of words are even closer to the golden section: the juncture occurs after 115 of 301 words, producing ratios of .6183 and .6179, and deviations of a miniscule .0003 and .0001. Calculations based upon the number of alphabet letters, however, are not close to section ratios, indicating that Milton did not locate the juncture by letter count—but why should he when there are less tedious ways? The structural and thematic break following line 26 occurs after 663 of 1705 letters (æ = two, œ = two, & = three), producing ratios of .6363 and .6111, with significant deviations of .0183 and .0069 (if æ, œ, and & are counted as single characters, not the common Renaissance practice, the juncture occurs after 655 of 1678 letters, producing ratios of .6403 and .6097, with the deviations of .0223 and .0083, the former a significant one). The juncture clearly is not defined by the number of alphabet letters, falling as it does after 1054 of 1706 letters, since this location, twelve letters before the structural and thematic break at the end of line 26, is of no significance.

25. Hugo Norden, "Proportions in Music," *The Fibonacci Quarterly* II (1964): 219. Using .62 and .38 would locate the section after 258 syllables (of 680), or two syllables *before* the juncture at the end of line 26; after 114 words (of 301), one word before the juncture; and after 25.84 lines (of 68), .16 of a line before the juncture.

26. Early luthiers also used the section, as well as other proportions, with great accuracy (Coates, *Geometry, Proportion*). It should be kept in mind that because the section is an irrational number, it can never be expressed exactly, and that whoever utilizes it must settle for an approximation. Proportions that are only generally approximate are "less than elegant" and not apt to impress (Kramer, "Fibonacci Series," p. 120). As a consequence, many composers wishing to avoid inexactitude with the proportion have resorted to the Fibonacci sequence of numbers whose relationships closely approximate the section, thus providing the precision, as well as convenience, of working with whole numbers (Lendvai, *Béla Bartók*, p. viii; Lowman, "An Example," p. 424). The Fibonnaci sequence (sometimes called the "golden mean series") is an additive or summation sequence in which each term (except 1) is the sum of the previous two terms: 1, 1, 2, 3, 5, 8, 13, 21, 34, 55. . . . Division of any term by the next highest term produces a quotient approximating the section; the larger the numbers, the closer the approximation. It might be noted that Bartók, for one, sought to follow nature in musical composition (Lendvai, *Béla Bartók*, p. 29), and that the Fibonacci series reflects the law of growth called phyllotaxis.

27. Perry-Camp, "Time and Temporal Proportion," notes the arbitrary nature of these figures (152). Her study of the golden section in Mozart stipulates that "a very rigid research attitude must be held" regarding accuracy, and she accepts a deviation of only ±.01 (that is, .01 either way), much more restrictive than most other researchers (p. 151). Johnson, *Wordsworth's Metaphysical Verse*, p. 60, accepts a deviation of ±.015; Rogers, "Rehearings," 246, a deviation of ±.02; Larson, "The Golden Section," 515, the same deviation; Fowler, *Spenser*, p. 253 (not pertaining specifically to the golden section), ±.025; and J. H. Douglas Webster, "Golden-Mean Form in Music," *Music and Letters* XXXI (1950): 248, a lenient ±.05.

28. While Renaissance authors almost never comment on their methods, a few hint at numerological structures in their work, such as Shakespeare and Chapman (Fowler, *Spenser*, pp. 250, 252). There might be such a hint in the full title of "*Eliensis*," which appears in both editions published in Milton's lifetime (1645, 1673): "*Anno ætatis 17. In obitum / Præsulis Eliensis.*" Its thirty-eight characters (alphabetical and numerical; æ = two) might be intended

to signify the use of this proportion within the poem; indeed, thirty-eight is a most appropriate number for the poem, since the poet locates the structural juncture at the minor mean, after 38 percent (.3824) of the work has transpired. Nevertheless, he does not appear to provide such hints in other works using the golden section.

29. Information about the life and death of Lady Jane Paulet may be found in William Riley Parker, "Milton and the Marchioness of Winchester," *MLR* XLIV (1949): 547–50.

30. The existence of an early manuscript version of this poem, not in Milton's hand, has long been noted. It is four lines shorter, and the structural reference point (that is, the initiation of the apostrophe, "Gentle Lady") begins at line 42, clearly not the mean of the poem (creating ratios of .6667 and .6000, with significant deviations of .0486 and .0180). This suggests the version is not in final form. For discussions of the version, see Parker, "Milton and the Marchioness"; and A.S.P. Woodhouse and Douglas Bush, *A Variorum Commentary on the Poems of John Milton*, 4 vols., gen. ed. Merritt Y. Hughes (New York, 1972), vol. II, pp. 193–97.

31. Lendvai, *Béla Bartók*, p. 22; Larson, "The Golden Section," 514–15. Lendvai calls the major-minor structure "positive," the minor-major "negative" (p. 21). The major-minor pattern corresponds with the standard structure of rising action in Shakespearean drama, the turning point or climax occurring most frequently in the third of five acts, followed by a dénouement. The minor-major pattern corresponds, in turn, with Greek drama, wherein the climax occurs before midpoint.

32. Nardo, *Milton's Sonnets and the Ideal Community* (Lincoln, Neb., 1979), pp. 147, 150.

33. An indication Milton did not employ other poetical units when calculating the location of this intersection may be noted by considering the following. The juncture falls after 68 of 114 words, creating ratios of .6765 and .5965, with significant deviations of .0585 and .0215 (it falls two words before the mean if computed in this manner); after 86 of 140 syllables, creating ratios of .6279 and .6143, with deviations of .0099 and .0037 (identical to the ratios and deviations derived when counting lines or metrical feet; but the juncture falls one syllable before the mean); and after 285 of 474 alphabet letters, creating ratios of .6632 and .6013, with deviations of .0452 and .0167 (the juncture falling eight letters before the mean).

"SUCH HEAV'N—TAUGHT NUMBERS SHOULD BE MORE THAN READ": *COMUS* AND MILTON'S REPUTATION IN MID–EIGHTEENTH-CENTURY ENGLAND

Don-John Dugas

FROM WHAT SOURCES did eighteenth-century Londoners derive their sense of "Milton?" Scholars investigating his reception during this period have identified the key sources as his major poems, criticism of those texts, biographies, illustrations, imitations, and—to a lesser extent—newspaper commentary.[1] In so doing, modern critics have privileged one group of historical records in an attempt to define how the eighteenth-century audience knew and understood Milton. However, another set of historical records—those of the London stage from 1738 to 1772—yield a very different interpretation of how Milton was seen in this time.

While much valuable work has been done to situate the reception of his individual works within the more general context of our ideas about Milton, the tremendous popularity of *Comus* on the eighteenth-century stage has received little attention since the work of John W. Good, David H. Stevens, and Alwin Thaler. In 1738 a young tutor named John Dalton adapted Milton's *A Mask Presented at Ludlow Castle, 1634* into a three-act mainpiece staged at the Drury Lane Theatre. But while Dalton's adaptation, called *Comus*, helped to change the title of Milton's work forever, it has gone largely unstudied. Exactly how successful was *Comus*? How did the eighteenth-century audience react to Milton on the stage? And, finally, how did *Comus* alter Milton's reputation in the eighteenth century?[2]

Comus was, in fact, a lasting success on the London stage, and its conspicuous place in the theater repertory meant that it almost assuredly contributed to any contemporary London theater-goer's or play-reader's conception of Milton. By examining the reasons behind Dalton's selection of *Comus* and how his version of it was regarded in 1738 and thereafter, we can establish the reception and popularity of the masque over time. Acknowledging the accessibility of *Comus* to Milton's eighteenth-century audience allows us to appreciate the long-neglected story of what is perhaps Milton's greatest popular success. It also changes our understanding of the poet's reputation during this time by identifying another means by which he was known to the general public.

I. MILTON IN THE 1730S

While not consciously or explicitly reiterating the value judgments of eighteenth-century commentators, most modern critics have made many of the same choices as their forebears in their selection of texts. This choice—privileging Milton's "major" works, particularly *Paradise Lost,* over the rest of his oeuvre—is by no means incorrect, considering that *Paradise Lost* was and is published more often than any of Milton's other works. However, such a filter makes complete representation of the sources of Milton's reputation in the eighteenth century impossible.

How was Milton regarded critically in eighteenth-century England? According to the standard critical interpretation, Milton was considered *the* English epic poet. After the poet's neglect during the Restoration—a result of the "degenerate" taste of that age—the English reading public of the first half of the eighteenth century was reintroduced to Milton through the writings of biographers and critics such as Joseph Addison, Sir Richard Blackmore, John Dennis, and Aaron Hill. According to Richard Blackmore,

It must be acknowledged that till about forty years ago Great Britain was barren of critical learning, though fertile in excellent writers; and in particular had so little taste for epic poetry and was so unacquainted with the essential properties and peculiar beauties of it, that 'Paradise Lost', an admirable work of that kind, published by Mr. Milton, the great ornament of his age and country, lay many years unspoken of and entirely disregarded.

As Blackmore indicates, *Paradise Lost* was revered above all of Milton's "major" works. Daniel Defoe considered it "the greatest, best, and most sublime Work now in the *English* Tongue," while Elijah Fenton called it "the noblest Poem, next to those of *Homer* and *Virgil,* that ever the wit of man produc'd in any age or nation." Good simply concludes that "With complete unanimity Milton's biographers exalt *Paradise Lost* as the greatest achievement of his life."[3]

But what of the "minor" works? Late seventeenth- and early eighteenth-century commentators devoted considerable attention to these texts. The early poems were basically regarded as means by which to trace the steps of Milton's greatness, a trail that leads us to the ultimate expression of the poet's genius, *Paradise Lost. Lycidas* and *A Mask* always received favorable comments from Milton's early biographers. In 1699, John Toland wrote that *Lycidas* was "one of the finest [poems] Milton ever wrote." As for *A Mask,* Toland believed that Milton made good his early ambition "in his inimitable poem *Paradise Lost*, and before this time in his *Comus*, like which piece in the peculiar disposition of his story, the sweetness of the numbers, the justness of the expression, and the moral it teaches, there is nothing extant in any language."[4]

However, in 1779—more than forty years after Dalton's *Comus* began its long run on the London stage—Samuel Johnson published his "Life of Milton," in which he became the first biographer-critic to object to *Lycidas* and *A Mask*. While Johnson attacked both of these, he did have a few good words for the latter, the "greatest of [Milton's] juvenile performances. . . . The dawn . . . of *Paradise Lost*," wherein Milton exhibited

his power of description and his vigour of sentiment, employed in the praise and defense of virtue. A work more truly poetical is rarely found; allusions, images, and descriptive epithets embellish almost every period with lavish decoration. As a series of lines, therefore, it may be considered as worthy of all the admiration with which the votaries have received it. As a drama it is deficient. The action is not probable.

Johnson almost certainly saw Dalton's *Comus* in performance, for he wrote a new prologue to the masque when it was performed at Drury Lane in 1750 for the benefit of Elizabeth Foster, Milton's only surviving descendant. However, Johnson must have been in the minority regarding the piece's dramatic virtues, for by the time he wrote the "Life of Milton," *Comus* had already been performed more than 150 times in London.[5]

At the time Dalton sat down to adapt *A Mask* for the eighteenth-century stage, Milton's masque was still held in high regard. Milton was being seriously compared with the greatest poets of all time. His "Whig" politics, so distasteful to the audience of the Restoration (and to Samuel Johnson), were so much in ascendancy that a monument was erected in Milton's memory in Westminster in 1737. Ironically, twenty-seven years earlier, the dean had refused to allow even Milton's name to be inscribed in the Abbey.[6] *Comus*'s time had come.

II. THE NATURE OF DALTON'S VERSION

Born in 1709, John Dalton was educated at Queen's College, Oxford. After having taken his bachelor of arts degree in 1730, he entered the service of the Duke of Somerset as tutor to the duke's only son, Lord Beauchamp, a position which he held full-time until 1735. According to the *Dictionary of National Biography*, "during the leisure which this employment afforded he amused himself with adapting Milton's masque of 'Comus' for the stage."[7] While we cannot know what professional aspirations Dalton held at this time, the fact that he did not take his master's degree from Oxford as soon as possible casts some doubt upon his dedication to entering the ministry.

Dalton may have toyed with the idea of becoming a professional play-wright—a fancy not unknown to students at Oxford and Cambridge since the 1580s. He certainly hoped to make a reputation for himself (and possibly some money) for his adaptation of *A Mask*, because he offered it for production at Drury Lane. But by the time he did, he was peddling his wares in a buyer's market—a situation produced by the radical changes that the passing of the Licensing Act effected on the London stage.

The Licensing Act of 1737 effectively limited production of legitimate drama in London to two patent theaters. After nearly a decade of theatrical experimentation initiated by the unprecedented successes of *The Beggar's Opera* and *The Provok'd Husband* during the season of 1727–28, the act returned the London stage to the conservatism that characterized the pre-1728 era. The act reestablished the monopoly created in 1660 for two patent theaters. This monopoly allowed these two theaters—Drury Lane and Covent Garden—to end the aggressive (and costly) competition that had marked the London stage in the early 1730s, the very factor that had fostered so many new and innovative plays. Without competition, the theaters could cut costs by reviving more stock pieces from the repertory. By producing old plays, Drury Lane and Covent Garden eliminated the expense (and rehearsal time) of working up new productions and paying authors for new plays.[8]

Arthur H. Scouten notes the impact of the Licensing Act on the repertory at Drury Lane for the season that immediately followed the passing of the act, where

an excellent company put on 58 different plays on 159 nights. They offered 3 new plays on 21 nights, one of which was *Comus*. Ten plays of Shakespeare were played on 26 nights, and 4 other Elizabethan plays on nine nights. A total of 22 Restoration plays were offered on 51 nights, with the remaining 52 nights devoted to 19 eighteenth-century plays.

Thus at Drury Lane during the season of 1737–38, 86 of the 159 acting nights were devoted to plays written before 1700. For an aspiring young writer, such a repertory presented a nearly insurmountable obstacle. In other words, after the Licensing Act was passed Dalton had exactly two potential venues for his work—neither of which was likely to take a chance on an unknown playwright or try a new play of any kind. Unless a playwright had a script with appeal instantly identifiable by one of the managers, he had no chance whatsoever. But Dalton did have four things that would have been of particular interest to one of the two patent houses: a play written before 1700, Milton's name, an exciting script that catered to the strengths of the company at Drury Lane, and the very latest continuation to what James Ogden has dubbed "the operatic wars of the 1730s."[9]

Dalton could have approached either Charles Fleetwood, the patentee of the Drury Lane Theatre, or Charles Macklin, the artistic manager. Alternatively, he may have shown the script to Thomas Augustine Arne, the most gifted and prolific English composer of the age, who was the composer-in-residence at Drury Lane in 1737. Dalton probably presented the manuscript in the summer of 1737 immediately after the passage of the Licensing Act and hence the worst possible time for a new play to be accepted in the whole eighteenth century. However, his libretto had a special advantage, for earlier that year a work similar to *Comus*—Paolo Rolli's Italian opera *Sabrina* (with a score by Porpora)—had been performed with success by the Opera of the Nobility at the King's Theatre, Haymarket, and published in Italian and English. For *Sabrina,* Rolli had taken the plot of Milton's *A Mask* and magnified it: en route to their double wedding, two brother-sister pairs (each brother affianced to the other's sister) are tempted by Comus. *Sabrina* premiered late in the 1736–37 season, but enjoyed a solid run until the theaters closed for the summer.[10]

Given the recent success of Rolli's version, whoever first read Dalton's manuscript at Drury Lane probably realized its potential. What Dalton had concocted was a longer version of Milton's text that relied heavily upon other early works of the poet. He had added two dances and nearly a score of songs (many adapted from *L'Allegro* and *Il Penseroso*), created or inserted new characters (most notably two more Attendant Spirits and Euphrosyne from *L'Allegro*), distributed the dialogue among more speakers, added a scene parallel to Comus's temptation of the Lady in which her brothers are similarly tantalized by a woman in Comus's crew, and omitted Milton's finale scene *"presenting* Ludlow Town *and the President's Castle."* By so doing, Dalton expanded Milton's original text into a three-act mainpiece that could be staged as an "English opera" (see table 1).[11]

At some point, Arne read the manuscript. The son of the upholsterer and box numberer at Drury Lane, Thomas Augustine Arne was born in 1710 and educated (he claimed) at Eton. After having left school, Arne was articled to an attorney, but continued to develop the extraordinary musical talent that he had first exhibited in his adolescence. In 1733 Arne composed his own setting for Addison's opera, *Rosamund,* a production that enjoyed moderate success, playing for seven nights at Lincoln's-Inn-Fields. Later that year, Arne adapted Fielding's *The Tragedy of Tragedies* into a musical burlesque. *The Opera of Operas* fared better than *Rosamund,* with eleven performances at the end of the 1732–33 season that attracted three royal visits. These works established Arne as a theatrical composer at the age of

TABLE 1.   COMPARISON BETWEEN DALTON'S *COMUS* AND MILTON'S *A MASK*

Action in Comus	Corresponding Lines in A Mask
Prologue	
Act 1 ("SCENE a wood near *Ludlow-Castle*")	
Dialogue between First and Second Attendant Spirits	1–92
Second Spirit leaves to guard over the Lady	—
Comus enters and speaks	93–127
Song ("Now Phoebus sinketh in the West")	—
Song ("By dimpled Brook, and Fountain Brim")	—
Comus's invocation of Night	128–42
Song ("From Tyrant Laws and Customs free")	—
Song ("By the gayly circling Glass")	—
Comus calls his crew to dance. Dismisses them at the Lady's approach	143–69
First conversation between the Lady and Comus	170–330
Song ("Sweet Echo, sweetest Nymph, that liv'st unseen")	230–43
Song ("Fly swiftly, ye Minutes, till Comus receive")	—
Act 2 ("Enter the two Brothers")	
The Brothers discuss darkness and loss of the Lady	331–489
First Spirit appears as shepherd and tells Brothers of Comus's palace	490–579
Enter Comus's crew, "revelling and by turns caressing each other"	—
The Brothers meet the crew	—
Brothers are tempted by a beautiful woman holding Comus's cup	—
Song ("Fame's an Echo, prattling double")	—
Song ("Would you taste the noontide Air?")	—
Song ("Live, and love, enjoy the Fair")	—
The Brothers resist temptation	—
Comus's crew departs	—
First Spirit agrees to guide Brothers to Comus's palace	580–658
Act 3 ("SCENE opens and discovers a magnificent Hall in Comus's palace . . . the Lady . . . seated in an enchanted Chair")	
Comus summons Euphrosyne to banish melancholy	—
Song ("Come, come, bid Adieu to Fear")	—
Comus orders Naiades to dance	—
Naiades dance	—

Action in Comus	Corresponding Lines in A Mask
Recicativo ("How gentle was my Damon's Air!")	—
Song ("On every Hill, in every Grove")	—
Recicativo ("Love, the greatest Bliss below")	—
Ballad ("The wanton God, that pierces Hearts")	—
Comus and crew prepare for a feast	—
Second Spirit descends, "invisible to Comus and his Crew"	—
Second Spirit comforts the Lady	—
Song ("Nor on Beds of fading Flowers")	—
Second Spirit "reascends"	—
Comus offers the Lady his cup	—
Second conversation between the Lady and Comus	663–813
Song ("Preach not me your musty Rules")	—
Song ("Ye Fauns, and ye Dryads, from Hill, Dale, and Grove")	—
Fauns and Dryads enter and dance	—
The Brothers rush in and drive Comus and his crew away	—
Second and Third Spirits arrive	—
Third Spirit invokes Sabrina to release Lady from the chair	814–59
Song ("Sabrina fair")	860–89
"Sabrina rises, attended by water-Nymphs"	—
Song ("By the rushy-fringed bank")	890–901
Recicativo ("Goddess dear")	902–21
Recicativo ("Shepherd, 'tis my Office best")	922–75
"Sabrina descends, and the Lady rises out of her seat"	—
The Brothers delight	—
First and Second Spirits "Epiloguize"	976–1023
Epilogue	—

Note: Corresponding lines in *A Mask* are approximate.

twenty-three. By 1738 he was "Composer to the Theatre Royal in Drury Lane." There he numbered among his colleagues two of his relatives: his sister, Susanna Maria Cibber, who was quickly becoming one of the leading actors of the company; and the noted singer Cecilia Young Arne, whom the composer had married the previous year.[12]

Arne would have recognized Dalton's script as an opportunity to pursue his cherished aim of creating a distinctively "English opera," a project to which several composers had applied themselves since the early 1730s. In his famous letter to Handel of 5 December 1732, the playwright and manager Aaron Hill suggested that the great composer should "deliver us from our *Italian bondage;* and demonstrate, that *English* is soft enough for Opera, when compos'd by poets, who know how to distinguish the *sweetness* of our tongue, from the *strength* of it, where the last is less necessary." Handel continued with Italian opera, but in 1732–33 Arne and two German-born composers—John Lampe and John Christopher Smith—attempted what Hill had in mind. They hoped to create full-length, all-sung English opera (as opposed to the ballad opera Gay had pioneered) capable of competing with the Italian opera that had dominated the London musical world since the early eighteenth century. Roger Fiske observes that "In less than fifteen months London was given no less than seven new full-length fully composed English operas—almost as many as were staged there in all of the remaining years of the century put together." Although the experiment was a financial failure, Arne was not to be deterred. With an English genre (the masque), a libretto and score by an English author-composer team, and a story by one of England's greatest poets, Arne almost certainly saw *Comus* as another way to compete against the Italians.[13]

Starting with *Comus* in 1738 Arne again devoted himself to English opera, developing three masques with varying degrees of success. As we shall see, *Comus* was a hit. The second production, an abbreviated version of *Rosamund* revived on 8 March 1740 at Drury Lane, was a modest success. The third production, *Alfred,* fared better than *Rosamund* though not as well as *Comus,* but introduced the song for which Arne is still known today, "Rule Britannia."

Comus was also a means to compete directly in the ongoing battle between the opera companies. Between 1732 and 1738, three theatrical groups—the Royal Academy of Music, the Opera of the Nobility, and ultimately Drury Lane—produced rival versions of the same story (see table 2). When Arne wrote the music for *Comus* we cannot be certain, but Fleetwood's letter to the censor requesting permission to perform *Comus,* dated 9 February 1737[/8], proves that the masque was complete at that time. As

TABLE 2. The "Operatic Wars" of the 1730s

Location	Production	Author	Year
Little Haymarket	*Acis and Galatea*	(pirated from) Gay/Handel	1732
King's Theatre, Haymarket	*Acis and Galatea*	Gay/Handel (completely revised)	1732
King's Theatre, Haymarket	*Polifemo*	Rolli/Porpora	1735
Covent Garden	*Alcina*	Handel	1735
King's Theatre, Haymarket	*Sabrina*	Rolli/Porpora	1737
Drury Lane	*Comus*	Dalton/Arne	1738

we can infer from the specific naming of songs and pieces in advertisements one month later, audiences were attracted by music. One of the songs from *Comus*, "The Noon-Tide Air," became a special favorite and was often performed on its own as an entr'acte piece into the 1740s.[14]

The Dalton-Arne *Comus* was quite different from Milton's original *A Mask* by the time of the first performance because the definition of masque had been completely altered since the 1630s. Strict definitions of theatrical categories were not a feature of the mid–eighteenth-century London stage, especially regarding productions that incorporated music. In 1755 Samuel Johnson defined a masque as "a dramatick performance, written in a tragick stile without attention to the rules of probability"—a definition that seems as useful as any other offered during this period.[15] The features that define the eighteenth-century masque—supernatural elements, pastoral settings, dialogue, dance, and song—were also characteristic of many operas of this period. Since definitions were by no means firm, and as the proportion of spoken dialogue to song varied tremendously between productions, a production in a "larger" genre might actually be less grand than another production in a "smaller" genre. Such was the case with Theobald's *Orestes* (1731)—advertised as an "Opera"—which had less music than *Comus*.

Fiske defines a masque in the 1730s as a musical production in which "classical deities played a major part and elaborate scenic effects were expected, usually with machines descending from the sky or ascending through traps." Because vocal and instrumental music, machines, and elaborate scenic effects were characteristic elements of non-Italian opera at this time, and because non-Italian opera assumed spoken dialogue between the songs, we should regard Dalton's *Comus* as a full-length English opera rather than as a "masque" in the pre-1642 sense.[16]

III. THE FIRST PRODUCTION OF *COMUS*

On Thursday, 2 March 1737/8, the *London Daily Post, and General Advertiser* ran an advertisement for the command performance of Sir John Vanbrugh's *The Relapse* at Drury Lane. At the bottom of the announcement was written: "On Saturday next will be performed a Masque (never acted before) call'd COMUS." Two days later, the same newspaper carried a full-sized advertisement for the eighteenth-century premiere of *Comus* (see fig. 1). The use of Milton's name from the first day of the production is striking here because a playwright's name hardly ever appeared in advertisements for his or her own play. Dalton's was not used, and Arne's was not added until the second performance two days later. Only well-known authors might hope to be named with some regularity in the notices for performances of their plays, and generally not for new ones. This practice can be

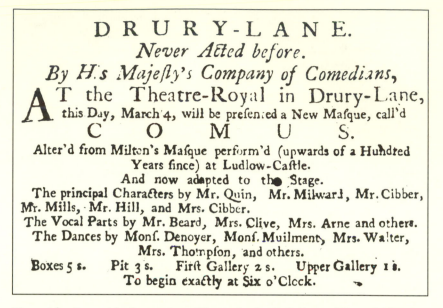

Fig. 1. Advertisement for the premiere of *Comus, London Daily Post, and General Advertiser,* 4 March 1737/8. Courtesy of The Pennsylvania State University Libraries.

seen in the advertisements for the offerings at Covent Garden and the Haymarket the night *Comus* premiered. At the former, Sir John Vanbrugh's *The Mistake* was performed, but the advertisements make no mention of the playwright's name. The production at the latter is simply listed as "ALESSANDRO SEVERO," again with no mention of either the librettist (probably Apostolo Zeno) or the composer (George Frideric Handel) of that opera. Two days later, the Haymarket was still performing *Alessandro Severo,* while Covent Garden performed "The Life of King HENRY the Fifth. *With the Memorable Battle of* Agincourt . . . Written by Shakespear."

　　Dalton's prologue, which relies exclusively upon Milton's fame as a poet of the first rank, is a distillation of the admiration that Milton enjoyed in 1738:

> *Our Stedfast Bard, to his own Genius true,*
> *Still bade his Muse fit Audience find, tho' few.*
> *Scorning the Judgement of a trifling Age,*
> *To choicer Spirits he bequeath'd his Page.*
> *He too was scorn'd, and to* Brittania's *Shame*
> *She scarce for half an Age knew* Milton's *Name.*
> *But now, his Fame by every Trumpet blown,*

We on his deathless Trophies raise our own.
Nor Art nor Nature did his Genius Bound,
Heav'n, Hell, Earth, Chaos, he survey'd around.
All Things his Eye, thro' Wit's bright Empire thrown,
Beheld, and made what it Beheld his own.
      Such Milton *was: 'Tis Ours to bring him forth,*
And Yours to vindicate neglected Worth.
Such Heav'n—taught Numbers should be more than read,
More wide the Manna thro' the Nation spread.
Like some bles'd Spirit he to Night descends,
Mankind he visits, and their Steps befriends,
Thro' mazy Error's dark perplexing Wood
Points out the Path of Truth and real Good,
Warns erring youth, and Guards the spotless Maid
From Spell of magick Vice, by Reason's Aid.
      Attend the Strains; and should some meaner Phrase
Hang on the Stile, and clog the nobler Lays,
Excuse what we with trembling Hand supply,
To give his Beauties to the publick Eye;
His the pure Essence, Ours the grosser Mean,
Thro' which his Spirit is in Action seen.
Observe the Force, observe the Flame Divine,
That glows, breathes, acts, in each harmonious Line.
Great Objects only strike the gen'rous Heart;
Praise the Sublime, o'erlook the mortal Part.
Be There your Judgement, Here your Candour shown;
Small is our Portion—and we wish 'twere none.

As the prologue indicates, Milton's "nobler Lays" were not seen by Dalton as a deterrent to an enjoyable night at the theater. Indeed, special care was taken to assure "the Publick Eye" that, owing to its pastoral setting, the masque offered something for everyone. *The Gentlemen's Magazine* commented that

The Masque of Comus, exhibited at *Drury-Lane*, was wrote by *Milton:* It is a *Pastoral* kind of poem, and some of as [sic] beautiful Descriptions and Images run thro' it, as are to be found in any of his other Writings. The Stile, as it is *rural*, is more *simple* and *plain* than that of his *Paradise Lost*, and tho' there is nothing but must give infinite Pleasure to the most exalted Genius, there is nothing beyond the Comprehension of a common Capacity.[17]

As the theater-going audience in London was more than large enough to support the two licensed theaters comfortably, Drury Lane and Covent Garden worked more in cooperation than in competition after 1737 by rarely accepting new plays. At these theaters, one factor seems pretty well to have governed repertory decisions at this time: commercial viability. Fleetwood, an inveterate gambler and spendthrift, was interested in the theater solely as a means of personal profit. *Comus* would have to be profitable or it would be no more.

Because there were only two potential outlets for his work and so few new plays were being produced in 1738, Dalton would probably have been extremely conscious of who might act in his masque. To write or adapt a play without parts for a company's best actors would make no sense at all for an aspiring professional writer, especially if he wanted his play to last. Looking at the cast will show us how Dalton used the star system to his advantage.

The cast for the first production of *Comus* was glamorous and talented. The principal roles, the Lady and Comus, were played by Mrs. Cibber and James Quin. Susanna Maria Cibber was the wife of Drury Lane's second leading man, Theophilis Cibber, and one of the greatest tragic actresses of the eighteenth century. In her tumultuous career on the London stage, Mrs. Cibber built up a repertory of parts "which in time included virtually all the great tragic roles written for women in the English dramatic canon . . . especially those roles in which pathos dominated."[18] These parts included Desdemona, Cordelia, Ophelia, Cleopatra in *All for Love,* Statira in Lee's *The Rival Queens,* and her renowned portrayals of Monomia in Otway's *The Orphan* and Belvidera in *Venice Preserv'd.*

Every contemporary source confirms that her ability to wring tears from her audience was unsurpassed. *A Guide to the Stage* (1751) declared that Mrs. Cibber, "taught by nature to lay every tumultuous passion, has the skill to attack the heart in the milder forms of pity, grief, and distress," while in 1747 Samuel Foote had observed that

This Lady . . . has almost all her Time reign'd unrival'd in the Hearts of the People. There is a Delicacy in her Deportment, and a sensible Innocence to her Counte-nance, that never fails to prejudice the Spectator in her favour, even before she speaks. Nor does Mrs. *Cibber's* subsequent Behaviour eraze these first Impressions. Her Expressions of the Passion of Grief, surpass every thing of the sort I have seen. There is a melancholy Plaintiveness in her Voice, and such a Dejection of Counte-nance, (without Distortion), that I defy any Man, who has the least Drop of the Milk of Human Nature about him, to sit out the distresses of *Monomia* and *Belvidera,* when represented by this Lady, without giving the most tender and affecting Testi-monies of his Humanity.

At the time of the original production, Mrs. Cibber was having an affair (arranged by her philandering husband) with a Mr. Sloper, an affair that was to result in a suit for "criminal conversation" in the autumn of 1738 when

Mr. Sloper stopped lending Mr. Cibber money and Cibber decided that he wanted his wife back. Although this case had become notorious by the autumn of 1738, the irony of the passionate Mrs. Cibber playing Milton's prudish Lady seems to have been lost on later audiences—a testimony to her powers of impersonation.[19]

James Quin was "the acknowledged male star" of the company. A veteran of the London stage since at least 1715, the "rough fantastic" veteran was a mainstay, both in tragic and comic productions, at Drury Lane. Among the many pre-1642 roles Quin played were Cymbeline, Hector and Thersites in *Troilus and Cressida*, Vincentio in *Measure for Measure*, King Lear, Henry VIII, Volpone, the ghost in *Hamlet*, Richard III, and Brutus. However, Quin's most famous role, and the part for which he received the greatest acclaim, was that of Falstaff. The robust, heavyset Quin played the role in every one of Shakespeare's plays in which Falstaff appears. As the testimonials of Reed, Thomas Davies, and Francis Gentleman indicate, as well as the many portraits and souvenir china statues of Quin as Falstaff prove, Quin was the mid–eighteenth-century face of Shakespeare's most celebrated rogue.[20]

Perhaps surprisingly, the other role for which he was most remembered was Comus. John Hill wrote that

thro' the whole part, [Quin] is something more than man: the majesty of the *Deity* he represents, dwells about him in every attitude, and in the pronouncing every period; with what a superior greatness does he introduce himself to us by his manner of delivering the glorious lines that open his part. . . . The manner in which he makes love to the lady, is of a piece with the rest. . . . To sum up the praise of this quality in the performer we are mentioning in this part, we shall not scruple to affirm, that if any thing claims title of being the greatest sentence, and most nobly pronounc'd of any on the *English* theatre, it is that threat of *Comus* to the lady, where, on offering to get up to leave him, he tells her

> Nay, lady, sit—If I but wave this wand,
> Your nerves are all bound up in alabaster,
> And you are a statue.[21]

Quin's size, stately bearing, famous temper, and deliberate (some said monotonous) delivery must have made him a dominating presence on the stage. Softened with a touch of Falstaff's humor, Quin's Comus must have been both imposing and compelling.

The supporting cast was no less impressive. The Brothers were played by Theophilis Cibber and William Milward. Cibber was a talented if troublesome leading man who specialized in comic roles, notably Pistol. Milward was one of the most promising young actors on the London stage in the mid-eighteenth century and was regarded as an early rival to David Garrick. The Attendant Spirits were played by Aaron Hill and William Mills. Hill, the nephew and namesake of his uncle, the playwright and manager, was probably the weakest member of the cast. Mills was Drury Lane's utility actor, who, like Cibber, specialized in comic roles.

The principal vocal roles were played by John Beard (Attendant Spirit and Bacchanal), Mrs. Clive (Euphrosyne), and Mrs. Arne (Sabrina and Pastoral Nymph). Beard is still considered one of the finest singers in English theatrical history. Singing under Handel at Covent Garden in the early 1730s, he had established himself as a popular and critical success before his twentieth birthday. Owing to his great popularity, Beard exerted a great deal of influence, for his name on an advertisement meant greater returns at the box office. Another favorite was the great Mrs. Clive as Euphrosyne—a role borrowed from *L'Allegro* with heavy singing demands in the highly musical act 3. Vastly popular for her wit and beauty, "Kitty" Clive was the "most vivacious comedienne and the best female comic singer on the London stage in the middle of the eighteenth century." Mrs. Arne played Sabrina, nymph of the Severn, as well as the Pastoral Nymph. Cecilia Arne was a singer of great distinction who had been trained by the great violinist, composer, and vocal coach Francesco Geminiani in the late 1720s. While her later career was to be marred by poor health and a failed marriage, in 1738 she was at the height of her powers as a singer.[22]

Apart from the music, another distinguishing feature of all theater at this time, be it masque, play, or opera, was a strong dance component. According to Arthur H. Scouten, a

survey of the Calendar of performances will show the great amount of singing, dancing, and music used in a night's production at a London theatre. Of this entertainment, dancing occupied the largest share. Formal ballet occurred in the pantomimes, and separate ballets were offered as entr'actes. In addition a profusion of individual named dances and hornpipes spiced every evening's program. . . . As the lists of the different companies are examined, the reader will find that sometimes one in three [cast members] was a dancer.

As William A. Sessions has demonstrated, dancing was by no means incompatible with Milton's masque, and the three dances inserted into Milton's text helped turn the production into the kind of multimedia show that theatrical audiences of the 1730s expected. Drury Lane employed many excellent dancers in the company, the most famous being the celebrated Denoyer. He was the Prince of Wales's own dancing master who, in "addition to the services he rendered to the royal family, danced frequently at Drury Lane." As Fiske comments, besides "being the leading dancer in *Comus*, Denoyer must also have been the choreographer." The announcement in the *London Daily Post, and General Advertiser* shows that the dancers in *Comus* were considered to have such drawing power that their names appeared in the advertisement when the names of adaptor and composer did not.[23]

What the original audience saw, then, was a spectacular musical production featuring many of the finest actors, singers, and dancers available—not unlike a musical such as *Showboat*. With the notable exception of Mrs. Cibber, the cast was predominantly composed of comic actors. While such a crew seems completely out of keeping with Milton's original masque to us, Drury Lane's all-star spectacular presentation of "Milton" proved hugely popular. Milton had—and has—never been so accessible.

IV. *COMUS* AND MILTON'S REPUTATION

Comus must have had a profound impact upon the popular conception of Milton for London theater-goers during the eighteenth century for the simple reason that, in one form or another, it held the stage well into the nineteenth century. To understand the impact of *Comus* on Milton's eighteenth-century reputation, we must measure the success of the masque over time by analyzing its performance history, examining contemporary reactions to the play, and evaluating its publication history.

With a highly respectable eleven performances during its first season, *Comus* proved to be what John Downes, the famous Restoration prompter, liked to call "a living play." Revived annually until 1752, Dalton's *Comus* played well throughout the 1740s (helped, no doubt, by the success of two Milton-inspired oratorios: Handel's *Samson* and John Christopher Smith and Benjamin Stillingfleet's *Paradise Lost*) and remained in the repertory for over a generation (see table 3). Apart from the great number of performances over such a long period of time—131 times over twenty-nine years—another way to measure the show's success was the readiness of the rival company to mount a production of its own. This occurred at Covent Garden on 3 March 1744. They, too, found *Comus* to be a popular success, reviving it almost annually until 1772.[24]

Contemporary reactions are useful in gauging the success of the production. While attached to the Prussian Embassy to the Court of St. James, Baron Friedrich von Bielfeld attended the Haymarket, Covent Garden, and Drury Lane theatres in 1741, performances that he commented upon in his letters. One of these was *Comus*. He wrote that: "They [Drury Lane] sometimes present charming *Operettes*. The other day I saw the one called *Comus* and I have never had so much pleasure. The words and the music are admirable, and I am going to learn all the airs from it by heart, all the more since they are not difficult to sing."[25]

TABLE 3. PERFORMANCES OF THE DALTON-ARNE *COMUS*, 1738–1772

Year	Performances	Year	Performances	Year	Performances
1738	11	1750	3	1762	5
1739	7	1751	1	1763	2
1740	7	1752	2	1764	5
1741	10	1753	1	1765	3
1742	5	1754	0	1766	2
1743	4	1755	1	1767	3
1744	3	1756	4	1768	0
1745	11	1757	0	1769	0
1746	2	1758	2	1770	0
1747	4	1759	3	1771	0
1748	5	1760	15	1772	0[a]
1749	3	1761	7		

Note: *Comus* was performed = 131 times.
a. Adapted by Colman

The overwhelmingly positive response to Arne's music continues to this century, for *Comus* proved to be the composer's first major success. In his biography of Arne, Hubert Langley wrote that, by composing the music for *Comus*,

Arne had found himself, and fixed a standard by which we can judge the whole of the rest of his work; for, although at times it is reminiscent of Handel, yet it has its own very decided individuality and spontaneous expression. There is a freshness and natural grace in all the airs, no striving after effect to please the ears of the groundlings, no sacrifice in taste in order to indulge in mere vocal display. It became a model for what was to be recognized for nearly a hundred years as typical English music.

In his entry for *Comus* in *The Companion to the Play-house* (1764), David Erskine Baker wrote that Dalton's adaptation was

a very judicious Alteration of *Milton*'s Masque at *Ludlow* Castle, wherein it is render'd much more fit for the Stage by the Introduction of many additional Songs, most of them *Milton*'s own, of part of the *Allegro* of the same Author, and other Passages from his different Works, so that he has rather restor'd *Milton* to himself than altered him. — It met with great Applause.

We have no way of proving that Baker actually attended a performance, but his pronouncement on the play has the tone of one who had seen and admired the show.[26]

Comparing the success of Dalton's *Comus* with other, similar productions, we discover some interesting figures. In his *The History of the The-*

atres (1761), the former actor, manager, treasurer, and playwright Benjamin Victor observed that Arne's *Alfred* was "well received." By my count, *Alfred* was performed a total of twenty-six times on the London stage in its seventeen-year life span. To say that Dalton's *Comus*—a production that was performed more than five times as much as *Alfred* over twenty-nine years—was "well received" would therefore be something of an understatement. Similarly, the authors of the *Biographical Dictionary* note that Arne's revival of Barton Booth's *Dido and Aeneas* in 1734 "was enormously successful, attaining seventeen performances." By contemporaneous standards, Dalton's *Comus* was a lasting triumph.[27]

Although the popularity of the masque began to wane in the 1760s, *Comus* by no means vanished from the London stage, for in 1772 George Colman the Elder made a two-act adaptation of the Dalton-Arne *Comus*. He retained almost all of Arne's score and reduced the dialogue by excising many of the descriptive passages in the text—both Milton's original words and Dalton's additions. Three-act musical mainpieces were changing in character, and "burlettas"—musical farces—were flooding the repertory. What Colman did was simply to recast the Dalton opera in a popular new form. Griffin mistakenly asserts that "Though never as successful as the Dalton version, the Colman-Arne *Comus* went through 23 performances in 1772."[28] In fact, Colman's *Comus* played only fourteen times that year, but proved even more popular than its predecessor, being performed nearly twice as many times as Dalton's *Comus* by the end of the eighteenth century (see table 4).

In his exhaustive *Some Account of the English Stage from the Restoration in 1660 to 1830*, John Genest indicates that Colman's *Comus* was still playing as late as 1830. In his entry for the play, Genest writes:

TABLE 4. PERFORMANCES OF THE COLMAN-ARNE *COMUS*, 1772–1800

Year	Performances	Year	Performances	Year	Performances
1772	14	1782	8	1792	4
1773	10	1783	14	1793	3
1774	8	1784	9	1794	2
1775	6	1785	9	1795	3
1776	8	1786	4	1796	1
1777	31	1787	17	1797	6
1778	17	1788	16	1798	2
1779	12	1789	5	1799	2
1780	27	1790	2	1800	1
1781	10	1791	5		

Note: Comus was performed 256 times.

Comus was adapted to the stage in 3 acts—this alteration was made by Dr. Dalton—it is a very judicious one—he has retained nearly the whole of the original—added or compiled the scene between the Brothers and Comus' Crew, and introduced a variety of songs to make it pass off better on the stage; the B.D. says they are taken from Milton's other works—the Prologue is modest and sensible. . . . Coleman, in 1772, compressed Dr. Dalton's 3 acts into 2, omitting great part of the dialogue and making Comus a Musical Entertainment—in this mangled state it still keeps possession of the stage.[29]

Through these two adaptations, Milton enjoyed one of the greatest theatrical successes in the history of the eighteenth-century stage: in one form or another, Comus remained in the theaters for almost one hundred years.

The final index to the play's success is its publication history in comparison to Milton's other works. An *English Short Title Catalogue* search reveals that Comus was published as a single edition more often in the eighteenth century than any of the poet's "major" works save *Paradise Lost*. Between 1738 and 1800 Comus was published at least forty-nine times in Great Britain and Ireland, proving noticeably more popular than *Samson Agonistes* (thirty-nine separate editions between 1743 and 1800, including oratorio versions), and substantially more so than *Paradise Regained* (five separate editions between 1752 and 1800).

How does the success of Comus alter our understanding of Milton's reputation during this period? Quite simply, we must conclude that in the eyes of many contemporary Londoners—and certainly most of the theatergoers—Milton was more than the epic poet: he was a dramatist, and a very successful one at that. Through the addition of more characters, dialogue, dances, and a musical score from the finest English composer of the age, Dalton transformed Milton into an eighteenth-century playwright and Comus into a contemporary entertainment of the first quality. When tastes and expectations changed in the later half of the century, Colman did exactly the same thing, turning Comus into an even bigger success. For London's theater-goers after 1738, "Milton" most likely meant an exciting and spectacular night's entertainment featuring outstanding music as well as some of the most talented singers, dancers, and actors to appear on the eighteenth-century stage. "Milton" meant a good time, and better yet he appealed to the moral tastes of the time by offering a story of evil resisted and virtue proved.

Because theater attendance patterns indicate that patrons often saw a production more than once, we can only speculate as to how many people actually saw Comus in the eighteenth century. However, the effect of 387 performances of Comus between 1738 and 1800 on the popular perception of Milton cannot be easily dismissed. From all of the evidence, we must conclude that *Comus* was a vital source for establishing Milton's reputation during the eighteenth century. Yet despite the masque's great popularity, eighteenth-century commentators after Johnson chose to ignore *Comus*. Since that time, critics have focused their efforts on *Paradise Lost* and, more recently, on *Samson Agonistes* and *Paradise Regained*. And yet, the people who wrote criticism and involved themselves with things literary in mid–eighteenth-century England must have been aware of the tremendous popularity of *Comus* on the London stage, for it was they who patronized the theaters. For us as literary critics, this has resulted in the dissemination of one set of records that tell us that Milton's reputation in the eighteenth century was based almost exclusively on *Paradise Lost*. However, the theatrical and cultural records tell us that a tremendous number of people over nearly one hundred years knew Milton through his ongoing presence in London's theaters. Thus, the current state of criticism on Milton's reception in eighteenth-century London does not accurately reflect the actual experience of eighteenth-century Londoners—a fact that should leave us with some unsettling doubts about the soundness of the critical picture we have inherited. No doubt Milton was the author of the great English epic, but he was also the writer associated with one of the most popular English operas of the eighteenth century.

The Pennsylvania State University

NOTES

I am grateful to Laura L. Knoppers and Robert D. Hume for their comments and suggestions.

1. Ants Oras, *Milton's Editors and Commentators from Patrick Hume to Henry John Todd, 1695–1801, A Study of Critical Views and Methods* (London, 1931); *Milton Criticism: Selections from Four Centuries*, ed. James E. Thorpe (New York, 1950); *Milton: The Critical Heritage*, ed. John T. Shawcross (New York, 1970); Bernard Sharratt, "The Appropriation of Milton," *Essays & Studies, 1982: The Poet's Power* (1982): 30–44; and Ernest W. Sullivan, II, "Illustration as Interpretation: *Paradise Lost* from 1688 to 1807" in *Milton's Legacy in the Arts*, ed. Albert C. Labriola and Edward Sichi, Jr. (University Park, 1988), pp. 59–92.

2. Good, *Studies in the Milton Tradition* (1915; rpt. New York, 1971); Stevens, *Milton Papers* (Chicago, 1927), pp. 21–35; and Thaler, *Shakespere's Silences* (Cambridge, Mass., 1929), pp. 232–57. Dustin Griffin, *Regaining Paradise: Milton and the Eighteenth Century* (Cambridge, 1986), pp. 67–68, devotes three paragraphs to *Comus*, essentially repeating Good's findings. Joseph Wittreich, *Feminist Milton* (Ithaca, 1986); p. 29, states, "That *Comus* should rival Milton's epic in popularity solidifies the impression of Milton as a poet of conventional moral virtue," but is otherwise silent on the masque. William A. Sessions, "Milton and the Dance," in *Milton's Legacy in the Arts*, offering a necessarily brief interpretation of the masque, argues that the success of *Comus* in the eighteenth century lay in the adaptors' ability to

manipulate "the basic dialectic of Milton's myth of temperance" p. 194. For the best discussion of Dalton's *Comus*, see Roger Fiske, *English Theatre Music in the Eighteenth Century*, rev. ed. (Oxford, 1986), pp. 179–88.

Roy Flannagan, "Comus," in *The Cambridge Companion to Milton*, ed. Dennis Danielson (Cambridge, 1989), sidesteps the title issue when he writes: "Not the least of critical problems with *Comus* is what to call it. It is not properly called Comus, because Milton gave it the generic name *A Mask presented at Ludlow castle, 1634.* When John Dalton rewrote the masque as a opera in 1738, he changed the name to that of its principal character and the name stuck, though calling *Comus 'Comus'* may be tantamount to calling *Paradise Lost 'Satan'*. Modern editors and critics would rather call the masque *A Mask*, but they are all forced by popular usage to call it *Comus*, if they want to be understood by a general audience" (p. 21). Dalton's *Comus* was not solely responsible for changing the name of *A Mask* to *Comus*, since John Toland refers to the masque by that title in his *The Life of John Milton* (London, 1699).

3. Blackmore, *Essays* (London, 1716); qtd. in C. W. Moulton, *Library of Literary Criticism*, 2 vols. (1910; rpt. Gloucester, Mass., 1959), vol. II, p. 258; Defoe, *A Review of the State of the British Nation*, 18 August 1711; Fenton, "Life" in his edition of *Paradise Lost* (London, 1725), p. xxi; Good, *Studies in the Milton Tradition*, p. 139.

4. Toland, *The Life of John Milton*, pp. 132, 36. Thomas Birch, another biographer and editor, also devotes considerable attention to *Lycidas* and *Comus* in *The Complete Prose Works of Milton, with An Account of the Life and Writings of Mr. John Milton*, 2 vols. (London, 1738), vol. I, pp. vii–xvi.

5. Johnson, *Lives of the English Poets*, 3 vols., ed. George Birkenbeck Hill (Oxford, 1905), vol. I, pp. 167–68. In 1749 William Lauder brought the plight of Milton's only surviving descendant, his granddaughter Elizabeth Foster, to the attention of the English public in his *Essay on Milton's Use and Imitation of the Moderns*. John Dalton, by then a distinguished clergyman, helped procure a benefit for the impoverished Mrs. Foster at Drury Lane on 5 April 1750. To generate interest in the performance, Samuel Johnson wrote a letter that appeared in the *General Advertiser* on 4 April 1750 that read "Whosoever then would be thought capable of pleasure in reading the works of our incomparable Milton, and not so destitute of gratitude as to refuse to lay out a trifle in a rational and elegant entertainment for the benefit of his living remains . . . should appear at Drury-Lane Theatre to-morrow." Johnson's prologue was spoken by the greatest actor of the eighteenth century, David Garrick. The benefit proved to be a success, for the profits of the night (and thus for Mrs. Foster) were £130, "the greatest benefaction that Paradise Lost ever procured the author's descendants," according to Johnson. See Johnson, *Poems*, Yale Edition of the Works of Samuel Johnson, vol. 6, ed. E. L. McAdam with George Milne (New Haven, 1964), pp. 239–40.

6. See Griffin's account of "Milton's Politics" in *Regaining Paradise*, pp. 11–21.

7. *Dictionary of National Biography*, 22 vols., ed. Leslie Stephen and Sidney Lee (1885–1901; rpt. Oxford, 1963–64), vol. V, p. 427.

8. For an excellent discussion on the effects of the Licensing Act, see Robert D. Hume, *The Rakish Stage: Studies in English Drama, 1660–1800* (Carbondale, Ill., 1983), pp. 270–311.

9. *The London Stage, 1660–1800. Part 3: 1729–1747*, 2 vols., ed. Arthur H. Scouten (Carbondale, Ill., 1961), vol. I, p. cxl. Ogden, personal communication.

10. Rolli, *Sabrina, a Masque: in three acts and in verse. Founded on the Comus of Milton* (London, 1737). *Sabrina* played ten times at the King's Theatre, Haymarket, in 1737: 26 April; 3, 7, 10, 14, 17, 21, 31 May; 7 and 11 June. It was revived once in the season 1737–38 (21 December), but its run was cut short by the untimely death of the queen.

11. *John Milton: Complete Poems and Major Prose*, ed. Merritt Y. Hughes (New York,

1957), p. 112. All references to Milton's works are to this edition. References to Dalton's adaptation are from his *Comus, a Mask* (London, 1738).

12. Philip H. Highfill, Jr., Kalman A. Burnim, and Edward A. Langhans, *A Biographical Dictionary of Actors, Actresses, Musicians, Dancers, Managers, and Other Stage Personnel in London, 1660–1800*, 16 vols. (Carbondale, Ill., 1973–1993), vol. I, p. 109.

13. Hill, *The Works of the Late Aaron Hill*, 4 vols. (London, 1753), vol. I, p. 116; Fiske, *English Theatre Music*, p. 132.

14. For the complete score, see Milton, Dalton, Arne, *Comus, Musica Britannica: A National Collection of Music*, vol. 3, ed. Julian Herbage (London, 1951). For a complete audio recording of the mask, refer to Thomas A. Arne, *Comus*, cond. Anthony Lewis, Ensemble Orchestral de l'Oiseau-lyre and the St. Anthony Singers, Editions de l'Oiseau-lyre, OL 500070-500071, 1954.

15. Johnson, *A Dictionary of the English Language*, 2 vols. (London, 1755), vol. II, s.v. "mask."

16. Fiske, *English Theatre Music*, p. 172.

17. "The Public Unjustly Blam'd for Want of Taste," *Gentlemen's Magazine* VIII (March 1738): 152.

18. Highfill et al., *Biographical Dictionary*, vol. III, p. 264.

19. *Guide to the Stage* cited in ibid., p. 265; Foote cited in ibid., pp. 274–75. For the complete story on the affair and suit, see ibid., pp. 267–70.

20. Highfill et al., *Biographical Dictionary*, vol. X, p. 6. For a good discussion of Quin as Falstaff, see Nancy A. Mace, "Falstaff, Quin, and the Popularity of *The Merry Wives of Windsor* in the Eighteenth Century," *Theatre Survey* XXXI (May 1990): 55–66.

21. Hill, *The Actor: A Treatise on the Art of Playing* (London, 1750), pp. 174–76.

22. Highfill et al., *Biographical Dictionary*, vol. III, p. 341.

23. Scouten, *The London Stage*, vol. I, p. clv; Sessions, "Milton and the Dance," pp. 181–203; on Denoyer, see Highfill et al., *Biographical Dictionary*, vol. IV, p. 332; Fiske, *English Theatre Music*, p. 186.

24. Although Fiske, *English Theatre Music*, states that there were no performances of *Comus* in the season 1738–39 (p. 181), the compilers of the *London Stage* record seven performances during that period. For more on Milton's success on the musical stage, see Stella P. Revard, "From the State of Innocence to the Fall of Man: The Fortunes of *Paradise Lost* as Opera and Oratorio," in *Milton's Legacy in the Arts*, pp. 93–134.

25. Baron Jacob Friedrich von Bielfeld, *Lettres familieres et autres de Monsieur le Baron Bielfeld* (La Haye, 1763), p. 269, dated 7 February 1741: "On nous donne aussi quelques fois des Operettes charmantes. J'ai vu l'autre jour celle de *Comus* & jamais je n'eus tant de plaisir. Les paroles & la Musique en sont admirables, & je vais en apprendre tous les airs par cœur, d'autant plus qu'ils ne sont pas difficiles à chanter." Von Bielfeld must have attended the performance of 31 January.

26. Langley, *Doctor Arne* (Cambridge, 1938), p. 22; Baker, *The Companion to the Playhouse*, 2 vols. (London, 1764), vol. I, s.v. "*Comus.*"

27. Victor, *The History of the Theatres of London and Dublin From the Year 1730 to the Present Time*, 2 vols. (London, 1761), vol. II, p. 126; Highfill et al., *Biographical Dictionary*, vol. I, p. 110.

28. Griffin, *Regaining Paradise*, p. 68.

29. Genest, *Some Account of the English Stage, From the Restoration in 1660 to 1830*, 10 vols. (Bath, 1832), vol. III, pp. 533–34.

WITHOUT CHARITY:
AN INTERTEXTUAL STUDY OF
MILTON'S *COMUS*

Hilda Hollis

T HE BIBLE HAS an authoritative position for Milton, and this makes any substantive alteration of it in his writing significant. While the Lady's cry in *Comus* has been frequently glossed over, it is actually very startling. The famous triad of 1 Corinthians, chapter xiii, "Faith, hope and charity," are replaced by faith, hope, and *chastity:* "O welcome pure-ey'd Faith, white-handed Hope, / Thou hov'ring Angel girt with golden wings, / And thou unblemish't form of Chastity."[1] This statement represents a double disruption and thus suggests an important site from which to begin an analysis of *Comus*. Until these words, the text functions within a classical frame and is without obvious Christian reference. This world of Greek mythology, however, is broken up by the words of Saint Paul which are themselves even more notably disrupted. Why does Milton interrupt his classical humanist text with this Christian allusion, and simultaneously break up the Christian text by omitting the crucial word that gives it meaning? Paul's words at the beginning of chapter xiii were well known by Milton and should not be ignored: "though I have all faith . . . and have not charity, I am nothing" (verse 2).[2] Milton's Lady, significantly, has all but charity.

Malcolm Ross's exclamation, "Faith, Hope, and *Chastity*. And the greatest of these is chastity!," is frequently cited only to be dismissed as an extreme and unfounded reaction to Milton's change.[3] I will argue that Ross's exclamation mark is appropriate, despite his inadequate interpretation of this substitution as a bungled attempt by Milton to valorize the Protestant ethic of chastity. Instead, this essay will suggest a well-developed progression through the text of *Comus*, from an inward-turning righteousness (chastity without charity) to a love for God (charity which produces chastity). Such a reading is clearly dependent on A.S.P. Woodhouse's groundbreaking discussion of *Comus* in 1941, but a crucial difference lies in my understanding of the substitution of *chastity* for *charity*.[4]

Focusing on the concept of chastity, Woodhouse sees this as the link between the natural world and the Christian one. This progression is evi-

159

denced as *Comus* moves through three stages. In Nature, the point of departure, there are natural laws of temperance and continence. In the second stage, these laws are transformed into a doctrine of chastity through Platonic idealism—an illumination of a higher order "whose note is not self-sufficiency, but self-surrender" ("Argument," 58). This, argues Woodhouse, is the point where the natural world and Christianity meet. The final stage of *Comus* moves into a period of Christian grace in which virginity replaces chastity as a symbol of all virtue. This is a "state higher and more dynamic than a merely self-dependent pursuit of Platonic idealism can afford" (*Variorum*, p. 804).

The movement from self-sufficiency to grace which Woodhouse proposes is helpful, but his scheme is extremely problematic both in the preeminent position which he gives chastity and virginity in Christian thought, and in his understanding of virginity in the final movement of the poem. He admits that his stress on virginity is "not directly stated and that one can deduce it only by a consideration of the poem as a whole, and by cross-reference to other passages" ("Argument," 60). A study of Milton's other writings will reveal that Woodhouse's link between chastity and virginity is fallacious. A much clearer sense of progression can be discerned in this poem when we start by inquiring about the significance of the Lady's distorted allusion to a key Christian text.

In order to understand the substitution of chastity for charity, I propose an intertextual study in which I will consider Saint Paul's text into which *chastity* has been inserted and also the text of *Comus* into which Paul's words have been introduced. The wider social and historical context which frames *Comus* will also form a part of this study. How were *chastity* and *charity* understood in Milton's society, and what issues informed Milton's first audience? The most valuable intertexts for this discussion, however, will be those which demonstrate Milton's own biblical interpretation in *Paradise Lost, Paradise Regained,* and the large body of his prose works, especially *Christian Doctrine.*

While most of Milton's works postdate *Comus*, this does not preclude their ability to indicate Milton's interpretation of the Bible and the importance he attaches to it. His clearest theological exposition is found in *Christian Doctrine.* Although it was not yet written in 1634, its conception was much earlier: "I began by devoting myself when I was a boy to an earnest study of the Old and New Testaments in their original languages."[5] This early emphasis on the Bible is evident in his mature work. He states in the introductory epistle to *Christian Doctrine* that he compiled it from biblical excerpts in order to be able to respond to contemporary issues from the only determinant of heresy (YP VI, p. 123). Milton structures *Christian Doctrine* deliberately in a manner which allows the greatest space to the text of the Bible: "I . . . have striven to cram my pages even to overflowing, with quotations drawn from all parts of the Bible and to leave as little space as possible for my own words, even when they arise from the putting together of actual scriptural texts" (p. 122). He continues, "I devote my attention to the Holy Scriptures alone" (p. 123).

After William B. Hunter's attack on the Miltonic authorship of *Christian Doctrine*, a reliance on this work, particularly the epistle, as evidence for Milton's beliefs may appear somewhat tendentious. Although the debate on its authorship is far from resolved, in this essay *Christian Doctrine* is treated as Milton's own. My argument, however, does not rest on this assumption, for if it is not written by Milton himself, *Christian Doctrine* functions at least as a text of society. Hunter notes that whoever "originated the work would have . . . shared Milton's minority ideas on divorce and on many of the basic beliefs held by the groups loosely titled radical puritans" (p. 139).[6] Its emphasis on the Bible, which is crucial to my argument, is consistent with Milton's other works. In her rebuttal of Hunter's position, Barbara Lewalski points to a striking parallel between the epistle's expression of the Bible's function and a passage in *A Treatise of Civil Power*: "then ought we to beleeve what in our conscience we apprehend the scripture to say, though the visible church with all her doctors gainsay . . . they who so do are not heretics, but the best protestants" (YP VII, p. 251).[7] In his discussion of scripture in *Of Reformation*, Milton, quoting Saint Basil, writes that "*it is a plain falling from the Faith, and a high pride either to make void any thing therin, or to introduce any thing not there to be found*" (YP I, p 565). The Bible, in Puritan circles and in Milton's thought, is clearly the final arbiter, and Saint Paul's words should not be subject to alteration.

The almost universal assumption among critics is that Milton replaces *charity* by *chastity* in *Comus* in order to give the latter the connotations of the former.[8] Most commonly, it is argued that charity and chastity were identified in Renaissance thought before Milton. Maryann McGuire proposes an example from Book I of Spenser's *Faerie Queene*: "Spenser synthesized the two in his depiction of Charissa, sister of Fidelia (Faith) and Speranza (Hope), as 'full of great love . . . chast in worke and will.' Charissa's roles as faithful wife and fecund mother draw on the traditional motif of the Christian soul bound by reciprocal love to Christ and reflecting that love in acts of virtue."[9] Spenser's text and McGuire's comments rightly demand a more comprehensive interpretation of chastity since it does not function only under the constraint of virginity. It is an expression of faith and not simply a signifier of a particular sexuality. Yet, although Charissa is chaste in work and will, no complete identification of chastity and charity is made.

The relationship is instead derivative; chastity arises from charity. McGuire further argues that chastity is substituted for charity in an effort to make a distinction from Anglican charity which, as a social virtue, had been made into an argument for conformity. She argues that in Puritan thought chastity became an inclusive virtue. (pp. 138–45). However, Milton's other writings, as we shall see, show the importance that he and other Protestants attach to charity, and suggest that he would teach a correct doctrine of charity rather than abandon the word. In fact, the second book of *Christian Doctrine* "is about THE WORSHIP OF GOD and CHARITY" (YP VI, p. 637). Milton in his English prose works uses *charity* 122 times, while *chastity* appears only eleven times. In none of these instances does chastity become an inclusive virtue.

Georgia Christopher argues that chastity and faith are virtually synonymous in reformation theology. Contending that Milton changes the triad "in order to maintain a key doctrinal distinction" between faith and love, she writes that working against Papist ideas, "Milton is attempting to preserve the virginity of the concept of faith against any contamination from works, even loving ones. If we keep in mind that chastity is a pervasive metaphor for faith among the Reformers and that they have a tendency to meld faith with hope, then the famous substitution of 'chastity' in line 215 becomes tantamount to a triple iteration of 'faith' for rhetorical effect."[10] Again, a consideration of *Christian Doctrine* makes it evident that Milton is capable of distinguishing between works of the law and works of faith. Charity is associated with the latter and thus fully compatible with Milton's reformed beliefs. Discussing the epistle to the Romans, Milton writes that Saint Paul does not say that man "is justified by faith alone, but *by faith working through charity*, Gal.v.6. Faith has its own works, which may be different from the works of the law" (YP VI, p. 490).[11]

Other commentators, like Woodhouse, argue that the substitution is natural, given the Platonic imagery underlying *Comus*. A. E. Dyson argues that "Chastity is, in fact, Virtue, given the context—and in Platonic terms a key virtue, because the essence of purity itself."[12] Milton's *An Apology for Smectymnuus* is the work most often advanced for this case. He remarks that he learned of "chastity and love" in "the divine volumes of *Plato*, and his equall *Xenophon*" (YP I, p. 891). The coupling of chastity and love in this context, however, in no way suggests that chastity can represent love. In contrast, Milton's view of charity goes far beyond sexual relations, which are clearly the subject of this tract. It may also be asserted with confidence (and with confirmation in the next paragraph from the same tract) that Milton does not think more highly of Plato than Saint Paul, and that he would not engage in the substitution of chastity for charity on the basis of Greek philosophy.

Although the above critics' comments on the value of chastity have merit, each of these critics simply accepts the substitution of chastity for charity. My contention is not that Milton is condemning the Lady because of her adherence to a doctrine of chastity.[13] Rather, he argues that while chastity is in itself good, it is not itself sufficient. Milton is not biblically superficial. He does not engage in wordplay on decontextualized verses of Scripture, but rather bases his work on a comprehensive understanding of the Bible. In the context of *Comus*, Milton's reverence for the Bible should not be dismissed lightly.[14] Attention must go beyond the final verse of Corinthians, chapter xiii, to the whole chapter, especially given its universal familiarity. In addition, William B. Hunter points out that this chapter was the New Testament lesson for evening prayer on the night before the first production of *Comus*. Any reading of the masque should first entail a reading of this chapter.[15]

The final verse of 1 Corinthians, chapter xiii, reads, "And now abideth faith, hope, charity, these three; but the greatest of these is charity" (13). Although this verse gives the preeminent position to charity, it does not suggest that faith and hope would be worthless without charity. The opening verses of this chapter, however, make such a claim:

Though I speak with the tongues of men and of angels, and have not charity, I am become as sounding brass, or as tinkling cymbal. And though I have the gift of prophecy, and understand all mysteries, and all knowledge; and though I have all faith, so that I could remove mountains, and have not charity, I am nothing. And though I bestow all my goods to feed the poor, and though I give my body to be burned, and have not charity, it profiteth me nothing. (1–3)

Far from being condemnable, these actions which Saint Paul contrasts with charity are virtues. Yet, they are worthless without charity. A tripling of faith, which Christopher suggests as Milton's rationale for substituting *chastity* for *charity*, cannot make up for this lack, nor can chastity itself. Milton describes *chastity* in *Christian Doctrine* as "forbearance from the unlawful lusts of the flesh; it is also called purity" (YP VI, p. 726). This is the full extent of his attention to chastity. It is identified as one among several special virtues whose function is to "regulate our appetite for external advantages . . . in relation either to the pleasures of the flesh or to the material possessions and distinctions of our life" (p. 724). Chastity's accompanying virtues include sobriety, modesty, decency, contentment, frugality, industry, elegance, humility and high-mindedness. It is one among many, not an extraordinary virtue. In contrast, charity is the controlling thought of Book II of *Christian Doctrine.*

Milton, discussing charity in *Christian Doctrine,* shows the importance he attaches to the first verses of 1 Corinthians, chapter xiii. He writes that charity "is nowhere more fully described than in 1 Cor. xiii" (YP VI, p. 717). Parts of the first three verses are quoted as least three times (pp. 566, 718, 791). In yet another instance, Milton interprets the story of the young man who is told to sell all he has and follow Christ (Matt. xix) in the light of 1 Corinthians, chapter xiii: "There was no perfection in selling all he had: men have done that without charity. The perfection lay in leaving his possessions and following Christ" (p. 643). The young man's sacrifice is worth nothing without a love for God. This same awareness of the importance of charity is also found in *Paradise Lost.* Michael says to Adam:

> only add,
> Deeds to thy knowledge answerable, add Faith,
> Add Virtue, Patience, Temperance, add Love,
> By name to come call'd Charity, the soul
> Of all the rest.   (*PL* XII, 581–85)

Michael defines love as charity, but clearly does not subsume faith, virtue, patience, or temperance under the label *charity.*[16] Rather, charity is their soul; it gives them meaning.

In *Christian Doctrine,* Milton delineates two types of charity based on Jesus' summary of the Decalogue: the love of God and the love of man. Charity displaces all legalistic fulfillments of the law: "For the works of the faithful are the works of the Holy Spirit itself. These never run contrary to the love of God and of our neighbour, which is the sum of the law" (YP VI, p. 640). Charity, Milton writes, arises "FROM A SENSE OF DIVINE LOVE WHICH IS POURED INTO THE HEARTS OF THE REGENERATE THROUGH THE SPIRIT" (p. 479).

Within the corpus of Milton's English prose writing, the idea of charity is most prominent in his various tracts or pamphlets on divorce. He argues in *Tetrachordon* that "the christian arbitrement of charity is supreme decider of all controversie, and supreme resolver of all Scripture" (YP II, p. 637). Because it is not the law but charity which is supreme, Milton argues that divorce should be allowed. Charity is the fulfilling of the law and nothing can stand in its stead: "Our Saviours doctrine is, that the end, and the fulfilling of every command is charity; no faith without it, no truth without it, no worship, no workes pleasing to God but as they partake of charity" (p. 637).[17]

In light of the high value which Milton places upon charity, it is reasonable to suppose that he is signaling a problem when the Lady disrupts Saint Paul's triad with chastity. The first mention of love is heard in Comus's speech: "*Venus* now wakes, and wak'ns Love" (124). Comus, whose name is a transliteration of the Greek *Kwmos*, meaning revels, is clearly not speaking of the love (*agape* or charity) that Paul advocates in his first epistle to the Corinthians. As Christopher suggests, his name is probably taken from Paul's list of the works of the flesh in Galatians V, 19.[18] These works of the flesh are contrasted with the "fruit of the Spirit" (Gal. v, 22), the first of which is love. It is easy to see that Comus is missing the mark, but why are the Lady's words problematic? She is chaste; her "virtuous mind . . . [is] attended / By a strong siding champion Conscience" (211–12). The problem does not lie in her virtue, but in a self-reliance which excludes a love for God.

The Lady does voice a trust in the "Supreme good" (217) to protect her, but this faith does not arise from a sense of personal limitation or from a devotion to God. Rather, she is confident of aid because of her own virtue. Her chastity is a bodily manifestation or reflection of the ideal. She expects help from a "glist'ring Guardian" (219) whose outward appearance would reflect her own shining virtue. It is notable that she stresses the outward, and thus potentially deceptive, qualities of the guardian. *Glister* in Milton's lexicon is sometimes associated with deception. In *Paradise Lost,* the serpent *glisters.*[19] Caution should be exercised in identifying the Christian God with the "Supreme good" (217) from whom this dazzling guardian would emanate. When the Lady makes her plea or prayer a few lines after this assertion of confidence, she does not invoke Jove, who has been shown through the prologue to be concerned with her plight. Instead, she calls upon Echo. In essence, she calls upon herself and expects to be able to rely on her own virtue. The error of the Lady is further evinced when the moon appears and she claims to see chastity. Here I am following Rosemond Tuve's identification of the moon ("chaste Diana") as the form of chastity visible to the Lady, who then wonders:

> Was I deceiv'd, or did a sable cloud
> Turn forth her silver lining on the night?
> I did not err, there does a sable cloud
> Turn forth her silver lining on the night. (221–24)[20]

The Lady is deceived, not because she sees the moon, but because she interprets it as a guarantor of unblemished chastity. Comus has already invoked the moon as Hecate for a very opposite purpose. Chastity without charity is indeed nothing.

The Lady's susceptibility to deception is evident when she does not

penetrate Comus's disguise and addresses him ironically as "good Shepherd" (307). Jesus calls himself "the good shepherd" (John x, 11), and his
sheep "follow him: for they know his voice. And a stranger will they not
follow, but will flee from him: for they know not the voice of strangers"
(4–5). The Lady's response to the disguised magician stands in marked contrast to Jesus' immediate recognition of the disguised devil in *Paradise Regained* (I, 348). In her last address to Comus before she sets off with him,
the Lady's problematic self-reliance becomes yet more evident. In the same
speech in which she professes a trust in Comus's "honest offer'd courtesy"
(323), she also addresses Providence in a way which significantly differs
from the Lord's Prayer. She prays: "Eye me blest Providence, and square
my trial / To my proportion'd strength. Shepherd lead on" (329–30). If she
were following the true shepherd she would have prayed his prayer: "And
lead us not into temptation, but deliver us from evil" (Matt. vi, 13). The
Lady does not ask for this absolute deliverance, but rather that her trial or
temptation will not be beyond *her* powers. She does not recognize that she
is already out of her depth.

The elder brother demonstrates an overconfident understanding of the
self-sufficiency of chastity which goes even beyond that of his sister. He
does not recognize any limits to his sister's self-sufficiency which Providence would be required to rectify. While his sister and younger brother
recognize physical vulnerability, he refuses to concern himself over the fate
of his sister:

> I do not think my sister so to seek,
> Or so unprincipl'd in virtue's book
> And the sweet peace that goodness bosoms ever,
> As that the single want of light and noise
> (Not being in danger, as I trust she is not)
> Could stir the constant mood of her calm thoughts.   (366–71)

He describes virtue as dependent on itself alone and on its own light rather
than the light of God: "Virtue could see to do what virtue would / By her
own radiant light, though Sun and Moon / Were in the flat Sea sunk" (373–
75). Virtue may have light, but the brother's words ignore the greater light
of God as he puts the individual and his or her virtue in the center: "He
that has light within his own clear breast / May sit i'th' center, and enjoy
bright day" (381–82). This description is reminiscent of the shepherd's description of a deity in *Arcades:* "This, this is she alone, / Sitting like a Goddess bright, / In the center of her light" (17–19). The elder brother makes
the virtuous individual into a god, guided by his or her own light. She does
not receive "Light from above, from the fountain of light" (*PR* IV, 289).

When the second brother voices his fear over his sister's safety, the elder one responds that "she has a hidden strength" (415). In an attempt to give this hidden strength the correct derivation, the younger brother asks whether his senior is referring to heaven. To this query, the elder brother gives a grudging acknowledgment to heaven, but reserves his finest praise for his sister and her chastity:

> I mean that [heaven] too, but yet a hidden strength
> Which if Heav'n gave it, may be term'd her own:
> 'Tis chastity, my brother, chastity:
> She that has that, is clad in complete steel. (418–21)

He draws on Greek myths and philosophy to show the power of chastity. Milton, as many readers have commented, surely intends irony in the younger brother's response:

> How charming is divine Philosophy!
> Not harsh, and crabbed as dull fools suppose,
> But musical as is *Apollo's* lute,
> And a perpetual feast of nectar'd sweets,
> Where no crude surfeit reigns. (476–80)

Divine philosophy appears able to ignore the problems of the real world. Chastity is attributed a type of magical power which can soothe away real danger.

In contrast, when a potential threat actually comes to the elder brother, he does not rely on the power of chastity. While no "savage fierce, Bandit or mountaineer / Will dare to soil" (426–27) his sister's virgin purity, as soon as he hears a "far-off hallo" (481), he prepares to draw his sword: "Come not too near, you fall on iron stakes else" (491). Either the elder brother is not chaste or he is a hypocrite. His self-righteousness is clear in his response to the Attendant Spirit's query about his sister: "To tell thee sadly, Shepherd, without blame, / Or our neglect, we lost her as we came" (509–10). While the brothers did not lose their sister wilfully or maliciously, their action could hardly be termed prudent. It is worth remarking that prudence is one of the "general virtues" discussed by Milton in *Christian Doctrine*, and that it is not given any lesser value than chastity, which is so highly prized by the brothers in their sister. It "is the virtue which allows us to see what we ought to do and when and where we ought to do it" (YP VI, p. 651). Leaving their sister alone in the woods at dusk, while they went off berry picking without marking a return trail, should prompt some remorse.

Although it comes from a much later period in Milton's life, Jesus' description of the Stoic in *Paradise Regained* is relevant to both the elder brother's philosophic pretensions and to his sister. Comus in fact regards the Lady's words as emanating from Stoic philosophy:

> O foolishness of men! that lend their ears
> To those budge doctors of the *Stoic* Fur,
> And fetch their precept from the *Cynic* Tub,
> Praising the lean and sallow Abstinence.   (706–09).

Milton's Jesus, like Comus, rejects such philosophy, although for very different reasons. He identifies it with a false and boastful virtue:

> The Stoic last in Philosophic pride,
> By him call'd virtue; and his virtuous man,
> Wise, perfect in himself, and all possessing
> Equal to God, oft shames not to prefer,
> As fearing God nor man, contemning all
> Wealth, pleasure, pain or torment, death and life,
> Which when he lists, he leaves, or boasts he can,
> For all his tedious talk is but vain boast.   (*PR* IV, 300–07)

The words of the young siblings indicate, to varying degrees, such a self-reliant understanding of virtue.

Milton's Jesus does not, however, in any way object to virtue, but rather censures an attitude which excludes love of God: "Much of the Soul they talk, but all awry, / And in themselves seek virtue, and to themselves / All glory arrogate, to God give none" (*PR* IV, 313–15). Jesus, however, does make one exception to his condemnation of Greek poetry: "Unless where moral virtue is express'd / By light of Nature, not in all quite lost" (*PR* IV, 351–52). Milton, in *Apology for Smectymnuus*, likewise finds a preliminary instructive value in the morals of the Greeks.

Jesus' exception in *Paradise Regained* is crucial for any understanding of *Comus*. Milton does not condemn the chastity of the Lady, but he recognizes its deficiency without divine grace and charity. When the Spirit informs the two brothers of the dire predicament of their sister, the younger accuses his senior of a false confidence in philosophy: "Alone and helpless! Is this the confidence / You gave me, Brother?" (583–84). The elder brother's response is significant and moves into the realm of allegory: "Yes, and keep it still, / Lean on it safely, not a period / Shall be unsaid for me" (585–87). His words are reminiscent of Jesus' discussion of the law: "Till heaven and earth pass, one jot or one tittle shall in no wise pass from the law" (Matt. v, 18; "Matt. v. 17, etc." cited in *CD*, YP VI, p. 531). The chastity described by the brother is derived from the natural law and has a parallel in the Hebrew one. This law is not abrogated by the coming of Jesus, but rather he and his love fulfill it. Milton, in his discussion of the law in *Christian Doctrine*, clearly understands charity as the fulfillment of the law. He quotes Jesus' words: *"on these two commandments,* that is, those which concern love for God and for our neighbour, *all the law and the prophets depend"* (YP VI, p. 532). Elsewhere in the same book, he writes that the overriding motive for keeping the law must be charity (p. 640). Similarly, chastity is not undermined by charity but is completed by it. Not a dot will be removed from either the Hebrew or the natural law, but both will be transformed by charity.

Difficulties naturally arise from the interweaving of the corporeal and the spiritual. On an allegorical level, Milton asks whether chastity or charity provides better protection against the devil, personified as a potential rapist. But allegory cannot be turned back into physical reality, and engaging in such a practice is dangerous; neither chastity nor charity provides adequate protection against rape. Milton seems to caution against this reversal. The irony in the older brother's naïveté comes from Milton's recognition of the difference between the two spheres and the elder brother's problematic confusion of them. His sister's comment that Comus can touch her body, but not her mind (663–64), and her reference to her body as "this corporal rind" (664) acknowledge that the key concern of the masque has moved into a spiritual dimension, away from the very real physical concerns of rape.[21]

In the sphere of theological allegory, preredemptive chastity does afford a modicum of protection to the Lady, but it is insufficient. She does not submit to drink Comus's potion, for she possesses a "well-govern'd and wise appetite" (705) and lives according to Nature's "sober laws, / And holy dictate of spare Temperance" (766–67). But, although she has the strength not to drink, Comus is able to bind her in "stony fetters fixt and motionless" (819). The stone tablets (*CD*, YP VI, p. 524; 2 Cor. iii, 3) of a law without charity are recalled. The Spirit of God enables a living response: *"for the letter kills, but the spirit gives life"* (*CD*, YP VI, p. 524; 2 Cor. iii, 6). While the law is the Lady's defense, or alternative to Comus's potion, it does not offer freedom. Chastity must be supported by charity for the attainment of this goal.

Grace, which brings with it charity and freedom, is achieved in two distinct stages in *Comus*. The Attendant Spirit, sent from Jove, has the function of drawing the children to the saving and liberating power of haemony and of Sabrina. Instead of a sword, he counsels the brothers to take up spiritual arms. His offering is a gift from a young shepherd lad "skill'd / In every virtuous plant and healing herb" (620–21). This young shepherd is a true shepherd, for he gives the Spirit a healing leaf "of *divine* effect" (630; my emphasis). It is of more effect than moly, the magic herb given to Odysseus by Hermes to protect him from the charms of Circe, which "was often allegorized in the Renaissance as temperance or prudence."[22] The name of the leaf is haemony and one derivation suggested by the *Oxford English Dictionary* is *haemonia*, or blood-red. The most obvious allegorical interpretation is Christ's blood.

While the derivation from *haemonia* is dismissed by some interpreters who claim it does not fit the description of the plant, it would seem that the match is more than obvious.[23] The following argument has been made by numerous critics with slight variations. In this discussion, I will follow their lead and also introduce some further understanding of Milton's allusions, particularly with regard to the root. This "small unsightly root / . . . of divine effect" (629–30) can be understood with reference to the well known description of the suffering servant in Isaiah liii, 2: "For he shall grow up before him as a tender plant, and as a root out of dry ground; he hath no form nor comeliness and when we shall see him, there is no beauty that we should desire him."[24] In Christian theology, the suffering servant is clearly identified with Jesus. In *Paradise Lost*, the Father identifies the Son as "a second root" (III, 288) into which the guilty will be transplanted and so receive new life. Milton is closely following Saint Paul's development of this image in the epistle to the Romans. Paul tells the branches, those who have been grafted into the church, not to be proud of their own righteousness: "But if thou boast, thou bearest not the root, but the root thee" (Rom. xi, 18).[25] This is the truth which the children, lost in the woods, have forgotten—they must rely on Christ's virtue. Cedric Brown's reading of *haemony* as "the word of God" is helpful in understanding this image, but it must be extended by recognizing the Bible's identification of Christ with the word of God (John i).[26] The children are not simply functioning without God's truth; they are without Christ. The Spirit further describes the plant: "The leaf was darkish, and had prickles on it, / But in another Country, as he said, / Bore a bright golden flow'r" (631–33). It does not demand overreading to conceive of a darkish leaf being the hue of blood. The prickles bring to mind the crown of thorns, and the golden flower recalls the crown of glory. The Spirit's comment that haemony is of more effect than moly is the crux of the mask; Christ's love is worth more than chastity.

With Christ's blood, figured as haemony, the brothers are able to assault and triumph over Comus. Although they win the battle, Comus, like the devil after Christ's crucifixion, is not killed, but is still at liberty to wreak harm. The "stony fetters" (819) of the Lady cannot, however, be freed until she receives baptism, the second opportunity of grace offered to her. Although it is not conventional, the baptismal significance of Sabrina and her triple sprinkling (in the name of the Father, the Son, and the Holy Ghost) is recognizable:

> Thus I sprinkle on thy breast
> Drops that from my fountain pure
> I have kept of precious cure,
> Thrice upon thy finger's tip,
> Thrice upon thy rubied lip. (911–15)[27]

Once these parts are thrice sprinkled, the Lady is able to follow the greatest commandment, which is "to love the Lord thy God with all thy heart, and with all thy soul [her breast], and with all thy strength [the action of her fingers], and with all thy mind [expressed through her lips]" (Luke x, 27). "Ensnared chastity" (909) becomes a free chastity founded on charity. While Milton in *Christian Doctrine* prefers immersion to sprinkling (550), the parallel to Milton's concept of baptism is striking in his preference for running water:

AT BAPTISM THE BODIES OF BELIEVERS WHO PLEDGE THEMSELVES TO PURITY OF LIFE ARE IMMERSED IN RUNNING WATER. THIS IS TO SIGNIFY OUR REGENERATION THROUGH THE HOLY SPIRIT AND ALSO OUR UNION WITH CHRIST THROUGH HIS DEATH, BURIAL AND RESUR-RECTION. (YP VI, p. 544)[28]

If this scene truly does represent a baptism, it is worth noting that, while all three children were protected by haemony, only the eldest is sprinkled by Sabrina, which is consistent with Milton's Anabaptist stance against the baptism of infants and children (*CD,* YP VI, pp. 544–52). The Lady has been tested and found faithful. She fully declares against Comus and by doing so pledges herself to "PURITY OF LIFE" (p. 544). She is then ready for baptism.

This preparation for baptism may be seen in the Lady's transformation from a reliance on the law of nature to a dependence on charity, as evidenced in her speech while enchained by Comus. In her final and lengthy soliloquy, she begins by asserting her adherence to Nature's sober laws and by accusing Comus of transgressing them. Her speech then becomes self-reflexive: "Shall I go on? / Or have I said enough?" (779–80). Her words mirror a change in her spiritual progression. She goes on, realizing that her speech has been insufficient, and moves beyond her own chastity to the "Sun-clad power of Chastity" (782). No longer is chastity lit up by its own light; it is instead clothed and illuminated by the "sun of righteousness" (Mal. iv, 2). Comus recognizes this transformation and no longer attributes her speech only to philosophy. Rather, he says, "She fables not, I feel that I do fear / Her words set off by some superior power" (800–01).

Evidence for a scheme of progression appears in the words of the Spirit after the Lady has been set free: "Come Lady, while Heaven lends us grace, / Let us fly this cursed place" (938–39). The Spirit remains the children's "faithful guide" (944) until they come to their "Father's residence" (947) in "holier ground" (943). At this point, the allegory operates on more obvious ground as the children progress toward heaven where they are presented as "Three fair branches" (969), not only of the family tree, but more significantly of the Christian tree of which Christ is the root.

The activity of the Attendant Spirit suggests Milton's conception of the Holy Spirit. He has been dispatched "by quick command from Sovran *Jove*" (41) to help them find their way through the "perplex't paths" (37) of the wood and to defend them.[29] In *Paradise Lost*, Milton describes the comforter:

> His Spirit within them, and the Law of Faith
> Working through love, upon their hearts shall write,
> To guide them in all truth, and also arm
> With spiritual Armor, able to resist
> *Satan's* assaults
>
> . . . .
>
> Baptiz'd, shall them with wondrous gifts endue.   (XII, 488–92, 500)

The spirit in *Comus* teaches the importance of the law of faith working through love, and he both arms and baptizes. In the 1634 manuscript of *Comus*, Milton identifies this actor as "a Guardian spirit, or Daemon," but in 1637 he becomes "the attendant Spirit."[30] This renaming removes the idea of a guardian angel or the connotations of Daemon's homonym, allowing an easier, though still inexplicit, identification with the Christian Holy Spirit.

The epilogue, like the whole mask, is couched in classical mythology, but it does not advocate the pursuit of Greek philosophy. The sensual Venus and Adonis are pictured well below the Celestial Cupid and "his dear *Psyche*" (1005), who are conjoined after Psyche's long wanderings. The eternal union of the soul and love (charity) is the goal of this poem, and this marriage is here pictured in a long tradition of allegorization.[31] The spirit enjoins his listeners to "Love virtue, she alone is free" (1019). Virtue, however, has been shown to be much greater than chastity. It can only emanate from a charity which is derived from God's concern and love: "Or if Virtue feeble were, / Heav'n itself would stoop to her" (1022–23).

The final text to consider in our study of *Comus* is that of society. Why is Milton particularly concerned with chastity? Is his purpose, as Woodhouse suggests, simply to demonstrate the compatibility between philosophic thought and Christianity, or even to show a theological improvement of philosophy? Or is he battling a false conception of chastity? It is this latter possibility which I take up. The body of Milton's work is didactic and polemic, and *Comus* is no exception. His argument is that chastity cannot be substituted for charity, but should emanate from it. Chastity without this ground is worth little or is even false.

Barbara Breasted points out that the sexual scandal for which the Earl of Bridgewater's brother-in-law was executed is relevant to any interpretation of *Comus*. The public display of the chastity of Bridgewater's young daughter would certainly carry overtones when one considers the blemished reputation of very close relatives. Scandal surrounded Bridgewater's wife's older sister, Anne, who was also his stepsister. In 1624, she married the Earl of Castlehaven. Four years later, her eleven-year-old daughter by a previous marriage, Elizabeth, was married to Castlehaven's son, also by a previous marriage. This son, in 1631, brought charges against his father for having Anne and Elizabeth raped, and for practicing sodomy with two male servants. Castlehaven was tried by twenty-one of his peers and eventually executed. In his discussion of the scandal, William B. Hunter notes that when civil war broke out, the record was used as propaganda against the nobility. Very shortly after Castlehaven's execution, his brother-in-law, the Earl of Bridgewater, was named the Lord President of Wales by King Charles. As Hunter suggests, Charles probably made this appointment to show his support for the Bridgewater family.[32]

A mask dealing with chastity, to distinguish his immediate family from the sensational sins of his brother-in-law, would be very appropriate for the occasion of Bridgewater's installation. His own children, contrary to convention, acted out the parts of the three children committed to chastity. But is Milton, as Breasted argues, being complimentary to the earl and his children in that she understands *Comus* as expressing "the family's need to see its last unmarried daughter enact sexual virtue and restraint," or is Milton's purpose, as I will argue, didactic or even polemic?[33]

In *Comus*, Milton differentiates between a true chastity, supported by charity, and one which would allow and cover up scandal. Among the nobility, and propelled by the example of King Charles and his wife, Henrietta Maria, a Neoplatonic cult of chastity flourished. Maryann McGuire describes it: "In most respects, the Caroline love cult differed little from the poetic Platonism that had flourished throughout Europe during the Renaissance. It was a literary style and a style of living and loving—a code of manners, of political behavior, and of courtship. . . . Two attributes, beauty and chastity, make the lady the heroic centre of her world."[34] Masks of this period reflect this love cult. Contemporary Puritans, however, George Sensabaugh argues, "condemned the cult on the ground, first, that all the pious talk of chastity merely served as a disguise for licentious behavior, and, second, that the cult fostered the idolatrous worship of women."[35] Milton clearly believed the latter, and it seems highly probable that he agreed with his fellow Puritans on the former point. While McGuire argues that Milton is distinguishing the Lady's chastity from the false courtly chastity, I suggest that it is precisely such a false chastity that the Lady is initially in danger of possessing. The Lady's chastity, though not completely identifiable with the Platonizing courtly chastity, resembles it. Since her chastity has no firm root in charity, it is not sufficiently distinguished from this cult. By showing the Lady's development of a true chastity through the progression of the mask, Milton offers an implicit critique of all chastity which is not grounded in Christian charity.

The peculiar circumstance of the Bridgewater family and McGuire's discussion of the Caroline love cult make important contributions to our understanding of the appropriateness of discussing chastity in this mask. What, therefore, is the significance of the omission of some key discussions of chastity from the Bridgewater manuscript, which is likely the script that was actually performed? In this copy of *Comus*, the Lady's soliloquy on chastity, which includes her famous substitution, is omitted. It is, however, present both in the original Trinity manuscript and in the printed version of 1637. McGuire does not deal with the changes in the manuscript at all. Hunter attributes this particular change to a performance on an outdoor stage instead of the expected indoor one, where it would have been possible to make a moon appear through artificial lighting. His own discovery of Milton's reliance on the lessons of evening prayer, from the previous day, is ignored by Hunter in this practical explanation for the passage's excision.[36] Why would Milton cross out words so carefully chosen to recall the biblical lesson rather than simply delete the allusion to the moon? The omission may seem relatively unimportant if we read *chastity* and *charity* as synonymous in the text, but this question becomes very significant if the lines are controversial. If Milton's intention is to demonstrate a lack in the Lady's understanding, is it surprising that the lines are deleted? Breasted attributes these cuts to their subject matter, but her argument is rightly criticized by John Creaser for inconsistency: "On the one hand she sees a pointed allusion to the scandal and an 'implicit contrast' between Lady Alice and her debauched cousin Elizabeth; on the other hand, passages apparently most relevant to that contrast—three passages of sexual consciousness, overture, and denial—were cut from the performance, so that memories of the scandal should not be evoked too vividly." In addition, Creaser notes that the haemony passage which is also deleted bears no relation to chastity. If Milton's original intention was criticism rather than adulation, however, Creaser's argument becomes less powerful. The lines concerning chastity may have been censored because they were offensively polemical.[37]

The other absent lines follow a similarly confrontational pattern. The Lady's simile of being "Like a sad Votarist" (189) is omitted, and S. E. Sprott suggests that this passage may have been cut "as Popish."[38] Comus's diatribe against virginity is also missing. These lines imply a criticism of the court: "Beauty is nature's brag, and must be shown / In courts, at feasts, and high solemnities" (745–46). The Spirit's comments on haemony are perhaps the most scathing lines of all that are omitted:

> But in another Country, as he said,
> Bore a bright golden flow'r, but not in this soil:
> Unknown, and like esteem'd, and the dull swain
> Treads on it daily with his clouted shoon,
> And yet more med'cinal is it than that *Moly*
> That *Hermes* once to wise *Ulysses* gave.   (632–37)

Adams comments on these lines that one "does not offhandedly tell the members of a Christian commonwealth that grace is unknown to them." It seems that somebody in 1634 agreed with Adams's sentiment.[39]

Taken together, the deleted passages all point to Milton, or to a concerned friend, perhaps Henry Lawes, having edited the original manuscript to render *Comus* more palatable to Milton's aristocratic patrons. The fact that these passages are evidently critical of court life, and that they were removed, suggests that their controversial nature was recognized in 1634, even though today they are frequently glossed over.[40] When these passages are reintroduced in 1637, Milton continues the Lady's soliloquy: "Shall I go on" (779–99). This continuation enables Milton to show her preparedness for baptism and a strong Christian commitment on the part of the Bridgewaters, thus also appeasing any personal offense Bridgewater might have taken by the reintroduction of the Lady's initial error.

In *Comus*, Milton shows that a self-reliant Platonic chastity can never be adequately substituted for charity. Only a love for God will bring about true virtue. Chastity is a virtue, but, as in 1 Corinthians xiii, 1–3, without charity it is nothing. Milton's mask engages the values espoused by the contemporary drama of his period and the values of court, but it is also didactic. It shows the children learning what true virtue is and demonstrates them finding a virtue which goes beyond superficiality. Milton interrupts his classical mask to introduce a Christian message which is interrupted in turn by Greek philosophy: faith, hope, and *chastity*. Christian imagery, however, insists on entering into the dialogue of the mask: haemony, baptism, grace. *Comus*, despite its classical language, must eventually be interpreted in Christian terms; Psyche and Cupid become Christian allegories. The soul must be engrossed by God's love. Without this Christian interpretation, the play is a meaningless medley of words, dance, and song. Without charity, Milton's mask is nothing.

McMaster University

NOTES

1. *Comus*, 213–15. All references to Milton's poetic works are from *John Milton: Complete Poems and Major Prose,* ed. Merritt Y. Hughes (Indianapolis, 1957). Subsequent citations will appear parenthetically in the text.

2. All quotations of the Bible are from the King James Version.

3. Malcolm Ross, "Milton and the Protestant Aesthetic: The Early Poems," *UTQ* XVII (1948): 355. Woodhouse quips that Ross exchanges "the text of *Comus* for *Pamela*" in *A Variorum Commentary on the Poems of Mr. John Milton: The Minor English Poems,* ed. A.S.P. Woodhouse and Douglas Bush (New York, 1972), vol. II, part 3, p. 808.

4. A.S.P. Woodhouse, "The Argument of Milton's *Comus.*" *UTQ* XI (1941): 46–71. This is followed up by *"Comus Once More," UTQ* XIX (1950): 218–23.

5. *Christian Doctrine,* YP VI, p. 119. All references to Milton's prose will be to *Complete Prose Works of John Milton,* 8 vols., ed. Don M. Wolfe et al. (New Haven, 1953–82), hereafter referred to in the text as YP.

6. William B. Hunter, "The Provenance of the *Christian Doctrine," SEL* XXXII (1992): 129–42, 139.

7. Barbara Lewalski, "Forum: Milton's *Christian Doctrine," SEL* XXXII (1992): 143–66.

8. A different approach is found in William Kerrigan's Freudian reading of *Comus* in *The Sacred Complex: On the Psychogenesis of "Paradise Lost"* (Cambridge, Mass., 1983), pp. 22–72. He finds a disjunction between virginity (chastity) and charity, but his identification of chastity with virginity, and charity with motherhood is limiting and ignores Milton's much larger theological understanding of these terms, which will emerge in this study.

9. Maryann McGuire, *Milton's Puritan Masque* (Athens, Ga.: 1983), p. 138.

10. Georgia Christopher, "The Virginity of Faith: *Comus* as a Reformation Conceit," *ELH* XLIII (1976): 485, 486.

11. Elsewhere in *Christian Doctrine,* Milton writes that "attention to the requirements of charity is given precedence over any written law" (YP VI, p. 532). He cites Romans viii, 10: "charity is the fulfilling of the demands of the law" (pp. 532–33).

12. A. E. Dyson, *Between Two Worlds: Aspects of Literary Form* (London, 1972), p. 29.

13. E.M.W. Tillyard, in *Studies in Milton* (London, 1951), pp. 94–95, comes close to this position: "The play concerns chastity and the Lady is the heroine. Comus advocates incontinence, Acrasia; the Lady advocates abstinence. The Attendant Spirit gives the solution, advocating the Aristotelian middle course, which for the Lady is the right one; and it is marriage."

Despite showing that chastity is not the best response by the Lady, Tillyard does not condemn her but merely contends that her actions are "not final."

14. Susan Felch, "The Intertextuality of *Comus* and Corinthians," *MQ* XXVII (1993): 59–70, without challenging the conventional interpretation of Milton's substitution, argues that the whole of 1 and 2 Corinthians is influential in Milton's composition of the mask.

15. William B. Hunter, *Milton's "Comus": Family Piece* (New York, 1983), p. 30.

16. It is worth noting that Milton specifically identifies this love as charity—*agape*, not *eros*.

17. See also *Tetrachordon*, YP II, p. 708; *Doctrine and Discipline of Divorce*, YP II, pp. 330–31.

18. Christopher, "The Virginity of Faith," 481–82, cites Luther's commentary on Galatians: "The word 'carousing' (*commessatio*), however, comes from the name Comus, who was called the god of festivity and of dissipation by the Greeks."

19. "So glister'd the dire Snake, and into fraud / Led *Eve* our credulous Mother" (IX, 643–44).

20. Rosemond Tuve, *Images and Themes in Five Poems by Milton* (Cambridge, Mass., 1957), p. 148.

21. Leah Marcus, "The Milieu of Milton's *Comus*: Judicial Reform at Ludlow and the Problem of Sexual Assault," *Criticism* XXV (1983): 293–327, relates the political overtones in *Comus* to the rape trial of Margery Evans. The argument of Milton's mask, however, appears to be theological and allegorical, not feminist. For other discussions of Marcus, see John Leonard, "Saying 'No' to Freud: Milton's *A Mask* and Sexual Assault," *MQ* XXV (1991): 129–40, and William Kerrigan, "The Politically Correct *Comus*: A Reply to John Leonard," *MQ* XXVII (1993): 149–55.

22. *John Milton*, ed. Stephen Orgel and Jonathan Goldberg (Oxford, 1990), p. 769.

23. Robert Adams, *Ikon: John Milton and the Modern Critics* (Ithaca, 1955), pp. 1–34, argues that the formalist argument made by Edward Le Comte, "New Light on the 'Haemony' Passage in *Comus*," *PQ* XXI (1942): 283–98, and followed by Cleanth Brooks and John Hardy, *Poems of John Milton: The 1645 Edition with Essays in Analysis* (New York, 1951), pp. 187–234, is implausibly elaborate. A thorough appreciation of all the classical allusions found by these scholars, however, is not necessary for understanding *haemony* as blood (Christ's) in opposition to moly, allegorized as temperance. Some of the readings that follow in my argument are summarised by Woodhouse, *A Variorum Commentary*, p. 929.

24. See also Isaiah xi, 10, Ephesians iii, 17, and Colossians ii, 7.

25. "OF INGRAFTING IN CHRIST, AND ITS EFFECTS" is the subject of chapter 21 of *Christian Doctrine*. Milton writes that "CHARITY AFFECTS THOSE WHO ARE IMPLANTED IN CHRIST" (YP VI, p. 479). He cites John xv, 5: "*I am the vine, and you are the branches*"; and more significantly Ephesians iii, 17: "*that Christ may dwell in your hearts through faith: so that rooted and grounded in charity, etc*" (YP VI, p. 480).

26. Cedric Brown, *John Milton's Aristocratic Entertainments* (Cambridge, 1985), pp. 104–11.

27. Although Milton exhibits subordinationist tendencies later in his life, at all points he shows a respect to the three persons of the Trinity. Especially since *Comus* (1634) is an early work it would be orthodox in its baptismal trinitarian formulation. In *Of Reformation* (1641), Milton invokes all three persons of the Trinity as "one *Tri-personall* GODHEAD" (YP I, p. 614). Even in the much later *Christian Doctrine* (YP VI, p. 544, cited below), Milton mentions the Spirit and the Son in conjunction with baptism.

28. Compare *Paradise Lost*: "Baptising in the profluent stream" (XII, 442).

29. Milton's conception of the Holy Spirit is far too complex to discuss here. It should

be noted, however, that this dispatch by "Sovran *Jove*" is not incompatible with the subordinationist tendency of *Christian Doctrine*.

30. S. E. Sprott, *A Maske: The Earlier Versions* (Toronto, 1973), pp. 42–43.

31. This reading is somewhat dependent upon J. H. Hanford: "The pagan image of the love of a mortal youth for a goddess draws insensibly nearer to the truth in the reversed symbol of the union of the God of love himself with Psyche, the human soul," cited by Woodhouse, "Argument," 65.

32. Barbara Breasted, "*Comus* and the Castlehaven Scandal," in *Milton Studies* III, ed. James D. Simmonds (Pittsburgh, 1971), pp. 201–24; Hunter, *Milton's "Comus,"* p. 28.

33. Breasted, "*Comus* and the Castlehaven Scandal," p. 202.

34. McGuire, *Milton's Puritan Masque*, pp. 131–32.

35. Sensabaugh cited in ibid., p. 135. Compare *Eikonoklastes:* "Examples are not farr to seek, how great mischeif and dishonour hath befall'n to Nations under the Government of effeminate and Uxorious Magistrates. Who being themselves govern'd and overswaid at home under a Feminine usurpation, cannot but be farr short of spirit and autority without dores, to govern a whole Nation" (YP III, p. 421). Or see God's chastisement of Adam in *Paradise Lost* X, 144–56.

36. Hunter, *Milton's "Comus,"* p. 55.

37. John Creaser, "Milton's *Comus:* The Irrelevance of the Castlehaven Scandal," *MQ* XXI (1987): 27, 29.

38. Sprott, *A Maske*, p. 22.

39. Adams, *Ikon*, p. 13. Brown, *John Milton's Aristocratic Entertainments*, p. 113, makes a similar observation.

40. Leah Marcus's anti-Laudian reading of *Comus* in *The Politics of Mirth: Jonson, Herrick, Milton, Marvell, and the Defense of Old Holiday Pastimes* (Chicago, 1986), suggests further reasons for the cuts. In light of jurisdictional contention between Bridgewater and Archbishop Laud, Marcus argues that *Comus* was designed "to encourage the Earl in his resistance to Laud and the central ecclesiastical authority" (177). Her identification of a subtle political critique of the Catholicism of the court would also comprehend the court's idealization of a false chastity. Marcus explains the changes in the text through her observation that, by 1637, the rift between Laud and Bridgewater was so open as to make caution superfluous.

THE WRITING POET:
THE DESCENT FROM SONG IN
THE POEMS OF MR. JOHN MILTON,
BOTH ENGLISH AND LATIN (1645)

Randall Ingram

T HE RECENT DEVELOPMENT of media that provide alternates to print have focused new attention on "the book." Jerome J. McGann, for instance, calls for more bibliographically sensitive reading, especially of poetry: "We must turn our attention to much more than the formal and linguistic features of poems or other imaginative fictions. We must attend to textual materials which are not regularly studied by those interested in 'poetry': to typefaces, bindings, book prices, page format, and all those textual phenomena usually regarded as (at best) peripheral to 'poetry' or 'the text as such.' " By juxtaposing bibliographic data and "formal and linguistic features," McGann implies a contrast between a formalist approach to poetry and bibliographically informed reading. Of course, Milton's critics have long read his books *as* books, and the critical histories of Milton's books indicate that careful attention to McGann's "bibliographic codes" often extends rather than disrupts formalism; the book can replace the poem as a self-contained object of close reading. For example, in his important reading of *The Poems of Mr. John Milton, Both English and Latin* (1645), a reading of both linguistic and bibliographic features that preceded McGann's admonition by more than twenty-five years, Louis L. Martz attempts to establish the coherence of *Poems,* arguing that "Milton's original arrangement creates the growing awareness of a guiding, central purpose that in turn gives the volume an impressive and peculiar sense of wholeness. In order to regain the significant integrity of the volume one must, now and then, go back to the original." Martz's reading represents an expansion of formalism, an analysis of "wholeness" and "integrity" in an entire book rather than in a single poem.[1]

But such an approach to seventeenth-century books imports the assumptions of late print into the study of early printed texts by objectifying books that were, for their authors, publishers, and readers, far less stable and far less sure of their format than later books. Early modern books often contain, as Walter J. Ong and Eric Havelock have chronicled, vestiges of orality that were erased, imperfectly, in later books, and this orality continually challenges readings of individual poems or entire books as fixed, spatial objects. Ong states that "oral habits of thought and expression" remained "in Tudor England some two thousand years after Plato's campaign against oral poets. They were effectively obliterated in English, for the most part, only with the Romantic Movement two centuries later." Ong argues that poetry continues even longer to imply "a feeling that one writing is actually speaking aloud." Although critical discussion of the "speakers" of poems recognizes the remnants of orality lingering even in the most recent poetry, the transition that Ong describes can be traced in such forms as the sonnet, which shifts from the "little songs" of quattrocento Italy to the "pretty rooms" of the English Renaissance, the spatial metaphor befitting the transmission of sonnets in manuscript and print. Milton's *Poems* represents this transition in miniature, as one poet, gradually and grudgingly, comes to accept the less powerful modes of writing and print.[2]

Usually, however, Milton's *Poems,* a book with "an impressive and peculiar sense of wholeness," is said to represent a different transition. The overwhelming majority of critics who discuss Milton's first book of poetry agree that it presents a "rising poet" to an international audience. The image of the "rising poet," which Martz uses for the title of his essay on *Poems,* occurs in the source of the book's famous motto: "Baccare frontem / Cingite, ne vati noceat mala lingua futuro" ("Encircle my brow with fragrant plants so that no evil tongue may harm the future bard") (Virgil, Eclog. 7).[3] Critics regularly cite the motto's emphasis on futurity and its Virgilian source, reading the motto, and the book itself, as a promise of the epic greatness to come. For critics like Richard Halpern, the volume of 1645, coherent in itself, is also part of a "coherent poetic *career*":

As the sonnets on his blindness (for instance) suggest, Milton tends to view himself from the projected point of a later reckoning. Almost all of the early poems insist on their place within a developing order, gesturing obscurely toward the accomplishment of some greater work or task. . . . The 1645 *Poems* opens with an epigraph in which Milton declares himself a "future bard," and thus at a stroke converts the entire contents of the volume into elements in a scheme of self-preparation.

For Halpern, the motto not only signifies the single-mindedness of the book, it is a "stroke" that "converts the entire contents" into a unified presentation of a poetic career. Even when they attempt to read the motto without retrospective recourse to the later works—"to understand Milton's actions of 1645," John K. Hale warns, "we had better play down our hindsight knowl-

edge of 1667"—critics generally invoke the motto to attribute an ambitious integrity to *Poems*.[4]

But what about the poet's vulnerability to an "evil tongue"? Though Martz quotes more fully from the eclogue, claiming that "the whole context is essential," he does so only to point out how neatly the motto anticipates the Virgilian themes of *Poems* and how it typifies the unity of the volume.[5] And yet the anxiety of the motto seems undeniable. The wreath here does not clearly denote the poetic triumph or supreme confidence of a rising poet; it is instead the talismanic safeguard of a nervous poet. The motto's imperative, *cingite,* asks for protection within an emblematic embrace. Only a readership biased by Milton's persistent popular image as a serenely self-assured titan could discuss the words *vati* and *futuro* at such length while overlooking the motto's main verbs: "Encircle so that I will not be harmed." The quotation from Virgil's seventh eclogue provides a fitting motto for *Poems,* not because both motto and book display a careerist integrity, but because the fearful image of an "evil tongue" anticipates the potency that characterizes oral utterance in the volume and the published poet's uneasy awareness of his medium's relative weakness. *Poems* complicates Milton's poetic annunciation because, especially in the English poems, it continually raises doubts about its format. This book questions books, distrusting the capacity of writing and print to capture what *At a Solemn Music* calls "divine sounds."

I. "Deliberate Sabotage"

A reader who opens Milton's *Poems* of 1645 will see, before its title page or the publisher's letter to the reader, its frontispiece, one of the most frequently discussed bibliographic details of the seventeenth century. The frontispiece features an engraving of Milton in academic robes, sitting before a window. Below the engraving is a quatrain in Greek, traditionally attributed to Milton, that invites readers to laugh at the engraver's ineptitude. David Masson's translation of the quatrain reads:

> That an unskilful hand had carved this print
> You'd say at once, seeing the living face;
> But, finding here no jot of me, my friends,
> Laugh at this botching artist's mis-attempt.

Martz describes the engraving in detail and links the frontispiece to the "theme" of "the entire volume":

The entire volume strives to create a tribute to a youthful era now past—not only the poet's own youth, but a state of mind, a point of view, ways of writing, ways of living, an old culture and outlook now shattered by the pressures of maturity and by the actions of political man. Even the frontispiece, by William Marshall, attempts to set this theme. The aim of the engraving is clearly to present the youthful poet surrounded by the Muses, with a curtain in the background lifted to reveal a pastoral landscape of meadows and trees, where a shepherd is piping in the shade, while a shepherd and a shepherdess are dancing on the lawn. The legend around the portrait identifies it as a picture of the poet in his twenty-first year—but in fact the portrait presents the harsh and crabbed image of a man who might be forty or fifty! Marshall could do better than this, as his engraving of the youthful Donne testifies; one almost suspects deliberate sabotage here.

Part of Marshall's engraving fits Martz's reading of the entire volume (the signs of nostalgic pastoral), and part does not (the "harsh and crabbed image" of the poet), leading him—or one—almost to suppose that Marshall intended to undermine the poetic authority that the volume ostensibly claims for Milton. Martz's baffled disappointment ("Marshall could do better than this") shows his discomfort with a frontispiece that mocks the poet, the engraver, and frontispieces in general. Since he cannot reconcile Marshall's engraving with his understanding of Milton's aims in *Poems,* Martz characterizes the engraving as an attempt to subvert those aims.[6]

Gary Spear also explores the tensions between the engraving and the quatrain, which figure, on a small scale, the struggle between early modern authors and countless other agents. Spear's reading parallels the work of critics like Paul Werstine who have begun to emphasize the contributions of "multiple and dispersed agencies" to Renaissance dramatic texts. Spear accordingly considers the frontispiece "a textual place where the materiality of authority and authorial identity appear as the *effects of the material circumstances* of textual production." Spear disagrees with Martz's reading of the frontispiece, making the important point that Martz attributes too much authorial autonomy to Milton: "Martz's formalist imperative compels him to see all of the features of the text including the frontispiece as a related, coherent, whole. Underlying this is the figure of Milton the author as completely autonomous: 'Milton designed his book with care.'" According to Spear, Milton attempts to prescribe the reading of a page not usually within the control of an early modern author—"The Greek epigram registers Milton's attempt to assert his own identity in this arena of authorial creation"—and Spear concludes that in early seventeenth-century England, "public identity was not always within the author's control."[7]

A belief that Milton sought to present a consistent, stable poetic identity in *Poems* informs both Martz's and Spear's readings of the frontispiece. Both

assume that Milton wrote the quatrain to wrest depiction of himself from Marshall and that, as Spear puts it, "Since apparently neither Moseley [publisher of *Poems*] nor Marshall could translate it, Marshall ended up copying the character of the epigram without realizing the critical thrust of the message." Both Martz and Spear divide elements of the frontispiece between contending authors, presuming that Milton must have wanted a more accurate or flattering representation of himself and that Marshall, more craftsman than artist, must have transcribed without understanding a self-indictment in Greek. But the frontispiece does in a page what the volume does in full: it destabilizes the authority of *Poems* by undercutting the nascent conventions of print, in this case the engravings of authors that had become a conventional feature of printed literary works. Spear argues that the opening pages of the book "deconstruct the very poetic authority that it is their explicit purpose to represent," but such an argument assumes that Milton, like Jonson before him, "constructed" his authority by manipulating the semiotics of early printed books, when in fact *Poems* portrays print itself as an enormous obstacle to his authority. The compatibility of the frontispiece with the book that follows suggests that a collaborative model of authorship might better describe the engraving and the quatrain of the frontispiece: Milton, Moseley, and Marshall created a book that deliberately sabotages any reading of it as a hypostatized representation of a poet's power.[8]

The pattern established by the engraving and the quatrain of the frontispiece, a pattern of claiming the authority associated with printed books for the *Poems* then disavowing it, recurs on the next page of the book, the title page. A number of the page's features assert the book's legitimacy: it identifies an author, makes the standard claim that the poems have been "Printed by his true Copies," and states the book's compliance with prevailing laws that regulated publication, "Printed and publish'd according to ORDER," the upper-case letters of the final word reinforcing the assurance that all is in ORDER. Other features dispute the book's authority, particularly the advertisement at the center of the page:

> The SONGS were set in Musick by
> Mr. HENRY LAWES Gentleman of
> the KINGS Chappel, and one
> of His MAIESTIES
> Private Musick.

Some critics, including Martz, have expressed surprise that this bit of marketing on the title page of Milton's first book of poems uses associations, however tertiary, with royalty to tantalize potential buyers.[9] More surprising, though, is that these words, set in the heart of the page that should proclaim the book's accurate representation of the poet's art, acknowledge that the "SONGS" of the volume were "set in Musick" before they were set in print, indicating that a musician can offer an alternative, if not a better, representation of the "SONGS." Like the frontispiece, which points away from the conventional engraving of the author to "the living face," the title page points away from the printed poems to the poems "set in Musick." This pointing away from writing and print to speech and singing is a gesture of "deliberate sabotage" that the *Poems* continually reenacts, perhaps most spectacularly in the book's first poem, *On the Morning of Christ's Nativity*.

II. BREATH AND LETTER

In his preface to the *Poems,* addressed to "the reader," Humphrey Moseley describes the book as a "birth":

> The Authors more peculiar excellency in these studies was too well known to conceal his Papers, or to keep me from attempting to sollicit them from him. Let the event guide it self which way it will, I shall deserve of the age, by bringing into the Light as true a Birth, as the Muses have brought forth since our famous Spencer wrote; whose Poems in these English ones are as rarely imitated, as sweetly excell'd. Reader if thou art Eagle-eied to censure their worth, I am not fearful to expose them to thy exactest perusal.

Moseley portrays himself as a midwife, "bringing into the Light" what was "too well known to conceal." As an established publisher with a deep intellectual and material investment in print, Moseley imagines publication in strikingly visual terms, as he exposes the *Poems* to the "exactest perusal" of "Eagle-eied" readers. For Moseley, the *Poems* are a set of stable, printed works that he can reveal to the scrutiny of discerning readers.

As the first poem of the book, *On the Morning of Christ's Nativity* continues the birth imagery of Moseley's preface, employs a stanza form that, in keeping with Moseley's claim, shows the influence of Spenser, and, as a number of critics have suggested, implies a parallel between Christ's birth and Milton's own poetic nativity.[10] But the poem, like many of the English poems in the volume, undermines the print-based visual imagery of Moseley's preface, offering instead poetry that attempts to break through the limits of a printed page by emphasizing aural over visual art, song over writing. The references to song begin almost as soon as the poem itself begins. Recalling that "the holy sages once did sing" of the Nativity (5), the poet invokes his "Heav'nly Muse":

> Say Heav'nly Muse, shall not thy sacred vein
> Afford a present to the Infant God?

Hast thou no vers, no hymn, or solemn strein,
To welcom him to this his new abode . . . ?   (15–18)

The current silence of the "holy sages," the Old Testament prophets who now only "sing" in printed Scripture, and the silence of the Divine ("Infant," being derived from *infans*, Latin for "unspeaking") create the need for the poet's song. In the next stanza, the Magi, reduced to "Wisards," provide an additional competitive motive for singing, and the poet implores his Muse in the last lines of the prologue: "Have thou the honour first, thy Lord to greet, / And joyn thy voice unto the Angel Quire, / From out his secret Altar toucht with hallow'd fire" (26–28). The last line clearly alludes to Isaiah vi, 6–7: "Then flew one of the Seraphims unto me, having a live coal in his hand, which he had taken with tongs from off the altar: And he laid it upon my mouth, and said, Lo, this hath touched thy lips; and thine iniquity is taken away, and thy sin is purged." The emphasis on lips and speech is repeated in Milton's other famous allusion to the same verses, a passage from *The Reason of Church-Government* in which Milton expresses his hope of composing "a true poem." In that passage, Milton contrasts hands, "the pen of some vulgar amorist," and mouths, the purified lips of the prophet/poet.[11] The opening stanzas of the Nativity ode similarly privilege song, as they struggle against the expectations set up by the format of the printed book generally and by Moseley's preface specifically: Moseley promised to reveal something to the reader's sight, but the poet appeals overwhelmingly to hearing.

Walter Ong outlines how the shift from orality and writing to print entailed a shift from "hearing-dominance" to "sight-dominance": "Hearing rather than sight had dominated the older noetic world in significant ways, even after writing was deeply interiorized. Manuscript culture in the west remained always marginally oral." Ong argues that print finally eliminated the residual orality of manuscript culture: "Eventually, however, print replaced the lingering hearing-dominance in the world of thought and expression with the sight-dominance which had its beginnings with writing but could not flourish with the support of writing alone." The Nativity ode strains against its format because, as critics have long noticed, hearing rather than sight dominates "The Hymn." Sigmund Gottfried Spaeth concludes that "from beginning to end, the Nativity Hymn is built up on suggestions of sound. Its lyric effectiveness lies largely in this preference of the audible to the visible." Spaeth divides "The Hymn" into three parts. The first, exemplified by the fourth and fifth stanzas, "creates a background of complete silence": "But peacefull was the night / Wherin the Prince of light / His

raign of peace upon the earth began" (61–63). The celestial music announcing Christ's coming breaks the silence in the ninth stanza:

> When such musick sweet
> Their [the shepherds'] hearts and ears did greet,
>   As never was by mortall finger strook,
> Divinely-warbled voice
> Answering the stringed noise
>   As all their souls in blissfull rapture took:
> The Air such pleasure loth to lose,
> With thousand echo's still prolongs each heav'nly close.   (93–100)

The celestial music, Spaeth observes, is interrupted by the defeat of the
pagan deities which is "portrayed chiefly by the silencing of characteristic
sounds connected with their rites." After stanza xix announces that "The
Oracles are dumm" (173), the vanquished deities raise a "loud lament" of
"weeping" and "sighing" in stanza cc. The cacophony continues throughout
the retreat of "the damned crew" (228); both their ringing "Cymbals" (208)
and their singing "Timbrel'd Anthems dark" (219) are dismissed as "in
vain." But, as Catherine Belsey points out, the Nativity ode is not simply a
description of sounds; it claims itself to be a sound, a voice joined to "the
Angel Quire": "The 'Ode' is to be part of the angelic consort, a voice in
the divine polyphony which is the bond between God and human beings,
the union of heaven and earth." Moreover, the poem not only, as Spaeth
argues, prefers "the audible to the visible," the introduction of visual imagery actually forces the end of the poem: "But see the Virgin blest, / Hath
laid her babe to rest. / Time is our tedious Song should here have ending"
(237–39). Once the seeing starts, the singing stops, emphasizing with finality
the antithetical relation between song and the printed poem that reveals a
scene to the reader's eyes.[12]

The brief picture of a "Virgin" laying "her Babe to rest" brings the
Nativity ode as close as it comes to what Martz has influentially described
as "the poetry of meditation." In fact, Martz selects the Nativity ode as an
instructive contrast to that poetry, and he uses it to delineate the differences
between "the spirituality of English Puritanism and the spirituality of the
Counter Reformation." Martz remarks that in the Nativity ode, "Milton puts
last the concrete scene which would normally begin a Catholic meditation
on this subject." He compares the Nativity ode to Crashaw's "Sung as by
the Shepherds," a poem thoroughly informed by visual imagery: "Crashaw,
through the shepherds, makes himself intimately present at the manger-
scene: 'We saw,' 'I saw'—those repeated words provide the dramatic focus
and create an intimate application of senses to the scene." Although he does

not discuss it at length, Martz seems to recognize the emphasis on visualization in meditative literature. Ignatius and the authors of meditative treatises who preceded and succeeded him stress the application of all the senses, but meditation often privileges visual imagery, as the visualized birth of Christ replaces visually apprehended text describing the birth. Meditative literature and the poetry based on it generally attempt to transport the meditator to a specific scene, but the performative song of the Nativity ode brings the scene to the singer. "The Hymn," united with the song of "the Angel Quire," can, as Belsey puts it, make all time "simultaneously present," from creation to the last judgment:

> XIV.
> For if such holy Song
> Enwrap our fancy long,
>   Time will run back, and fetch the age of gold,
> And speckl'd vanity
> Will sicken soon and die,
>   And leprous sin will melt from earthly mould,
> And Hell it self will pass away
> And leave her dolorous mansions to the peering day.
>
> XV.
> Yea Truth, and Justice then
> Will down return to men.   (133–42)

Meditative poems often record exploration of the "inner world" opened by writing and print, but the singer of the Nativity ode shapes the outer world—indeed, the cosmos—through the potent orality of "holy Song."[13]

The companion poem to the Nativity ode, *The Passion*, begins with the same emphasis on song and refers directly to the ode:

> Ere-while of Musick, and Ethereal mirth,
> Wherwith the stage of Ayr and Earth did ring,
> And joyous news of heav'nly Infants birth,
> My muse with Angels did divide to sing.   (1–4)

After this reminder of the earlier song, the poet prepares for sadder music: "For now to sorrow must I tune my song, / And set my Harpe to notes of saddest wo" (8–9). The poet looks for appropriate musical instruments in the fourth stanza—"Me softer airs befit, and softer strings, / Of Lute, or Viol still, more apt for mournful things" (27–28)—but the poem soon stops describing itself as a song. By the end of the fifth stanza, the "Muse" disappeared, as has the pretense of "Ethereal" song, and an "I" appears to lament the difficulties of writing: "The leaves should all be black wheron I write, /

And letters where my tears have washt a wannish white" (34–35). Harold Bloom's Milton is the consummate "strong poet," a source of tremendous anxiety for his successors, but this "I" is himself anxious. As he imagines pages blackened to suit his grief and blackened by the ink of his predecessors, he can only imagine a writing that is also a painful erasing. After the opening stanzas, the poem is agonizingly aware of itself as a written text. William R. Parker contends that Milton *"was writing a poem about himself writing a poem; in every stanza except the third he had described himself in the process of composition."*[14]

If the third stanza does not mention the process of writing the poem, it does begin a series of visual images that bear a much closer resemblance to other meditative poems than to the Nativity ode: "He sov'ran Priest stooping his regall head / That dropt with odorous oil down his fair eyes" (15–16). The poem continues to foreground "holy vision"; the sixth stanza, for instance, depicts one of the "scenes" which "confine my roving vers" (22):

> See see the Chariot, and those rushing wheels,
> That whirl'd the Prophet up at *Chebar* flood,
> My spirit som transporting *Cherub* feels,
> To bear me where the Towers of Salem stood,
> Once glorious Towers, now sunk in guiltles blood;
>   There doth my soul in holy vision sit
> In pensive trance, and anguish, and ecstatick fit.   (36–42)

This stanza clearly diverges from the Nativity ode's precedent: it enjoins readers to "see see" rather than hear; the poet of *The Passion* is transported to the site of the Crucifixion by the chariot "that whirl'd" Ezekial, but the song of the Nativity ode brings the familiar scene, and all history, to the present; the poet of *The Passion* sits in silence, "in holy vision," "in pensive trance," writing rather than singing. William Shullenberger concisely summarizes the poet's struggle: "Music and masquelike ritual are abandoned for the attempt to compose an imaginative space in which the poet can witness the Passion." The poet never situates himself adequately to view the Passion, even though, as Shullenberger states, "Milton resorts to virtually every strategy in the poetic repertoire in order to broach his subject."[15] After eight stanzas the poem stops abruptly: *"This Subject the Author finding to be above the years he had, when he wrote it, and nothing satisfi'd with what was begun, left it unfinisht."*

The inclusion of this fragment in *Poems* is perplexing, especially, as Martz notes, because Milton would have had other poems available for the collection, "the more interesting and at least completed English poems that he added in 1673: the poem *On the Death of a Fair Infant,* and the lines from the *Vacation Exercise."* Martz proposes that *The Passion* serves "a clear function" in the book: "to stress the immaturity of these opening pieces, to suggest the ambitious young man outreaching his powers, and achieving poetical success only when he can subject his muse to some deliberate limitation."[16] The scope of *The Passion* seems severely circumscribed, however—"These latter scenes confine my roving vers, / To this Horizon is my *Phoebus* bound" (22–23)—whereas the Nativity ode ranges freely from the beginning of human history to its end. A surfeit, rather than a lack, of "deliberate limitation" stifles the poem. *The Passion* makes explicit what is implicit in the Nativity ode: the struggle against the limits of writing. *The Passion* must end because it is smothered by the material difficulties of writing, imagined as writing on surfaces that resist inscription, black pages and rock, and because it refuses an iconic visual representation of the suffering Christ that the medium seems to encourage. Including *The Passion* discovers a fear that the Nativity ode attempts to suppress, namely, that writing will rob the poet of his poem.

Although *Poems* features no shaped poems like Herbert's "Easter Wings" or Herrick's "Pillar of Fame," works comfortable with the new visual and poetic potential of typography, other English poems, such as *On Shakespeare* and the epitaphs for Hobson, reflect less anxiety than the Nativity ode and *The Passion* about their status as written and printed texts. Crossing the divide of *Poems* into the Latin poems, readers encounter poems that, unlike the Nativity ode or *The Passion,* accept their format, distanced from the power of song.

III. BOTH ENGLISH AND LATIN

Poems is, as Milton called it in his ode addressed to John Rouse, a "twin book," a book of English followed by a book of Latin poems, each complete with its own title page, commendatory poems, and pagination. Though miscellanies of poems in both English and Latin had been published often, such as *Justa Eduardo King* in which *Lycidas* first appeared, Milton's was the first book by a single author to include poems, as the title page announces, "BOTH / ENGLISH and LATIN" by a single author.[17] Despite the title of the book and Milton's reference in the Latin poem to Rouse, critical discussions of *Poems* often slight the Latin works. The Noel Douglas Replicas facsimile edition of *Poems,* published in 1926, omits the Latin poems without explanation. Cleanth Brooks and John Edward Hardy's *Poems of Mr. John Milton: The 1645 Edition with Essays in Analysis* also does not reproduce the Latin poems, even though Brooks and Hardy stress the importance of *Poems* as a whole: "The book is, in the first place, an edition of the poems which Milton chose to print in 1645. That volume was, needless to say, an important one, and from the viewpoint of literary history, there are clear reasons for preserving and emphasizing it as a volume in its own right, keeping the arrangement which Milton himself made." Brooks and Hardy include the Italian poems from the English half of *Poems*, but leave out the Latin and Greek poems that made up the second half "for obvious reasons": "Most readers simply lack the equipment to handle them as poetry, and in this edition we are interested primarily in poetry."[18] Whatever the insensitivities of twentieth-century readers to the nuances of seventeenth-century Latin poetry, and whatever the aesthetic weaknesses of the *Poemata*, the Latin works can disturb readings of *Poems* as the annunciation of a "rising poet"; the problems they raise for paradigmatic narratives of Milton's career have doubtless contributed to the Latin poems' omission from some discussions of Milton's first book of poetry.

Since Renaissance Latin developed primarily, though by no means exclusively, as a written language, it should probably come as no surprise that the *Poemata* consistently refer to themselves as written documents, most often letters. Ong's description of learned Latin—"devoid of baby-talk, insulated from the earliest life of childhood where language has its deepest psychic roots, a first language to none of its users, pronounced across Europe in often mutually unintelligible ways but always written the same way"[19]—contrasts sharply with Milton's greeting to English in the *Vacation Exercise*, added to the *Poems* of 1673:

> Hail native Language, that by sinews weak
> Didst move my first endeavouring tongue to speak,
> And mad'st imperfect words with childish tripps,
> Half unpronounc't, slide thorough my infant-lipps,
> Driving dum silence from the portal dore
> Where he had mutely sate two years before.   (1–6)

Here Milton associates English with an orality that precedes writing, but in the *Poemata* he associates Latin with conspicuously written texts. The singer of the Nativity ode claims for himself the oral force of prophetic song, but the Latin poems tend to sever song from poem. *Ad Leonoram Romeae Canentem (To Leonora, Singing at Rome)*, provides a clear instance of the separation of written texts and heavenly song in the *Poemata*:

> Angleus unicuique suus (sic credite gentes)
> Obtigit aethereis ales ab ordinibus.
> Quid mirum, Leonora, tibi si gloria maior,
> Nam tua praesentem vox sonat ipsa Deum.

Aut Deus, aut vacui certe mens tertia caeli
Pertua secreto guttura serpit agens;
Serpit agens, facilisque docet mortalia corda
Sensim immortali assuescere posse sono.
Quod si cuncta quidem Deus est, per cunctaque fusus,
In te una loquitur, caetera mutus habet.

[To every one, so let men believe, there is allotted a winged angel from out the hierarchies of heaven. What wonder, Leonora, if yours should be a greater glory, for your voice itself proclaims the presence of God. Either God, or surely a third mind that has deserted heaven, with secret power gently breathes through your throat—gently breathes, and easily teaches mortal hearts little by little to become accustomed to immortal sound. But if in truth God is all things, and is through all things diffused, yet in you alone does he speak; all the rest of his being is mute.][20]

Following, as it does, the Nativity ode, *Ad Leonoram* is almost poignant: the singer of the ode helps to unite heaven and earth with his song, but the poet of the epigram can only observe how Leonora's "voice itself proclaims the presence of God"; in the ode angelic song rings over the silenced false deities, as in the epigram the "secret power" channeled through Leonora's voice renders all creation "mute," including, presumably, the poet who responds with a written text.

Besides praising the oral performances of others, as they often do, the Latin poems can point toward the poet's own songs, but performance of those songs necessarily occurs elsewhere, outside what Ong calls the "chirographically controlled" province of learned Latin.[21] For example, like many of the Latin poems, the *Elegia Sexta,* addressed to Charles Diodati, asserts its physical existence as a written text. The headnote to the poem explains that when Diodati wrote to Milton describing how holiday festivities had sapped Diodati's creativity, *"hunc habuit responsum"* ("he received the following reply"). The poem is thus a part of a written correspondence, but at the end of the poem Milton describes a "song" usually taken to be the Nativity ode:

At tu siquid agam, scitabere (si modo saltem
Esse putas tanti noscere siquid agam)
Paciferum canimus caelesti semine regem,
Faustaque sacratis saecula pacta libris,
Vagitumque Dei, & stabulantem paupere tecto
Qui suprema suo cum patre regna colit.
Stelliparumque polum, modulantesque aethere turmas,
Et subito elisos ad sua fana Deos.

Dona quidem dedimus Christi natalibus illa,
Illa sub auroram lux mihi prima tulit.
Te quoque pressa manent patriis meditata cicutis;
Tu mihi, cui recitem, judicis instar eris.   (79–90)

[But if you will know what I am doing—if indeed you think it of consequence to
know that I am doing anything—I am singing of the peace-bearing King of heavenly race, and of that happy age promised in the sacred books, of the infant cries of
Jesus, and his shelter beneath the humble roof, who with his father now dwells in
the realms above. I sing of the star-bearing firmament and melodious hosts in the
heavens, of the gods suddenly shattered in their fanes. This is the gift that I have
offered to Christ on his natal day, when the first light of dawn brought me my
theme. These strains composed on my native pipes await you in close keeping,
when I recite them to you, you will be my judge.] (P. 101)

Rather than affixing a copy of the ode to his letter or assuring Diodati that
he will show him the poem, Milton promises to recite it later, implying that
this song demands oral performance and that its ideal form cannot be cap-
tured by ink and paper. The Latin poems thus tend to distance themselves
from the potency of song by ascribing it to another singer and by postponing
performance.

Martz reverses the order of *Poems* in his reading of the book, considering the Latin poems first and then the English poems—significantly, the
Nativity ode last. Despite his championing of "Milton's original arrangement," his discussion of the *Poems* is, in the Renaissance sense, preposter-
ous: what should be "pre" becomes "post." Martz's arrangement lends itself
easily to the narrative of a "rising poet," a poet who admires the power of
song in others, looks forward to his own oral performance, and finally joins
his prophetic voice to a choir of angels. The arrangement of these works in
Poems, however, hints at the opposite story, that of a falling (and fallen)
poet. If Milton's first book of poetry shows any progress—and that "if"
needs much emphasis—it shows the progress of a poet not rising but descending, from angelic song to the materiality of the written or printed page.

IV. THE WRITING POET

The Latin poem *Ad Patrem* (*To My Father*) exemplifies particularly well the
descent from song in *Poems*. At first the poem would seem to be an exception to the generalizations above since it calls itself "*carmen / Exiguum*"
(6–7), as MacKellar translates, a "trifling song" (p. 143). But a few lines later
it fixes itself firmly upon a page: "Sed tamen haec nostros ostendit pagina
census / Et quod habemus opum charta numeravimus ista" (12–13) ("Nevertheless this page displays my resources, and all my wealth is set forth on
this paper") (p. 143). As the poem continues, it justifies the poet's choice of

career by appealing to his father's fame as a composer of music. The poem makes clear that the elements of song, words and music, have undergone a separation:

> Nunc tibi quid mirum, si me genuisse poetam
> Contigerit, charo si tam prope sanguine juncti
> Cognatas artes, studiumque affine sequamur:
> Ipse volens Phoebus se dispertire duobus,
> Altera dona mihi, dedit altera dona parenti,
> Dividuumque deum genitorque puerque tenemus. (61–66)

[Now, if it has happened that I have been born a poet, why is it strange to you that we, so closely joined by the loving bond of blood, should pursue related arts and kindred ways of life? Phoebus, wishing to divide himself in two, gave some gifts to me, others to my father; and we, father and son, possess the divided god.] (P. 147)

In this pagan reenactment of the Incarnation, the god divides his divinity between father and son, each receiving fragmentary, separate powers — "Altera dona mihi" torn away, as in line 65, from "altera dona parenti." Rather than Incarnation, this dissolution suggests the Fall, the loss of perfect communication with the Divine. As Jacques Derrida puts it in a discussion of Edmond Jabès's *Le livre des questions*, "The difference between speech and writing is sin, the anger of God emerging from itself, lost immediacy, work outside the garden."[22] *Ad Patrem*, like *At a Solemn Music*, records how "disproportion'd sin" "Broke the fair musick that all creatures made / To their great Lord" (19, 21–22). This separation of gifts explains why the fallen poet writes: he can create words or music, but he cannot reunite the divided god in song.

If Milton imagines in *Ad Patrem* a primal splitting apart of word and music, in works like *At a Solemn Music*, *Poems* continually looks forward to a time of reuniting humanity and God, words and music:

> O may we soon again renew that Song,
> And keep in tune with Heav'n, till God ere long
> To his celestial consort us unite,
> To live with him, and sing in endles morn of light. (25–28)

Moving from the Nativity ode, to *At a Solemn Music*, to *Lycidas*—following without mentioning it the order of *Poems*—Catherine Belsey observes how angelic song which asserts the presence of the Divine retreats from the earth into heaven between the Nativity ode and *Lycidas*. Rather than the withdrawal of the Divine, *Poems* seems to show the poet's growing awareness of the separation between heavenly song and humanity, a separation reflected in poetry from the start of the book. Belsey points out that even the Nativity ode, the work in all of *Poems* that proclaims most insistently its status as a song and its ability to make its subject present, is betrayed by an inability to transcend the limits of writing. The singer attempts to appropriate the immediate presence associated with speech, but the text repeatedly declares the singer's absence from the song's cosmic scenes. This undermining of the singer's authority is signified typographically by parentheses: "Such Musick (as 'tis said) / Before was never made, / But when of old the sons of morning sung" (117–19). "As 'tis said" indicates that the singer does not know first-hand the relation between the hymns at the Nativity and at the Creation; the parentheses deny the singer the authority of one who is present. They similarly question his ability to participate in—or even hear—the music of the spheres: "Ring out ye Crystall sphears, / Once bless our human ears, / (If ye have power to touch our senses so)" (125–27). Considering these passages, Belsey concludes that this inconsistency "within the speaking voice of the text, these uncertainties and hesitations, come close momentarily to identifying the authority of the poem as imaginary." Since the poet's fallen nature already necessarily permeates the Nativity ode, *Poems* seems to show not the opening of a chasm between human and divine, but the growing awareness of a preexisting separation and a reluctant, partial acceptance of less powerful modes of communication—writing and print rather than angelic song—that such a separation requires. *Poems* portrays not the Fall but the poet's realizing the effects of the Fall for his poetry.[23]

This realization continues in the Latin poems, culminating in *Epitaphium Damonis (Damon's Epitaph)*, the last work of *Poems*. Critics frequently read the epitaph for statements of Milton's epic aspirations. Martz concentrates on lines at the center of the poem:

> O mihi tum si vita supersit,
> Tu procul annosa pendebis fistula pinu
> Multum oblita mihi, aut patriis mutata camoenis
> Brittonicum strides, quid enim? omnia non licet uni
> Non sperasse uni licet omnia.   (168–72)

[Ah! then if life remain, you, my pipe, shall hang on some aged pine far off and forgotten, unless forsaking your native songs you shrilly sound a British theme. Why not a British theme? One man cannot do all things, cannot hope to do all things.] (P. 169)

According to Martz, "the poet is contemplating deeper themes, British themes, and themes composed in English."[24] Martz overlooks the conditional clause that begins these lines, thereby eliding the possibility that the plans that follow may not be the poet's ideal choices; given that he has an abundance of life left (the prefix *super* connotes an excess), the poet considers his options. The poem's view, however, and that of *Poems* generally, seems to extend far beyond Milton's late epics. The real exercise of poetic power within the epitaph is Damon's; because "purum colit aethera Damon" (203) ("Damon dwells in the purity of heaven"), he achieves song that *Poems*, by its very existence as a printed book, suggests cannot be sung on earth:

> Ipse caput nitidum cinctus rutilante corona,
> Letaque frondentis gestans umbracula palmae
> Aeternum perages immortales hymenaeos,
> Cantus ubi, choreisque furit lyra mista beatis,
> Festa Sionaeo bacchantur & Orgia Thyrso.   (215–19)

[Your {Damon's} noble head bound with a glittering wreath, in your hands the glad branches of the leafy palm, you shall for ever act and act again the immortal nuptials, where song and the lyre, mingled with the blessed dances, wax rapturous, and the joyous revels rage under the thyrsus of Zion.] (P. 173)

These are the final lines of *Poems,* and they celebrate not the rising poet but the ascended poet; to the extent that they look forward to Milton's career at all, they look forward to his career after he leaves the earth to sing where he can "for ever act and act again the immortal nuptials" of words and music. These last lines of the book invite a rereading of some of the first lines: when is the "future" of the motto's "future bard"? Maybe 1667, but *Poems* looks forward more consistently to song "unexpressive" on earth, song that cannot be represented in writing, print, or any earthly medium.

But back on earth, near the end of 1645, the living poet John Milton used the press to circulate his poetry. *The Poems of Mr. John Milton, Both English and Latin* reveals that even before *Eikonoklastes,* when he scorned another of Marshall's frontispieces, Milton was very suspicious of the iconic potential of print. Later readers of *Areopagitica* may worship books, Stanley Fish writes, but Milton refuses to because "Milton is continually alert to the danger of reifying some external form into the repository of truth and value."[25] Consequently, his first book of poetry repeatedly calls attention to its failures: the failure of a graven image to capture even a "jot" of the poet; the failure of a spatial, visual format to reproduce the temporal, aural arrangements of Henry Lawes; the failure of print to capture the poet's song (the Nativity ode) and the failure of the poet's song to fit into print (*The Passion*); and, above all, the fallen poet's failure to escape the materiality of writing and bring heavenly song to earth. That these failures have been frequently overlooked illustrates very clearly the historical, cultural gap separating a yearning for song from an unquestioning acceptance of print and separating makers of iconoclastic books from readers of verbal icons.

Davidson College

NOTES

1. McGann, *The Textual Condition* (Princeton, 1991), p. 13; Martz, *Milton: Poet of Exile*, 2nd ed. (New Haven, 1986), p. 31. Martz's essay, "The Rising Poet, 1645," first appeared in *The Lyric and Dramatic Milton: Selected Papers from the English Institute*, ed. Joseph H. Summers (New York, 1965), but my article cites the most recent version (1986) throughout.

2. Ong, *Orality and Literacy: The Technologizing of the Word* (London, 1982), p. 26. Eric Alfred Havelock, *The Muse Learns to Write: Reflections on Orality and Literacy from Antiquity to the Present* (New Haven, 1986).

3. The version of *Poems* (1645) cited is the facsimile in *John Milton's Complete Poetical Works, Reproduced in Photographic Facsimile*, ed. Harris Francis Fletcher (Urbana, 1943), vol. I. All translations of Milton's Latin poetry come from *The Latin Poems of John Milton*, trans. Walter MacKellar (New Haven, 1930), and subsequent page references will appear in the text.

4. Halpern, "The Great Instauration: imaginary narratives in Milton's 'Nativity Ode,'" in *Re-membering Milton: Essays on the Texts and Traditions*, ed. Mary Nyquist and Margaret W. Ferguson (New York, 1987), pp. 3–4; Hale, "Milton's Self-Presentation in *Poems . . . 1645*," *MQ* XXV (1991): 37.

5. Martz, *Milton*, p. 34.

6. Masson, *The Life of John Milton: Narrated in Connexion with the Political, Ecclesiastical, and Literary History of His Time*, (London, 1896), vol. III, p. 459; Martz, *Milton*, p. 33.

7. Werstine, "Narratives About Printed Shakespearean Texts: 'Foul Papers' and 'Bad' Quartos," *Shakespeare Quarterly* XLI (1990): 86; Spear, "Reading Before the Lines: Typography, Iconography, and the Author in Milton's 1645 Frontispiece," in *New Ways of Looking at Old Texts: Papers of the Renaissance English Text Society, 1985–1991*, ed. W. Speed Hill (Binghamton, 1993), pp. 187, 189, 192, 193.

8. Spear, "Reading Before the Lines," pp. 193, 188.

9. Martz, *Milton*, p. 34.

10. See, for instance, C.W.R.D. Moseley, *The Poetic Birth: Milton's Poems of 1645* (Aldershot, 1991).

11. *Complete Prose Works of John Milton*, 8 vols., ed. Don M. Wolfe et al. (New Haven, 1953–82), vol. I, pp. 820–21.

12. Ong, *Orality and Literacy*, pp. 119, 121; Spaeth, *Milton's Knowledge of Music: Its Sources and Its Significance in His Works* (Princeton, 1913), p. 92; Belsey, *John Milton: Language, Gender, Power* (London, 1988), p. 4.

13. Louis L. Martz, *The Poetry of Meditation: A Study in English Religious Literature of the Seventeenth Century* (New Haven, 1954), p. 165; Belsey, *John Milton*, p. 2.

14. Parker, *Milton: A Biography* (Oxford, 1968), vol. I, p. 72.

15. Shullenberger, "Doctrine as Deep Structure in Milton's Early Poetry," in *A Fine Tuning: Studies of the Religious Poetry of Herbert and Milton*, ed. Mary A. Maleski (Binghamton, 1989), pp. 198–99, 196.

16. Martz, *Milton*, pp. 50–51.

17. Hale, "Milton's Self-Presentation in *Poems . . . 1645,*" 38.

18. Brooks and Hardy, *Poems of Mr. John Milton: The 1645 Edition with Essays in Analysis* (New York, 1951), p. vi.

19. Ong, *Orality and Literacy,* p. 113.

20. *The Latin Poems of John Milton,* p. 111.

21. Ong, *Orality and Literacy,* p. 113.

22. Derrida, *Writing and Difference,* trans. Alan Bass (Chicago, 1978), p. 68.

23. Belsey, *John Milton,* pp. 31, 22.

24. Martz, *Milton,* p. 38.

25. Fish, "Driving from the Letter: Truth and Indeterminacy in Milton's *Areopagitica,*" in *Re-membering Milton,* p. 236.

DONNE'S *BIATHANATOS* AND *SAMSON AGONISTES*: AMBIVALENCE AND AMBIGUITY

George F. Butler

CRITICS HAVE REPEATEDLY added Donne's *Biathanatos* to a canon of works providing a context for Milton's *Samson Agonistes*, for both texts examine Samson's suicide. Most scholars have held that Donne had little impact on Milton's views, and that each author approached Samson's suicide differently. The customary reading of *Biathanatos* is that Donne departed from Augustine's influential commentary on Samson's death in *The City of God* (I, 21), that he firmly believed Samson's destruction of himself and the Philistines was not divinely inspired, and that he thought Samson deliberately sought his own death. In contrast, Milton's Samson, like Augustine's, seems to have been moved by God. But neither Donne nor Milton maintains these positions fervently, and both authors approach Samson's death in surprisingly similar ways. Milton would have had access to *Biathanatos* prior to the composition of *Samson Agonistes*. Because of the significance of suicide as a Renaissance theological issue, the centrality of the hero's death in the Samson legend, the popularity of Donne in seventeenth-century England, and the comprehensive discussion of self-killing in *Biathanatos*, he would have had good reason to consult Donne's book. In *Biathanatos*, Donne summarizes various commentaries on Samson's suicide. He recites and rejects several views, but nevertheless reads the story of Samson ambivalently. In *Samson Agonistes*, Milton, like Donne, recounts several interpretations of Samson's death. He ultimately leaves certain issues unresolved and writes the story of Samson ambiguously. He considers the same arguments as Donne and in roughly the same order, so that the conclusions of Manoa and the Chorus parallel the arguments cited in *Biathanatos*. Some views considered by Donne and Milton are found in earlier sources, but others do not appear in major Renaissance dramatic analogues of *Samson Agonistes* or in the annotations of the Geneva Bible. And while his poetic style is inherently different from the prose of *Biathanatos*, Milton's language occasionally recalls Donne's phrasing.

Donne has long been mentioned in connection with *Samson Agonistes*. In a note on lines 1664–65, Merritt Y. Hughes comments in his edition that "Milton challenges the view of those who agreed with Donne that Samson's death seemed perilously like suicide." F. Michael Krouse cites Donne's work along with the writings of Thomas Hayne, Cornelius à Lapide, Cajetan, and other Renaissance and seventeenth-century authors whose writings on Samson were popular in Milton's time. Don Cameron Allen, in a discussion of the Miltonic Samson's despair, says Donne uses Samson's death as an example of justifiable suicide, but then adds that for Milton's hero, "death by suicide is never in his mind." Joseph Wittreich gives passing attention to Donne's treatment of Samson's death, while Gregory F. Goekjian briefly mentions *Biathanatos* but does not specifically link it to Milton's tragedy. Most critics have simply mentioned Donne's work without asserting or denying Milton's use of it; some have indicated superficial differences between Donne and Milton and then summarily dismissed Donne as an influence; while none have argued that Milton drew upon Donne's book.[1]

The composition and publication histories of *Biathanatos* and *Samson Agonistes* indicate Milton had ample opportunity to consider Donne's treatise. According to Ernest W. Sullivan II, who has dated virtually every stage of the composition and publication of the work, Donne finished the manuscript for *Biathanatos* between 1607 and 8 July 1608, and the volume was published by 19 October 1647. Milton likely wrote *Samson Agonistes* after *Biathanatos* was published. Allan H. Gilbert's study of the draft plans for five Samson plays in the Trinity manuscript shows that Milton was thinking about *Samson Agonistes* in the 1640s. William Riley Parker has noted that the play was written without the knowledge of Edward Phillips, and that Milton's earliest opportunity to have completed it would have been between 1647 and 1648. In a detailed consideration of the composition date of *Samson Agonistes*, Mary Ann Radzinowicz has stated that most modern Miltonists believe the play was composed between 1667 and 1670 and that objective evidence, stylistic elements, thematic similarities between *Samson Agonistes* and *Paradise Regained*, autobiographical matter, and allusions to current affairs support that date. Milton conceived *Samson Agonistes* shortly before the 1647 publication of *Biathanatos*, as the Trinity manuscript shows, but the tragedy was far from finished. Between the 1640s and the publication of *Samson Agonistes* in 1671, he clarified his views and refined his work in response to the intellectual currents of his era. Before completing the poem between 1667 and 1670, he had sufficient opportunity to study Donne's book.[2]

Certainly the subject of *Biathanatos* would have interested Milton. Suicide was an important intellectual, legal, and theological concern throughout the Renaissance and seventeenth century. In Tudor and early Stuart England, it was a form of murder and thus a criminal offense. Suicides were tried by a coroner's jury, and if convicted, their heirs were harshly punished by the state. Victims found guilty were punished by the church, which denied them Christian burial. Between 1485 and 1660, more than 95 percent of people who committed suicide were judged to have been of sound mind and were thus convicted of self-murder. Before the sixteenth century, suicide was rarely punished, and after 1660, it was gradually decriminalized.[3] Religious writers such as Richard Greenham (1599), George Abbot (1600), and John Sym (1637) viewed suicide as a response to despair and thus the devil's work. In his Commonplace Book, Milton provides an entry for suicide in which he praises Dante's punishment of that sin in the *Inferno* and writes that self-killing is "disputed with exquisite reasoning" in book 4 of Sir Philip Sidney's *Arcadia*. And in *Paradise Lost*, Adam and Eve consider whether to kill themselves after the Fall (X, 1001–28). While writing *Samson Agonistes*, Milton would not have overlooked contemporary theological debates on suicide. As Goekjian has commented, "To consider the story of Samson in the mid-seventeenth century is virtually to consider the nature of suicide."[4]

Such discussions took place with good cause, for suicide was widespread in the sixteenth and seventeenth centuries. There was a marked increase in cases reported to the King's Bench during this period. From 1500 to 1509, sixty-one cases of self-killing were ruled self-murders, while one was not, due to the victim's mental condition at the time of death. Between 1610 and 1619, shortly after Donne had written *Biathanatos*, 967 cases were declared self-murders, while only one person was acquitted. From 1640 to 1649, a period encompassing the publication of *Biathanatos* and Milton's initial work on *Samson Agonistes*, the number of cases declined to 328 self-murders, and an additional twenty-two victims were judged mentally incapable of having murdered themselves. And from 1670 to 1679, during the time *Samson Agonistes* was published, 409 of those who committed suicide were judged guilty of self-murder, while fifty-one additional suicides were acquitted.[5] The number of those convicted peaked in the earlier decades of the seventeenth century. In later decades, the proportion acquitted for psychological reasons increased substantially. The trend suggests that suicide grew as a topic of interest and condemnation until the middle of the seventeenth century, and that society then became more forgiving of those who took their own lives. The prevalence of suicide in the age of Donne and Milton prompted William Gouge to comment in his preface to Sym's 1637 *Lifes Preservative Against Self-Killing*, probably the first book published in English on the subject, "I suppose, that scarce an age since the beginning of the World hath afforded more examples of this desperate inhumanity than this our present age."[6]

Though there is some debate over Donne's intentions, *Biathanatos* was an early and influential consideration of suicide. Some scholars have called it a parody of scholastic argumentation that Donne did not intend to be taken seriously.[7] On the other hand, Michael Rudick and M. Pabst Battin have argued in their edition of *Biathanatos* that Donne succeeds in presenting a logically consistent defense of suicide under certain circumstances. Sullivan acknowledges that Donne may have had suicidal thoughts, but he sees *Biathanatos* as an example of Donne's wide-ranging interests in casuistry, law, and theological controversies (*B*, p. ix). He also holds that while Donne's treatise is not a defense of suicide in all cases, it is "a general plea for charity toward suicides and a proof that no set of rules can govern all instances" (*B*, p. xxx). In comparing the similarity of *Biathanatos* to the "serious intention of *Pseudo-Martyr*," written on the Oath of Allegiance, Sullivan adds that the parallels between the works "should give pause to those eager to read *Biathanatos* as something other than it appears, a limited defense of suicide" (*B*, p. xix). More recently, MacDonald and Murphy have provided a balanced summary of the present academic dispute over Donne's intentions, thus indicating that scholars have not yet reached a consensus.[8]

Milton's contemporaries read *Biathanatos* as a serious justification of self-killing. Shortly after *Biathanatos* was published, Sir William Denny, in his 1653 *Pelecanicidium: or the Christian Adviser against Self-Murder*, alluded to it as a defense of suicide. In his 1674 *Self-homicide-murther*, Thomas Philipot briefly cited Donne's book as an apology. Charles Blount, in his 1680 *The Two First Books of Philostratus*, argued that *Biathanatos* offers a successful vindication of self-killing. In 1692, Ezra Pierce mentioned *Biathanatos* in his *A Discourse of Self-Murder;* and around 1700, John Adams specifically attacked *Biathanatos* as a defense of suicide in his *An Essay Concerning Self-Murther. Wherein is endeavour'd to prove, That it is Unlawful According to Natural Principles. With Some Considerations upon what is pretended from the said Principles, by the Author of a Treatise, intituled, Biathanatos, and Others* (*B*, pp. xxiii–xxiv, xxxii–xxxiii).[9] The prevalence of such works has led Sullivan to state that seventeenth-century readers typically considered *Biathanatos* a defense of suicide, that most published attacks on suicide challenged *Biathanatos* and commented on its standing as an apology for self-killing, and that no serious flaw in Donne's reasoning was demonstrated (*B*, p. xxvi).

The strong response to *Biathanatos* underscores its popularity. Sullivan counts 104 extant copies of the 1647 first edition, a number unusually large for a book published before the Great Fire of 1666. The 1647 first issue was followed by a second issue in 1648, further attesting to the book's appeal (*B*, pp. vii, xlviii–xlix). Philipot justified his 1674 condemnation of suicide by emphasizing the powerful influence of *Biathanatos* in the seventeenth century, and MacDonald and Murphy note that *Biathanatos* was widely read. Given Donne's standing as a religious leader, Milton and others may have been further encouraged to examine his views. "Donne was the only English clergyman of his era," MacDonald and Murphy firmly state, "to suggest in print that suicide might be defensible."[10]

Milton attended St. Paul's School when Donne was dean of St. Paul's Cathedral; and Parker, C.W.R.D. Moseley, and John T. Shawcross have conjectured that Donne's sermons may have had a lasting impact on him. Donne and Milton shared the same publisher and at roughly the same time. Humphrey Moseley solicited and published Milton's *Poems* of 1645, to which he affixed a preface honoring Milton's work. He published many of Donne's writings, including the 1648 second issue of *Biathanatos* (*B*, pp. l–li). Given his relationship with Moseley, Milton could have easily obtained a copy of Donne's book. Ernest W. Sullivan II has pointed to the need to reassess the magnitude of Donne's impact on his contemporaries: "Through acknowledged or unacknowledged intertextuality," Sullivan asserts, "Donne's verse became part of the discourse of an entire society." Sullivan further notes that in addition to his uncollected printed verse, Donne's poems enjoyed extensive circulation in manuscript form. Among the various works containing adaptations of Donne's verse, Sullivan includes the 1638 *Justa Edovardo King naufrago, ab Amicis mœrentibus, amoris*, the collection in which Milton's *Lycidas* first appeared. The legacy of Donne's poetry underscores his popularity and suggests that his prose works, such as *Biathanatos*, may also have exerted a considerable and underestimated influence on his contemporaries.[11]

The most convincing evidence that Milton was not interested in *Biathanatos* is the absence of a reference to it in his Commonplace Book. But the entry for suicide also ignores Luther, the church fathers, the sermons of Milton's contemporaries, and Spenser's argument against despair and suicide in *The Faerie Queene* (I, ix, 28–54). James Holly Hanford has established that as there are only three quotations from the classics and none from the Bible, Milton did not use his Commonplace Book to record items from works he frequently used. Rather than cite all material he found potentially interesting, he used the Commonplace Book to organize topics systematically, with the aim of using that material to champion his civil, religious, and domestic causes. Because Donne does not thoroughly condemn self-killing, Milton would have found *Biathanatos* inappropriate to mention in an entry on suicide as a sin. Milton most likely wrote the entry between 1641 and 1642 (YP I, p. 371n2). After 1644, he only occasionally made new entries; and he rarely used the Commonplace Book after 1648. By the publication of *Biathanatos* in 1647, he had stopped regularly recording material and would not have habitually added Donne's book to his entry on suicide, even if he thought it belonged there.[12]

In itself, Milton's likely familiarity with *Biathanatos* does not prove that he drew upon it in *Samson Agonistes*. A cursory reading of the two works suggests that Donne and Milton differ, and that Milton was more likely influenced by Augustine. On the surface, Milton apparently thinks Samson's self-destruction was prompted by divine inspiration. Samson tells the Chorus, "Be of good courage, I begin to feel / Some rousing motions in me which dispose / To something extraordinary my thoughts" (1381–83). Augustine similarly argues that Samson's death was divinely inspired. "Nor is Samson acquitted of guilt on any other plea," writes Augustine, "inasmuch as he crushed himself by the collapse of the house along with his enemies, than the plea that the Spirit who through him had been working miracles, had secretly ordered this."[13] In contrast to Augustine, Donne is generally skeptical of divinely inspired suicides, and he notes that the Bible provides no textual evidence for Augustine's reading of the Samson legend (*B* III, v, 4).

But a closer look shows Milton's tragedy has more in common with *Biathanatos* than is initially apparent. Donne holds that if Samson's suicide had been divinely inspired, then the Bible would probably have been explicit. After discussing 1 Kings xx, 35–37, where God tells the son of a prophet to seek his own death, Donne writes: "it is not without some boldnesse, if others affirme without authority of the text, that the death of *Samson* and others had the same foundation, where it appeares by this, that God, when he would haue it vnderstood so, is pleasd to deliuer it playnly and expressly" (*B* III, v, 2). In words that echo *Biathanatos*, Milton restates Donne's point: "Let us assume that, appropriately enough, when God wants us to understand and thus believe in a particular doctrine as a primary point of faith," says Milton in *Christian Doctrine*, where he discusses the Holy Spirit, "he teaches it to us not obscurely or confusedly, but simply and clearly, in plain words" (YP VI, p. 287). In *Biathanatos* and *Samson Agonistes*, Donne and Milton apply the same principle of scriptural clarity to the same text, the story of Samson in the Book of Judges. As a result, they arrive at similar understandings of the Samson legend. In *Samson Agonistes*, Milton does not insist that Samson received special instruction from God to destroy the temple and end his life in the process. In *Biathanatos*, Donne does not deny that Samson may have somehow been inspired, though he doubts God told Samson specifically how to act.

Donne's understanding of inspiration is complex, and he argues against the likelihood of God ever inspiring a specific suicide. In discussing the suicides of the virgin martyrs, he says that Augustine's solution is to "retire

to that poore and improbable defence, That it was done by diuine instinct"
(*B* II, vi, 8). And in discussing Jonah's suicidal inclination, he claims there
is no reason "to admit any such perticular impulsion of Gods spirit" (*B* III,
v, 3). But Donne questions Augustine's position more than he condemns it,
for what is "poore and improbable" is not impossible. Though it may show
"boldnesse" to argue for divine inspiration without clear scriptural support
(*B* III, v, 2), there is a difference between being bold and being wrong. In
saying that Samson's inspiration "may with the same easinesse be refusd, as
it is presented," Donne asserts that Augustine's claim for divine inspiration
may be accepted or rejected with equal ease, not that it must be denied (*B*
III, v, 4).

On the other hand, Donne grants that God sometimes inspires people
to act in a generally holy manner. Jonah was "aduisd, and ordinate, and
rectified" in seeking his own death, even if he was not specifically inspired
to do so (*B* III, v, 3). Donne remarks that God owns each person's life; that
each person may properly return that life if called upon to do so; and that
such a calling would more likely be an inspiration to act virtuously, rather
than a divine request to take one's own life either incidentally or intention-
ally:

But we are still vpon a safe ground, That whensoeuer I may iustly depart with this
Life, it is but a Summons from God: And it cannot then be imputed to any Corruption of my will; for *velle non creditur qui obsequitur Imperio.* Yet I exspect not euer
a particular inspiration or new Commission, such as they are forced to purchase for
Samson, and the rest, but that resident and inherent Grace of God, by which he
excites vs to works of morall, or higher vertues. And so when it is so called for againe
it were a greater Iniustice in vs to deny, or withold any thing of which we were
depositaryes, then if we were Debtors. (*B* II, iv, 7)

Because God "excites" or inspires people to act virtuously, suicide may be
the proper response to God's motions, even if self-killing is not specifically
ordered. Though he doubts Samson's specific inspiration, Donne believes
he acted out of religious zeal. Does Samson's success prove "any impulsion,
and incitement, and preuention of the holy Ghost, to that perticular act,"
Donne asks, "or rather onely an habituall accompanying and awaking him,
to such actions, by which, God might be honord and glorified, whensoeuer
any occasion should be presented?" (*B* III, v, 4). For Donne, Samson was
inspired to punish the Philistines for their sins. But he was probably not
inspired to do so in the manner that he did, nor in any other manner, for
that matter.

Donne's position ultimately dignifies the individual's subjective understanding of God's will. In his strongest defense of Samson's suicide, he

claims that a personal belief in inspiration, rather than an objective confirmation of God's motions, is sufficient justification. "If then a man after requisite, and convenient diligence, despoyld of all humane affections, and selfe interest and *Sancto bonæ Impatientiæ igne exardens* (as *Paulynus* speaks) do in his Conscyence beleeue that he is invited by the Spirit of God to do such an act," writes Donne, "as *Ionas, Abraham,* and perchance *Samson* was, who can, by these Rules, condemne this to be Sinne?" (*B* II, vi, 8). By emphasizing the individual's subjective state, Donne admits that a particular instance of divine inspiration, however unlikely or improbable, may nevertheless be real. The conditions Donne attaches to feelings of inspiration screen genuinely inspired acts from delusions. Each person must certify that there are no personal motives for suicide; that the action and circumstances have been sufficiently contemplated; and that the deed will further God's will. Because the motives and inspiration of a suicide can be known only by the victim, a spectator, like Donne, should be ambivalent in assessing the holiness of any self-killing.

Donne's views unfold in his extended account of Samson's death (*B* III, v, 4). He begins by identifying Samson as the first suicide mentioned in Scripture, as an exemplar of virtue, and as a type of Christ. He adds that Samson's suicide is celebrated by the church as an act of martyrdom, and that Saint Paul and others have praised the hero's death. He then introduces the problem of interpreting Samson's demise: "And this generall applause and concurrence, in the prayse of the fact, hath made many thinke, or at least write, that he purposd not to kill himselfe: being loth either to depart from theyr opinion who extoll him, or to admit any thing which may countenance that maner of dying" (*B* III, v, 4). According to Donne, some people have been reluctant to deny Samson was virtuous, or they have refused to write anything that will sanction suicide. As a result, these people have chosen to argue that Samson did not purposely kill himself.

The inevitability of Samson's death, says Donne, is used to defend the virtue of his actions: "But, besides that such an exposing of himselfe to vneuitable danger is the same fault as *self homicide*," he argues, "When there is any fault in it, the very text is against them" (*B* III, v, 4). Eleazar's death is another example of an unavoidable consequence of a virtuous act (1 Macc. vi, 42–46). "For the passiue action of *Eleazar* none denyes, but that that endangering of himselfe was an Act of Vertue," Donne remarks; "yet it was a forsaking and exposing himselfe to certayne Destruction" (*B* III, v, 8). Eleazar's death, says Donne, "was a direct killing of himselfe, as expressly as *Samsons* pulling downe the house" (*B* III, v, 8). Donne's general principle is that when death is the inescapable effect of an act resulting in some greater good, then such a death is morally excusable. To summarize his position, he cites Cajetan's commentary on the death of Samson in Judges xvi:

That to expose our selues to certayne death, if our first end be not our owne death but common good it is Lawfull; for, sayth he, our actions, which be Morally good, or bad, must be iudged to be such, by the first reason which moues them, not by any accident or concomitance, accompanying or succeeding them, tho necessarily. (B III, v, 8)

Though the deaths of Eleazar and Samson are unavoidable consequences of virtuous actions, they stem from choices and thus are suicides.

Because of Samson's prayer to die among his enemies, Donne thinks his death may have been both inevitable and volitional. He reads the prayer not as a wish to die for death's sake, but as a conscious decision to embrace the inevitable result of a virtuous deed. Commentators on the prayer have argued that Samson "intended not his owne death principally, but accidentally," notes Donne. "For we say the same," he explains, "That this may be done onely, when the Honor of God may be promou'd by that way and no other" (B III, v, 4). But Donne also grants that Samson may have only been willing to die accidentally. In his final sermon, *Death's Duel* (1632), he states his ambivalence toward Samson's intent: Samson died "in such a manner (consider it actively, consider it passively in his own death, and in those whom he slew with himself) as was subject to interpretation hard enough."[14] He does not debate whether Samson deliberately ("actively") killed himself, or whether his death was an accidental ("passive") consequence. Instead, he stresses the difficulty of interpreting Samson's motives.

In a new paragraph, Donne discusses two arguments generally offered to support Augustine's position: Samson's prayer for revenge and the return of his strength. "O Lord God, remember me, I pray thee," says Samson in Judges xvi, 28, "and strengthen me, I pray thee, only this once, O God, that I may be at once avenged of the Philistines for my two eyes." According to Wittreich, "From St. Augustine onward, this prayer provided the crucial piece of inferential evidence that Samson's acts were divinely sanctioned."[15] But Donne does not offer the prayer as unmistakable proof that God told Samson how to act. In Samson's words, says Donne, "you may obserue much humanity, and weaknesse, and selfe respect" (B III, v, 4). He does not think the prayer proves divine intervention, but neither does he say it rules out inspiration. Donne acknowledges that Samson's petition for renewed strength was efficacious: "When therefore he felt his strength in part refresh'd," he explains, Samson "by prayer intreated the perfecting thereof" (B III, v, 4). The prayer is not necessarily followed by a divine command. But it is succeeded by an "inspiring" or "breathing in" of physical strength and religious zeal, so that Samson will have the force and courage to carry out an action of his own choosing. Donne questions whether Samson's success proves "that God restor'd him his strength to that end which he ask'd it" (*B* III, v, 4). Samson's hair had already begun to grow back, Donne notes, and thus his strength had partially returned. He further asks whether a miraculous increase in Samson's strength would prove that God told him to kill himself (*B* III, v, 4). In doing so, he questions the logical fallacy that because Samson's strength grew, it did so because God wanted him to use it in a particular way.

The commentary ends with some remarks about the virtue of Samson's death. Donne first repeats the argument of Franciscus Georgius Venetus, that Samson had the same authorization to kill himself as to kill the Philistines (*B* III, v, 4). Recognizing that his foes "tooke continuall occasion from his deiection to scorne and reproche his God," Donne writes, Samson sought "to remoue the wretched occasion thereof," and thus had "the same reason to kill himselfe, which he had to kill them, and the same authority, and the same priuilege, and safeguard from sinne" (*B* III, v, 4). According to Donne, the "occasion" of Samson being enthralled by the Philistines gave his captors evidence that God was equally subject to Dagon. By ending his own life, he could prevent himself from being used as proof of God's subjection. Donne closes by saying that Samson died "with the same Zeale as *Christ* vnconstraynd; for *in this maner of dying, as much as in any thing ells, he was a type of Christ*" (*B* III, v, 4). His conclusion recalls that Samson's death was the logical and unavoidable consequence of his massacre of the Philistines, for he considers this idea in his discussion of the death of Christ. "That that is a braue death, which is accepted vnconstraynd," says Donne of Christ's crucifixion, "And that it is a Heroique act of fortitude, if a Man when an vrgent occasion is presented, expose himselfe to a certayne and assured Death, as he did" (*B* III, iv, 5). Samson is a type of Christ, for through his death he exposed himself to "vneuitable danger" to advance God's greatness.

In *Samson Agonistes*, Milton dramatizes the ambivalence and uncertainty of those who must interpret Samson's death. Like Donne, Milton believes the truth of Samson's inspiration can be found only in the hero's mind, if anywhere at all. The tragedy is fraught with ambiguity, and Milton tells the reader little about the hero's motives. Manoa and the Chorus hear a "hideous noise" (1509) that is "Horribly loud" (1510) and full of "Blood, death, and deathful deeds" (1513). Manoa thinks the Philistines have killed his son (1515–16). The Chorus thinks Samson has killed the Philistines (1517–18). The Messenger, who has witnessed the "horrid spectacle" (1542), says Samson has died "By his own hands" (1584). Milton refrains from saying what actually happened. Instead, he relates the perceptions of the Messenger and the interpretations of Manoa and the Chorus. As they respond in diverse ways to Samson's death, Manoa and his countrymen construct a history of what took place at Gaza, why it took place, and what it signifies, and their queries and conclusions amount to the genesis of the Samson legend. That legend was current in the seventeenth century, and in *Biathanatos*, Donne writes what is virtually an encyclopedia entry summarizing how Samson's death was understood by theologians. In writing his story of the creation of the Samson legend, Milton addresses the same issues as Donne and in roughly the same order, so that his version parallels Donne's retrospective. And while his poetry and dramatic dialogue will not allow an extensive appropriation of Donne's prose, Milton sometimes recalls Donne's phrasing.

Milton generally follows the structure of Donne's argument. Manoa, the Messenger, and the Chorus briefly discuss Samson's slaughter of the Philistines (1557–81). They then question Samson's suicidal intent (1582–95), and whether his death was an unavoidable consequence of his actions (1586–89). Like Donne's paragraph break, Manoa's questioning of the Messenger shifts to the witness' extended narrative of what happened during Samson's final moments (1596–1659). Throughout the passage, Milton offers a sustained but implicit consideration of Samson's intent and inspiration. As the Messenger speaks, Milton, like the Bible, does not say Samson was inspired. But Milton considers Samson's prayer (1630–38) and the return of his strength (1623–28, 1643–56). The Chorus and Manoa, like Donne, finally conclude that Samson was a glorious champion of his faith (1660–1758).

Manoa and his companions begin by praising Samson's slaughter of the Philistines and speculating that God has miraculously restored his vision (1517–33). When Manoa learns his son has died, he wants to know how, for "death to life is crown or shame" (1579). His comment shows his predisposition to see Samson's death as a glorious achievement. He confirms this inclination when he asks, "What glorious hand gave *Samson* his death's wound?" (1581). When the Messenger responds that Samson died "By his own hands" (1584), Manoa is confused. His questions reveal his perplexity: "Self-violence? what cause / Brought him so soon at variance with himself / Among his foes?" (1584–86). Like the interpreters of Samson in *Biathanatos*, Manoa has difficulty reconciling his son's self-inflicted death with the image of Samson as the glorious deliverer of Israel.

Manoa's term, "Self-violence," recalls the title of Donne's treatise, which literally means "violent (*bia*) death (*thanatos*)." Milton again evokes the title of Donne's work when Manoa exclaims, "O lastly over-strong against thyself!" (1590). Manoa's emphasis on Samson's strength reminds us that his death was forceful, violent, and full of βία. The first quotation cited by the *Oxford English Dictionary* for "self-violence" is Milton's use of the term in *Samson Agonistes*. The lack of cited precedents suggests the title of Donne's book, rather than some other source, may have inspired Milton to choose "Self-violence" to describe Samson's death; he does not use the term elsewhere. In his Commonplace Book he calls suicide *"Mors Spontanea,"* the equivalent of "unaided death." In his discussion of self-hatred being opposed to self-love, he says in *Christian Doctrine* that suicides belong to the class of people who hate themselves. "Quo in numero habendi sunt qui mortem sibi consciscunt," Milton writes, with *"mortem sibi consciscunt"* being an accepted Latin phrase for "inflicted death on themselves." In *Paradise Lost* he calls "suicide" "self-destruction" (X, 1016); and he similarly uses "self-kill'd" (1664) and "self-offence" (515) to describe suicide in *Samson Agonistes*. As the *Oxford English Dictionary* notes, "self-killed," "self-killing," and "self-killer" had been used by Shakespeare in 1600, Edmund Bolton in 1618, and Thomas Browne in 1658. Perhaps an even more popular term, and one not used by Milton, was "self-murder," for which the *Oxford English Dictionary* cites John Foxe (1563), Spenser (1590), Donne (1631), William Lithgow (1632), and Thomas Gage (1648). Shakespeare had used "self-slaughtered" in 1593. "Suicide" had been used in 1651 by Walter Charleton, and Thomas Blount had listed it in his 1656 *Glossographia, or a dictionary interpreting such hard words . . . as are now used*. Given the many popular terms for "suicide" that Milton could have employed, his choice of "Self-violence" in *Samson Agonistes* invites attention.[16]

Milton also examines Samson's death as an unavoidable consequence of a virtuous deed. Like the authorities cited by Donne, the Messenger argues that Samson's death was an inescapable result of his intended action. When Manoa asks the cause of Samson's "Self-violence," the Messenger responds, "Inevitable cause / At once both to destroy and be destroy'd" (1586–87). Milton's "Inevitable cause" is a borrowing of Donne's "vneuitable danger" (*B* III, v, 4). The Messenger uses similar phrasing when he speaks of "inevitable destruction": *"Samson* with these immixt, inevitably / Pull'd down the same destruction on himself" (1657–58). The Chorus rephrases the Messenger's remark: Samson is "self-kill'd / Not willingly, but tangl'd in the fold / Of dire necessity" (1664–66). The phrasing of the Chorus echoes Donne's restatement of Cajetan, that to expose oneself to certain death must be judged by one's true intention, *"tho necessarily"* death may follow (*B* III, v, 8).

While both Donne and Milton discuss Samson's death as an inevitable consequence, the argument is not paralleled in the major dramatic analogues of *Samson Agonistes*. In his 1547 *Samson, Tragoedia Nova*, Hieronymus Zieglerus's hero resigns himself to die among his enemies. But Zieglerus does not discuss Samson's death as an inescapable consequence of his action. Marcus Andreas Wunstius, in his 1604 *Simson, Tragoedia Sacra*, has Samson say it is sweet to die among the slaughtered Philistines. But the priest who interprets his death stresses only that all humans must inevitably perish:

> Nay, rather, recognize the will of God
> By whose unchanged, inevitable law,
> At the due hour that He has ordained,
> A life is born, a life is blotted out.

Theodorus Rhodius, in the 1625 version of *Simson*, has the hero willingly accept death, provided that he may obtain vengeance. But there is no argument that Samson's death should inevitably result from his revenge. Vincenzo Giattini, in his 1638 *Il Sansone: Dialogo per Musica*, has Samson seek death among his enemies, and his demise seems more deliberate than unavoidable. And Joost van den Vondel, in his 1660 *Samson, of Heilige Wraeck, Treurspel*, has a Messenger "gather" that "A heavy stone . . . crushed his heart / And put it out of misery." Though the questioning of the Messenger by the Chorus is analogous with the equivalent exchange in *Samson Agonistes*, there is no mention of Samson's death being the inevitable result of his massacre of the Philistines.[17]

In *Samson Agonistes* as in *Biathanatos*, there is no indisputable proof of whether Samson prayed to die with the Philistines or of what he intended to accomplish, for the hero does not express himself directly. The Messenger's version of what occurred (1596–1659) comes after Manoa's remarks about "inevitable cause," rather than before Manoa's reaction to the death of his son. While the Messenger could have described Samson's death prior to Manoa's speculations, Milton instead follows Donne's order of presentation. In the Messenger's narrative, Milton explores Samson's inspiration, just as Donne does in his second paragraph (*B* III, v, 4). On the one hand, we know that Samson felt some "rousing motions" before being led away to the temple (1382). The Chorus links these "rousing motions" to divine inspiration by telling him, "Go, and the Holy One / Of *Israel* be thy guide" (1427–28); and by wishing that "that Spirit that first rusht on thee / In the camp of *Dan* / Be efficacious in thee now at need" (1435–37). On the other hand, we have no direct knowledge of Samson's death; we never see or hear the Spirit prompt him to do anything; and the Chorus is predisposed to believe Samson was inspired. Understandably but nonetheless conspicuously, the Messenger does not say he witnessed God command Samson.

With evidence neither for nor against inspiration, the Messenger must respond to Samson's death as Donne does in discussing Augustine. The Chorus, following its earlier inclination to believe in Samson's inspiration, says in unison: "Living or dying thou hast fulfill'd / The work for which thou wast foretold" (1661–62). The first Semichorus suggests God had inspired the Philistines to induce their own death:

> Among them hee a spirit of frenzy sent,
> Who hurt thir minds,
> And urg'd them on with mad desire
> To call in haste for thir destroyer.   (1675–78)

The second Semichorus adds that Samson acted "With inward eyes illuminated" (1689). Manoa follows the sentiments of the Chorus by saying that his son acted "With God not parted from him, as was fear'd, / But favoring and assisting to the end" (1719–20). The Chorus finally concludes that God "to his faithful Champion hath in place / Bore witness gloriously" (1751–52).

While dramatic conventions sanctioned Milton's use of a messenger to relate the carnage, the ambiguity surrounding Samson's suicide is a deliberate exploration of how witnesses respond to events. While Augustine is emphatic in claiming Samson was divinely inspired, Milton leaves much room for the reader to interpret Samson's feelings. Samson does not reveal what he thinks his "rousing motions" mean, and his words suggest he does not fully know himself. The motions dispose him to "something extraordinary," but he does not explain what that "something" is (1383). When he says, "If there be aught of presage in the mind, / This day will be remarkable in my life / By some great act, or of my days the last (1387–89), he reveals that he is not sure if there is "presage" in his mind; that he does not know what "great act" will make this time so remarkable; and that he is uncertain the day really will be his last.

Milton carefully questions whether every "rousing motion" felt by Samson is an instance of divine inspiration, and whether true inspiration may be determined. In discussing his marriage to the woman of Timna, Samson tells the Chorus that his parents "knew not / That what I motion'd was of God" (221–22). Because his Philistine wife proves herself false, there is reason to believe the marriage was not urged by the Lord. On the other hand, Judges xiv, 4, says the marriage was God's will. The Bible shows his parents cannot determine when he is divinely inspired. If that is the case, then Manoa and the Chorus cannot assess his inspiration to destroy the temple. Their conclusions, whether right or wrong, are only speculation. In *A Defence of the People of England* (1651), Milton reveals his own ambivalence toward Samson's inspiration. Like Donne in *Death's Duel*, he will not say whether Samson was "prompted by God or by his own valor" to slay the Philistines and kill himself in the process (YP IV, p. 402).

The hero's "rousing motions" are best read in light of *Paradise Regained*, where the Son of God, of whom Samson was a type, has similar feelings. The Son enters the desert, "the Spirit leading" (I, 189). He spends his time "Musing and much revolving in his breast" how to begin his mission as Savior (I, 185). As he ventures into the desert, he does not know what the future holds:

> And now by some strong motion I am led
> Into this Wilderness, to what intent
> I learn not yet; perhaps I need not know;
> For what concerns my knowledge God reveals.   (I, 290–93)

And he is confounded by his feelings:

> O what a multitude of thoughts at once
> Awak'n'd in me swarm, while I consider
> What from within I feel myself, and hear
> What from without comes often to my ears,
> Ill sorting with my present state compar'd.   (I, 196–200)

The Son's "strong motion" and swarming "multitude of thoughts" are the work of the Spirit who has led him into the desert. They are like the "rousing motions" felt by Samson. But the Spirit tells the Son neither what will happen nor how to proceed. Samson likewise knows neither his fate nor his proper course of action. The Spirit does not give him a special directive, as Augustine would insist upon. Samson and the Son, humans and angels, are all made "Sufficient to have stood, though free to fall," says Milton in *Paradise Lost* (III, 99). While God might inspire his creatures with a zeal to act virtuously, it would be a dangerous affront to free will for the Creator to urge particular deeds.

In its ambiguity, Milton's handling of Samson's inspiration is a departure from the dramatic analogues with which he may have been familiar. In Zieglerus's straightforward account, Samson, tired from entertaining his captors, leans against the pillars, prays for God to restore his strength, and succeeds in collapsing the temple. His success is proof that God renewed his strength. Wunstius's Samson similarly prays for strength and then destroys the edifice. A priest explains to Samson's mother that "God Himself, in that last victory, / Poured out on Samson's frame a power divine / More notable than all he knew before." In Rhodius's version, the Messenger testifies: "I saw his strength return / And pour into his body like a tide." After praying to God for strength, Giattini's Samson feels "My vanished valour /

Flood into my heart," and in Vondel's tragedy, Samson's strength apparently returns to him suddenly and after prayer, though before he entertains at Dagon's temple. The Messenger who recounts Samson's destruction says he stood burning "With an exalted soul, a power divine, / Strength greater than that lately taken from him." He describes Samson's terrifying roars, and he recites an outward sign of the hero's returning strength: "The hair on Samson's head / Seemed suddenly to grow."

These analogues never claim that God told Samson to collapse the temple. But each indicates God approved of Samson's choice and renewed his strength so that the hero could accomplish his objective. In *Samson Agonistes,* Milton provides no apparent sign of God commanding or approving Samson's actions. Even Samson's success in buckling the columns could be attributed to a return of his strength unrelated to his possible prayers. Before he is led to Dagon's temple, the Philistine Officer tells him, "Thy strength they know surpassing human rate, / And now some public proof thereof require" (*SA* 1313–14). And prior to destroying the building, he performs feats of extraordinary might (*SA* 1626–27). The remark of the Philistine Officer, followed by Samson's exhibition, shows the hero may have retained unusual strength throughout his captivity.

The prayer for revenge is closely linked with Samson's inspiration, and Milton follows Donne by next considering Samson's request for vengeance. Donne treats both components in the same paragraph, and Milton likewise groups the two complementary issues together in the Messenger's narrative. Milton's hero never utters the words from Judges xvi, 28, and there is some doubt whether he prays before his death· at all. The Messenger says that with "eyes fast fixt he stood, as one who pray'd, / Or some great matter in his mind revolv'd" (1637–38). For Milton, there is a difference between silent contemplation and prayer, though the two may look alike. By not revealing Samson's thoughts, he neither affirms nor denies the hero's supplication. To compound matters, the Messenger repeats Samson's last words, which suggest the destruction of the building was the hero's own choice and not necessarily God's. In the Messenger's account, Samson says he will act "of my own accord" (1643). Neither the reader nor the Chorus knows the accuracy of the Messenger's speech. If Samson's deed really is done of his "own accord," then Milton follows Donne by suggesting that Samson freely chose to collapse the temple. Milton's ambiguous handling of Samson's prayer contrasts with his straightforward claim in *A Defence of the People of England,* where he states that Samson slew the Philistines after "having first made prayer to God for his aid" (YP IV, p. 402). In *Samson Agonistes,* Milton instead focuses on the private nature of Samson's contemplation and thus recalls Donne's views on the subjectivity of inspiration.

After finishing his meditation, Samson tells the Philistines that he will show them an example "of my strength, yet greater" (1644). He then buckles the columns, collapses the building, and kills his enemies. He may mean that he will show his captors an even greater feat of strength. Or he may mean that his prowess is "yet greater" than before his moment of silent reflection, as if he had been strengthened by God. Milton follows *Biathanatos* more closely here than the Bible. Donne says that "his hayre before that tyme was begunne to be growne out againe and so his strength somewhat renewd" (*B* III, v, 4). Milton agrees that Samson's strength at least partially returned with the growth of his hair. Before he is led to the temple, Samson asks the Chorus if he should "abuse this Consecrated gift / Of strength, again returning with my hair" (1354–55). And during his spectacle, "To heave, pull, draw, or break, he still perform'd / All with incredible, stupendious force" (1626–27). But the Book of Judges never says that Samson's strength was restored prior to the destruction of the temple. Judges xvi, 22, reads, "Howbeit the hair of his head began to grow again after he was shaven." It says nothing about the return of his might. In fact, we know that he was not utterly weakened, for before his hair grew back, "he did grind in the prison house" (Judges xvi, 21). Judges xvi, 23–25, tells how the Philistines called Samson to make "sport" at the temple. But Judges does not say that his "sport" included prodigious feats of strength. The Geneva Bible even says that Samson's strength did not return with his hair. "Yet had he not his strength againe," reads the gloss on Judges xvi, 22, "till he had called vpon God, and reconciled himselfe."[19] His request that God strengthen him "only this once" (Judges xvi, 28) suggests that he had not yet regained his strength and that he sought it only to demolish the temple.

In his handling of the return of Samson's strength, Milton departs from other dramatic versions of the Samson legend. While Milton's hero performs mighty feats for his captors, Zieglerus's Samson dances for them. In Wunstius's version, "bands of youths / Plucked insolently at his hair and tunic / And uttered brutal jokes about his blindness." Rhodius says the Philistines mockingly asked Samson to sing of his love affairs, famous exploits, and Hebrew God. Giattini's Samson is left at the foot of the pillars so that he may suffer by listening to the Philistines celebrate Dagon. And in Vondel's tragedy, the Philistines taunt Samson, and Noëma plans to trick him into waving incense before Dagon's throne.[20]

Manoa espouses an argument similar to Donne's questioning of whether Samson's renewed strength proves inspiration. "And I persuade me God had not permitted / His strength again to grow up with his hair," says Manoa, "Garrison'd round about him like a Camp / Of faithful Soldiery, were not his purpose / To use him further yet in some great service" (1495–

99). He believes Samson's strength has returned because God wants him to use it for some cause. He continues to reason that because Samson's lost strength had nothing to do with his blindness, the return of his prowess will renew his vision: "And since his strength with eyesight was not lost, / God will restore him eyesight to his strength" (1502–03). There is no logic to Manoa's words, nor is there evidence that Samson's eyesight ever came back. Samson's strength and his eyesight are two unrelated matters that Manoa has joined together. His argument is only a human interpretation of Samson's actions, and his erroneous reasoning reminds us that God did not necessarily restore Samson's strength for some later purpose.

Like Donne, Milton suggests that Samson's life in captivity elevated Dagon and that his death benefited God, regardless of how few or how many Philistines he killed. On Dagon's feast day, the Philistine Officer summons Samson to give "some public proof" of his renowned strength, "To honor this great Feast, and great Assembly" (1314–15). Samson shows his unwillingness to dishonor God by doing so: "Thou knowst I am an *Ebrew*, therefore tell them, / Our Law forbids at thir Religious Rites / My presence; for that cause I cannot come" (1319–21). "To show them feats, and play before thir god," says Samson, would be "The worst of all indignities" (1340–41). And though the Chorus cautions him that his refusal will bring him worse punishment, he still refuses:

> A *Nazarite* in place abominable
> Vaunting my strength in honor to thir *Dagon?*
> Besides, how vile, contemptible, ridiculous,
> What act more execrably unclean, profane?   (1359–62)

He recognizes that even to perform feats of strength at Dagon's festival is to give the Philistines "occasion" to "scorne and reproche his God," as Donne would put it (*B* III, v, 4). Though he distinguishes between idolatry and the slave labor he provides at the mill, the Chorus notes a similarity: "Yet with this strength thou serv'st the *Philistines*, / Idolatrous, uncircumcis'd, unclean" (1363–64).

In his eventual decision to accompany the Philistine Officer, Samson seems guilty of failing God and of promoting Dagon's worship. Manoa, having heard that Samson will be entertaining the Philistines, has run to the Chorus, "Lest I should see him forc't to things unseemly" (1451). And the Messenger relates that Samson's performance inspires the Philistines to clamor "thir god with praise, / Who had made thir dreadful enemy thir thrall" (1621–22). But Samson repeatedly stresses that though he will be in Dagon's temple, he will not denounce his God. Before he agrees to leave with the Officer, he vows to do nothing "Scandalous or forbidden in our

Law" (1409). "Happ'n what may," he says as he leaves, "of me expect to hear / Nothing dishonorable, impure, unworthy / Our God, our Law, my Nation, or myself" (1423–25). His justification for accompanying the Officer and performing for his enemies is that he will have the simultaneous opportunity to deny them the future "occasion" to use him, while he also exacts God's vengeance. As he makes clear to the Chorus, his ends will ultimately justify his means: "Yet that he may dispense with me or thee / Present in Temples at Idolatrous Rites / For some important cause, thou needst not doubt" (1377–79). His presence at Dagon's temple will be forgiven because it is for the "important cause" of destroying God's foes.

In *Samson Agonistes,* the Chorus does not have the same perspective on Christian history as Donne has, and so it cannot look back at both Christ and Samson. Nonetheless, Milton follows Donne by indirectly comparing Samson to the Savior. To avoid the temporal constraints of his tragedy, he alludes to the phoenix, a symbol of Christ's resurrection and triumph (1699–1707). "The Chorus uses the phoenix image without being fully aware of its most important implications for a Christian audience," observes Anthony Low, "resurrection and personal immortality, but Milton's readers were bound, and presumably intended, to think of these additional implications."[21] The simile that comes near the close of the poem is a veiled prefiguration of the Son, so that Milton, like Donne, ends his history by saying that Samson was a type of the Messiah. Manoa will build him a monument, "With all his Trophies hung, and Acts enroll'd / In copious Legend, or sweet Lyric Song" (1736–37). Like the saints that did not yet exist, he would serve as a model for "all the valiant youth" (1738), who would remember his deeds and be inspired "To matchless valor, and adventures high" (1740). The final lines of the tragedy emphasize Samson's death is an example:

> His servants he with new acquist
> Of true experience from this great event
> With peace and consolation hath dismist,
> And calm of mind, all passion spent.   (1755–58)

The end of the poem amounts to a canonization of the blind but victorious hero, much as Donne concludes that Samson is a type of Christ *"in this maner of dying, as much as in any thing ells"* (B III, v, 4).

In *Biathanatos,* Donne questions the claims the church had attached to Samson's suicide since the time of Augustine. In *Samson Agonistes,* Milton demonstrates how such claims may have arisen in the first place. Milton's likely familiarity with *Biathanatos;* the emphasis of Donne and Milton on free will; the structural and verbal parallels between *Samson Agonistes* and Donne's treatise; the similar handling of Samson's religious zeal, specific inspiration, prayer, intent, and returning strength in both texts; Milton's departure from major Renaissance dramatic analogues on certain points common to *Biathanatos* and *Samson Agonistes;* and the willingness of both authors to explore traditional interpretations of the Samson legend without providing a definitive reading indicate that *Biathanatos* influenced Milton's tragedy. Milton's likely indebtedness to *Biathanatos* partially accounts for the intellectual background and pervasive ambiguity of *Samson Agonistes,* adds to our knowledge of the scope of Donne's influence, and further illuminates the relationship of the two most important poets of the seventeenth century.

Fairfield, Connecticut

NOTES

1. *John Milton: Complete Poems and Major Prose,* ed. Merritt Y. Hughes (Indianapolis, 1957), p. 591n. Milton's poetry is hereafter cited parenthetically in the text from this edition. Krouse, *Milton's Samson and the Christian Tradition* (1949; rpt. Hamden, Conn., 1963), pp. 67–75; Allen, *The Harmonious Vision: Studies in Milton's Poetry,* enlarged ed. (Baltimore, 1970), pp. 83–84; Wittreich, *Interpreting "Samson Agonistes"* (Princeton, 1986), pp. 252–53; Goekjian, "Suicide and Revenge: *Samson Agonistes* and the Law of the Father," in *Milton Studies,* vol. XXVI, ed. James D. Simmonds (Pittsburgh, 1990), pp. 256–57.

2. *Biathanatos,* ed. Ernest W. Sullivan II (Newark, Del., 1984), pp. xxxiv, l–li; hereafter cited parenthetically in the text as *B* and followed by part, distinction, and section. Roman numeral page numbers refer to the editor's introduction. Gilbert, "Is *Samson Agonistes* Unfinished?," *PQ* XXVIII (1949): 98–106; Parker, "The Date of *Samson Agonistes," PQ* XXVIII (1949): 145–66, and *Milton: A Biography* (Oxford, 1968), pp. 903–17; Radzinowicz, *Toward "Samson Agonistes": The Growth of Milton's Mind* (Princeton, 1978), pp. 387–407. Christopher Hill, *The Experience of Defeat: Milton and Some Contemporaries* (New York, 1984), p. 314, concurs with Radzinowicz and adds, "Parker's eccentric attempt to date *Samson Agonistes* early is now, I think, generally rejected."

3. Michael MacDonald and Terence R. Murphy, *Sleepless Souls: Suicide in Early Modern England* (Oxford, 1990), pp. 15–16.

4. Greenham, *The Works of the Reverend and Faithfull Servant of Jesus Christ M. Richard Greenham* (London, 1599), p. 239; Abbot, *An Exposition Upon the Prophet Jonah* (London, 1600), pp. 125–35; Sym, *Lifes Preservative Against Self-Killing,* ed. Michael MacDonald (1637; rpt. London, 1988), pp. 246–47; all cited in MacDonald and Murphy, *Sleepless Souls,* pp. 30–34. Milton's prose is from *Complete Prose Works of John Milton,* 8 vols., ed. Don M. Wolfe et al. (New Haven, 1953–82), vol. I, p. 371, hereafter cited parenthetically in the text as YP. Goekjian, "Suicide and Revenge," p. 256.

5. MacDonald and Murphy, *Sleepless Souls,* pp. 29, 122.

6. Sym, preface, sig. A4ᵛ, qtd. in ibid., p. 239.

7. Richard E. Hughes, *The Progress of the Soul: The Interior Career of John Donne* (New York, 1968), p. 150; Joan Webber, *Contrary Music: The Prose Style of John Donne* (Madi-

son, Wis., 1963), p. 11; Evelyn M. Simpson, *A Study of the Prose Works of John Donne*, 2nd ed. (Oxford, 1948), p. 159.

8. John Donne, *Biathanatos: A Modern-Spelling Edition*, ed. Rudick and Battin (New York, 1982), pp. lxxxii–lxxxiv; MacDonald and Murphy, *Sleepless Souls*, pp. 91–92.

9. See also Geoffrey Keynes, *A Bibliography of Dr. John Donne, Dean of St. Paul's*, 4th ed. (Oxford, 1973), pp. 116–17; S. E. Sprott, *The English Debate on Suicide from Donne to Hume* (La Salle, Ill., 1961), pp. 68–70; MacDonald and Murphy, *Sleepless Souls*, p. 151.

10. Philipot, sig. A₂, cited in MacDonald and Murphy, *Sleepless Souls*, p. 151, 92.

11. Parker, *Milton: A Biography*, pp. 60–61; Moseley, *The Poetic Birth: Milton's Poems of 1645* (Brookfield, Vt., 1991), pp. 24, 81, 95n1; Shawcross, "The Life of Milton," in *The Cambridge Companion to Milton*, ed. Dennis Danielson (New York, 1989), p. 3; Sullivan, *The Influence of John Donne: His Uncollected Seventeenth-Century Printed Verse* (Columbia, Mo., 1993), pp. 2–3, 21–22, 169–70.

12. Hanford, *John Milton: Poet and Humanist* (Cleveland, 1966), pp. 80–81, 103; John T. Shawcross, *John Milton: The Self and the World* (Lexington, Ky., 1993), pp. 77, 124.

13. Augustine, *The City of God Against the Pagans*, trans. George E. McCracken (Cambridge, Mass., 1957), book I, chapter 21, pp. 95–97.

14. Donne, *Devotions Upon Emergent Occasions, Together with Death's Duel* (Ann Arbor, 1959), p. 180.

15. Biblical quotations are from the King James Version. Wittreich, *Interpreting "Samson Agonistes,"* p. 75.

16. *The Works of John Milton*, 20 vols., ed. Frank Allen Patterson et al. (New York, 1931–40), vol. XVIII, p. 133; vol. XVII, p. 200. Some classical precedents include Cicero, *Tusculanae disputationes*, I, xxxiv, 83–84; *De officiis*, I, xxxi, 112; Caesar, *De bello Gallico*, I, iv; Livy, *Ab urbe condita*, III, lviii, 6; XLV, v, 12.

17. References to Zieglerus, Wunstius, Rhodius, Giattini, and Vondel are from Watson Kirkconnell, *That Invincible Samson: The Theme of "Samson Agonistes" in World Literature with Translations of the Major Analogues* (Toronto, 1964), pp. 9–11, 55, 64, 74–75, 139 and 134–40, respectively.

18. The following are cited in ibid.: Zieglerus, pp. 8–9; Wunstius, pp. 52–53; Rhodius, p. 64; Giattini, p. 74; Vondel, pp. 120–21, 137, 138.

19. *The Geneva Bible: A Facsimile of the 1599 Edition* (Pleasant Hope, Mo., 1990).

20. The following are cited in Kirkconnell, *That Invincible Samson*: Zieglerus, pp. 7–8; Wunstius, p. 50; Rhodius, p. 64; Giattini, p. 71; Vondel, pp. 136–37.

21. Low, "The Phoenix and the Sun in *Samson Agonistes*," in *Milton Studies*, vol. XIV, ed. James D. Simmonds (Pittsburgh, 1980), p. 225.